FOREWORD FROM GEKKO GLOBAL MARKETS

Last year Gekko Global Markets (Gekko) launched its state of the art investment and trading execution engine, TradeHub®. As hopefully you have discovered, TradeHub® provides a revolutionary new trading and investment experience; it is elegant, easy on the eye and simple to use. In addition, TradeHub® gives you the option of choosing variable margin (up to 100%), the ability to input notional trade values, extremely low lifecycle costs and top quality institutional research.

I am delighted to say that since launch, TradeHub® has won a number of awards but more importantly it is responsible for the business enjoying a 700% increase in daily transactions.

As financial markets in the UK, across Europe and throughout the world seem to be slowly and surely unwinding from their brush with financial disaster, Gekko and its sister companies continue to go from strength to strength. Gekko is at the centre of a portfolio of companies (which we call an ecosystem) that already has and which continues to create and acquire hi-tech solutions to empower and satisfy the future self-directed investment needs and wants of clients.

For the Gekko client, this means we are able to bring you the most advanced tools available – from StockPulse sentiment analysis to social trading from ayondo, which allows you to connect with expert traders from all around the world. We believe these technologies are not only leading the way in financial product innovation but will also revolutionise the way you approach your trading and investment decisions.

I sincerely hope you will continue to use and recommend others to use TradeHub® going forward (www.gekkomarkets.com) and please, always feel free to let me know what further improvements you feel we could make.

Robert Lempka
Executive Chairman
Gekko Global Markets

HARRIMAN HOUSE LTD

3A Penns Road

Petersfield

Hampshire

GU32 2EW

GREAT BRITAIN

Tel: +44 (0)1730 233870

Email: enquiries@harriman-house.com

Website: www.harriman-house.com

First edition published in Great Britain in 2004

This 7th edition published in 2013

Copyright © Harriman House Ltd

The right of Stephen Eckett to be identified as the author has been asserted in accordance with the Copyright, Design and Patents Act 1988.

978-0-857193-421

British Library Cataloguing in Publication Data

A CIP catalogue record for this book can be obtained from the British Library.

Hh Harriman House

CONTENTS

INTRODUCTION

Welcome to the 2014 edition of the *UK Stock Market Almanac* where we celebrate the Efficient Market Theory – or rather, the failure of the theory. This book could alternatively be titled, *The Inefficient Almanac*, as it revels in the trends and anomalies of the market that the Efficient Market Theory says shouldn't exist.

New in the 2014 Almanac

New research

Studies appearing in the *Almanac* for the first time include:

- **FTSE 100/250 Monthly Switching Strategy** – on the back of research into the comparative monthly performance of the FTSE 100 and FTSE 250, a strategy of switching between the two markets is found that greatly outperforms either index individually. [p. 94]
- **Day Of The Week Strategy** – a strategy exploiting the day of the week anomaly is presented; it significantly outperforms the FTSE 100. [p. 60]
- **Monthly Share Momentum Strategy** – in the previous edition of the *Almanac* a monthly rebalanced momentum portfolio of FTSE 100 stocks beat the market by an average of 1.1 percentage points per month. This strategy is now applied to FTSE 350 stocks and the outperformance is found to increase to 2.9 percentage points per month. [p. 38]
- **Monthly Share Bounceback Strategy** – this is the opposite of the above momentum strategy; in this case the 10 worst performing stocks were selected for the monthly rebalancing. This strategy not only beat the FTSE 350 but also beat the momentum strategy. [p. 40]
- **Monthly seasonality of sectors** – analysis of the monthly performance of FTSE 350 sectors reveals the strongest and weakest sectors for each month. [p. 18]
- **Strong/weak shares by month** – analysis of FTSE 350 shares reveals those that have performed consistently strongly or weakly for each month for the past ten years. Some shares have risen (or fallen) in a specific month for every year since 2003. [pp. 4 and 44]
- **Average market behaviour by month** – by taking the average performance of the market on each day of a month it is possible to create a chart of the average performance of the market for that month. This has been done for all 12 months and an aggregate average chart for the whole year produced. [p. 6]
- **Good trending shares** – a system is presented for ranking high-return, low-volatility shares. [p. 96]
- **Daily volatility of the stock market** – is October really the most volatile month? [p. 82]
- **Exxon v Shell pairs trading** – analysis of the monthly comparative performance of Exxon and Shell. [p. 26]
- **Correlation between UK and international markets** – new analysis of the correlation of the UK with six overseas stock markets. [p. 163]
- **FTSE 100 v CAC40** – analysis of the comparative monthly performance of the UK and French markets. [p. 16]
- **Monthly seasonality of the Brazil market** – January and October are the strongest months for the Brazilian stock market. [p. 56]
- **FIFA World Cup** – how does hosting and winning the World Cup affect stock markets? [p. 52]
- **The Scottish Portfolio** – what would an independent Scotland look like to investors? (Shh, don't mention the banks.) [p. 76]
- **Monthly seasonality of gold** – February, September and November have historically been strong months for gold. And a chart of the FTSE All-Share priced in gold is shown. [p. 24]
- **Monthly seasonality of GBPUSD** – strong months for sterling against the dollar have been April and October. [p. 66]

New features in the diary

We've added some new features to the month summary pages in the diary:

1. Alongside the chart of the performance of the market in the month there's now an average performance chart for the month. This is calculated by taking the average performance of the market on each day in the month since 1985 and using these to create a cumulative performance chart for the month to give an idea of the behaviour of the market over the 22 or so trading days of each month. [More information on this can be found on p. 6.]

2. In the summary table, the first row gives the three main statistics that describe the historic performance of the market in that month: the average return, the percentage of months where the return is positive and the ranking among the 12 months. [More information on this can be found on p. 84.]

3. In the summary table, the second row displays the sectors that have been historically strong (and weak) that month. [More information on this can be found on p. 18.]

4. In the summary table, the third row displays the shares that have been historically strong (and weak) that month. [More information on this can be found on p. 4.]

As in the previous edition, the top right box on the month summary pages gives the Sinclair numbers for the FTSE 100, FTSE 250, S&P 500 and Nikkei 225. [More information on this can be found on p. xii.]

Updated strategies and studies

The 2014 *Almanac* also updates some of the studies of seasonality trends and anomalies that have featured in previous editions, including:

- **Quarterly Sector Strategy** – the strongest/weakest sectors for each quarter are identified and the Quarterly Sector Strategy continues to beat the market. [p. 42]

- **FTSE 100/S&P 500 Switching Strategy** – the strong/weak months for the FTSE 100 relative to the S&P 500 are identified and a strategy of switching between the two markets is found that produces twice the returns of either market individually. [pp. 70 and 106]

- **Low/high Share Price Strategy** – a portfolio of the 20 lowest priced shares in the market has outperformed a portfolio of the 20 highest priced shares by an average 49.4 percentage points each year since 2002. [p. 102]

- **Tuesday Reverses Monday Strategy** – since the year 2000 market returns on Tuesdays have been the reverse of those on Monday. A strategy using this effect has significantly outperformed the FTSE 100 over this period. [p. 124]

- **Market seasonality (day/week/month)** – December is still the strongest month in the year for the stock market, while September is the weakest. The greatest change from five years ago has been the fall of January from fourth to ninth in the month rankings. Analysis is also updated for weekly and daily performance of the market (Sinclair Numbers) [pp. 30, 68 and 84]

- **Day of the week performance** – Wednesday is the new weakest day of the week (Monday used to be), and the strongest days are Tuesday and Thursday. [p. 58]

- **Market momentum** – a reference grid is presented giving the historic tendency of the market to rise (fall) following a series of consecutive daily/weekly/monthly/yearly rises (falls). As before, it is found that trends become more established the longer they last and the market displays greater momentum for longer frequencies. [pp. 116-7]

- **FTSE 100 quarterly reviews** – as before, it is found that share prices tend to rise immediately before a company joins the FTSE 100 and are then flat or fall back. Before a company leaves the index share prices tend to fall and then rise after the exit. [pp. 22 and 100]

- **FTSE 100 and FTSE 250** – the trend continues for the FTSE 100 to greatly underperform the mid-cap index in January and February and outperform it in September and October. [p. 14]

- **Small Cap Stocks in January** – on average small cap stocks significantly outperform large cap stocks in January and underperform in October. [p. 8]

- **Turn of the month** – the market tends to be weak a few days either side of the turn of the month, but abnormally strong on the first trading of the new month (except December). [p. 123]

- **First/last trading day of the month** – the first trading days of April and July are found to be unusually strong, while that of December is weak. The last trading of October is found to be the year's strongest, and the weakest are those for February and November. [pp. 12 and 88]

- **Holidays and the market** – in the last ten years the market has been significantly strong on the days immediately before and after holidays and weak fours days before and three days after holidays. [p. 32]

- **Triple witching** – the three days around triple witching have higher volatility than other days and the FTSE 100 return on triple witching days is abnormally strong. [p. 122]

- **Volatility** – studies have been updated for the analysis of intra-day volatility and the performance of the market following very large one-day moves. [p. 120]

- **UK and US markets** – the correlation between the UK and US markets has been increasing since the 1950s and in the years since 2010 has been stronger than ever. [p. 162]

- **The Long-Term Formula** – the formula that describes the long-term trend of the stock market and gives a forecast for the FTSE 100 in December 2063. [p. 167]

- **Ultimate death cross** – the last edition of the *Almanac* left readers on a cliffhanger as the market was about to form an *ultimate death cross* – find out what happened next! [p. 165]

Six-month effect

The extraordinary **six-month effect** (also called the *Sell in May effect* in the UK and the *Halloween effect* in the US) remains as strong as ever. Since 1982 the market in the winter months has outperformed the market in the summer months by an average 9% annually! The **six-month strategy** is therefore still performing well – beating the market (inc. dividends) by 40% since 1994. [p. 74]

In the previous edition of the *Almanac* a method was presented to improve the returns on the six-month strategy by using the MACD indicator. In this edition we look at another simple way of enhancing returns, by recognising that October is now a strong month and therefore switching to a **5/7-month strategy**. [p. 78]

And also…

The *Almanac* also includes many further statistics and analyses that aim to help understand the nature of stocks and market indices.

Finally, a few not so serious studies:

- **Pontifical analysis** – new research into the surprising relationship between the papacy and the stock market.
- **Under pressure** – forget sun hours, it's the pressure that affects markets!
- **The Wimbledon Indicator** – Andy Murray has followed in the footsteps of Fred Perry; will this cause the stock market to crash?
- **Chinese calendar and the stock market** – do stocks like horses?

Quantitative analysis

It should be noted that the type of quantitative analysis contained in the *Almanac* in some cases is best exploited by an arbitraged or hedged strategy, not a simple long position. For example, to exploit the strong shares identified for January [p. 2], it would be best to short the FTSE 100 or the weak shares against a portfolio of long positions in the strong shares.

Outlook for 2014

At the time of writing the only notable event scheduled for 2014 is the FIFA World Cup; no major elections or celebrations are planned. But no doubt some unforeseen things will pop up, it's strange the way that happens.

Having said that, the United Nations *will* be celebrating the Year of Crystallography in 2014 (good to see the UN keeping their eye on the important issues). Elsewhere, 2014 will mark the 100th anniversary of Charlie Chaplin appearing in his first film, the 200th anniversary of the Great Stock Exchange Fraud in London (the cynics among you may think that the word "Great" doesn't narrow the reference down much) and the 1000th anniversary of Cnut being declared King of England.

Coincidentally, the Decennial Cycle and the Chinese Calendar are in fairly close agreement on the forecast for the market in 2014. Since 1801 the average performance of the 4th year of the decade has been 6.2%, while the Year of the Horse (starting January 2014) has seen an average market return of 6.6%. But the Long-Term Formula (the equation of the long-term trend line of the stock market since 1920) forecasts a FTSE 100 level of 6498 by December 2014.

The financial word of 2013 must be "taper". After Ben Bernanke used the word in testimony before Congress in May 2013, all subsequent market commentaries seemed to contain the T word. This is likely to continue into 2014 – when to taper or not to taper will be the question. Interestingly, a computer programming language called CodeIgniter has an error code 2014 that alerts with the message:

you can't run this command now

Many investors will be hoping that an error code 2014 will apply to any taper commands in the near future.

Stephen Eckett

PREFACE

Definition

> *almanac (noun): an annual calendar containing dates and statistical information*

What the book covers

Topics in the *Almanac* cover a wide spectrum. The diary includes essential information on upcoming company announcements and financial events such as exchange holidays and economic releases. There are also the results of a unique seasonality analysis of historic market performance for every day and week of the year – our Sinclair numbers. Besides this, there is information of a lighter nature, such as important social and sporting events and notable events in history.

Accompanying the diary is a series of articles about the stock market. Many of these articles focus on seasonality effects, such as the likely performance of the market in each month, momentum effects, and the difference in market performance between summer and winter.

In short, the *Almanac* is a unique work providing everything from essential reference information to informative and entertaining articles on the UK stock market.

How the book is structured

The *Almanac* has three major parts:

1. **Diary**

   The Diary is in a week-per-page format. (See the next page for a detailed explanation of the layout of each diary page.) Opposite each diary page is a short article about the stock market. These articles are strategy-oriented – they aim to reveal trading patterns and anomalies in the stock market that investors and traders can exploit to make money.

2. **Statistics**

   This section contains further seasonality and anomaly studies as well as background information on the profile characteristcs of the market – the indices, the sectors and companies.

3. **Reference**

   The Reference section includes background information about UK and international stock indices, and a look at the original constituents of the FT 30 of 1935 and the FTSE 100 of 1984.

Supporting website

The website supporting this book can be found at **stockmarketalmanac.co.uk.**

UNDERSTANDING THE DIARY PAGES

A

B

C

JUNE

33, -0.9, 1.8 ⬇

Week 25

JUNE

Mon — 2nd weakest market week

16

2013: It is announced that the Co-Operative Bank will be floated on the stock exchange after it is agreed with a City regulator that the bank has a £1.5bn hole in its balance sheet.

↗

FTSE 100	65	0.2	0.5
FTSE 250	47	0.0	0.5
S&P 500	62	0.1	0.8
NIKKEI	50	0.1	1.5

Tue — Two-day FOMC meeting starts
Horseracing: Royal Ascot, Ascot Racecourse (until 21 June)
ECB Governing Council Meeting

17

1867: Joseph Lister performs the first operation under antiseptic conditions on his sister Isabella, at the Glasgow Infirmary.

↗

FTSE 100	67	0.3	0.9
FTSE 250	60	0.1	0.8
S&P 500	51	0.1	0.8
NIKKEI	48	0.1	1.3

J

D

Wed — MPC meeting minutes published
ECB General Council Meeting
30th anniversary of the Battle of Orgreave

18

1928: Aviator Amelia Earhart becomes the first woman to fly in an aircraft across the Atlantic Ocean (she is a passenger, Wilmer Stultz is the pilot and Lou Gordon is the mechanic).

↘

FTSE 100	41	-0.3	0.7
FTSE 250	35	-0.2	0.7
S&P 500	41	-0.1	0.7
NIKKEI	41	0.1	1.4

I

Thu Golf: US Women's Open, Pinehurst, North Carolina (until 22 June)
25th anniversary of the LSE flotation of Templeton Emerging Markets Investments Trust.

19

1997: Sir Andrew Lloyd Webber's *Cats* becomes the longest running Broadway musical upon its 6138th performance.

→

FTSE 100	45	-0.1	1.0
FTSE 250	50	0.0	1.2
S&P 500	53	-0.1	0.8
NIKKEI	50	-0.2	1.5

Fri Triple Witching

20

1960: Nan Winton becomes the first woman to read the national news on BBC television.

↘

FTSE 100	36	-0.4	1.0
FTSE 250	30	-0.3	0.9
S&P 500	46	-0.1	0.8
NIKKEI	59	0.0	1.0

E

H

Sat 21 Summer Solstice, also known as Midsummer or Litha

Sun 22

COMPANY NEWS

Interims Bankers Investment Trust, Chemring Group, Crest Nicholson Holdings Ltd
Finals Ashtead Group, Berkeley Group Holdings, Fidelity China Special Situation, Imagination Technologies Group, Micro Focus International, Utilico Emerging Markets Ltd

"I'm spending a year dead for tax reasons."
Douglas Adams

51

F

G

A – Diary page title

The diary is a week-per-page format.

B – Weekly performance analysis (Sinclair numbers)

These figures and arrow show the results of the analysis on the historic performance of the FTSE 100 during this week. The ten best performing weeks are marked with a square box around the Sinclair arrow here. The ten worst performing weeks are marked with a circle around the arrow. [See the next page for further explanation and the Statistics section for full data tables of FTSE 100 daily, weekly and monthly Sinclair numbers.]

C – Week number

The week number of the year is indicated at the top right of every diary page.

D – Social and sporting events

Notable social and sporting events, including public holidays, are included each day.

E – Daily performance analysis (Sinclair numbers)

These figures and arrow show the results of the analysis on the historic performance of four world stock indices on this calendar day. The ten best performing days for the FTSE 100 are marked with a square box around the Sinclair arrow here. The ten worst performing weeks are marked with a circle around the arrow. [See the next page for further explanation and the Statistics section for full data tables of FTSE 100 daily, weekly and monthly Sinclair numbers.]

F – Likely company announcements

The box at the foot of each page contains a list of companies expected to announce interim or final results during the week. The list is only provisional, using the date of announcements in the previous year as a guide.

G – Quotation

A fun financial quote to end the week.

H – On this day

Events that happened on this calendar day in history.

I – Anniversary

Significant anniversaries that occur on this day.

J – Financial events

Indicates days of financial and economic significance. For example, exchange holidays and important economic releases.

Abbreviations

FOMC – Federal Open Market Committee
MPC – Monetary Policy Committee

Sinclair numbers

We have conducted a unique analysis of the historic performance of four stock indices – the FTSE 100, FTSE 250, S&P 500 and Nikkei 225 – for each day, week and month of the year.

This analysis produces three numbers (which we call Sinclair numbers) for each day, week and month:

1. **Up(%)**

   The percentage of historic moves in this period (day, week or month) that were up. For example, in our sample the FTSE 100 increased 13 times on this day out of a total of 19 market days on 2 April, so the Up(%) is 68%. If you flick to Week 14 in the diary you will see this 68% recorded in the Sinclair table in the FTSE 100 row.

2. **Avg Change(%)**

   The average percentage change of the market in this period. For example, on 2 April, the market has risen 0.7% on average on the 19 market days.

3. **StdDev**

   This is the standard deviation of all the changes in this period away from the average. For example, for 2 April, the standard deviation is 1.2. This means that 66% of all the market moves on 2 April fell between -0.5% and +1.9% (i.e. average move of 0.7% -/+ standard deviation). The standard deviation measures how closely all the moves in the period cluster around the average. A high number for standard deviation suggests that clustering was not close, and therefore confidence in future moves being close to the average is decreased. Conversely, a low standard deviation figure suggests good clustering and increases one's confidence in future moves being close to the calculated historic average.

Sample data

- **FTSE 100 Index**: from April 1984
- **FTSE 250 Index**: from December 1985
- **S&P 500 Index**: from January 1950
- **Nikkei 225 Index**: from January 1984

Sinclair arrows

The figures for Up(%) are displayed for the respective days and weeks on the Diary pages employing the following arrow symbols:

Daily arrows

↑   the Up(%) is over 74%

↗   the Up(%) is 63% to 74%

→   the Up(%) is 41% to 63%

↘   the Up(%) is 30% to 41%

↓   the Up(%) is under 30%

Weekly arrows

↑   the Up(%) is over 70%

↗   the Up(%) is 60% to 70%

→   the Up(%) is 50% to 60%

↘   the Up(%) is 40% to 50%

↓   the Up(%) is under 40%

These daily ranges were calculated on the following basis: the average Up(%) for all days in the year is 52% and the standard deviation is 11. Adding two standard deviations to the average gives 74, adding one standard deviation gives 63, subtracting one standard deviation gives 41 and subtracting two standard deviations gives 30. The weekly ranges have been modified slightly from these figures so as to present the data with more variation.

The top ten days and weeks – with the highest Up(%) – are highlighted with a square box around the arrow and the weakest ten days and weeks – with the lowest Up(%) – are highlighted with a circle.

See the Statistics section for full data tables of FTSE 100 Sinclair numbers.

I
DIARY

JANUARY MARKET

Market performance this month

Since 1984 the market has risen in 59% of all years in January, with an average return of 0.5%. This makes the month 9th in the ranking of monthly performance. Interestingly, it is the month whose performance has changed the most over the last few years – in 2007 the month ranked fourth and has since fallen five places.

FTSE 100	59	0.5	5.2
FTSE 250	61	1.9	4.7
S&P 500	62	1.2	4.9
NIKKEI	59	0.9	6.0

As can be seen from the average chart, historically the euphoria of December (the strongest month of the year) carries over into January as the market continues to climb for the first couple of days. But by around the fourth trading day the exhilaration is wearing off and the market then falls for the next two weeks – the second week of January has been the weakest week for the market in the whole year. Then, around the middle of the third week, the market has tended to rebound sharply.

The month is better for mid-cap and small-cap stocks (called the January Effect). On average, since 2000 the FTSE 250 has outperformed the FTSE 100 by 2.3 percentage points in January – the best outperformance (with February) of all months. Small caps do even better, outperforming the FTSE 100 by an average 3.7 percentage points in the first month.

A famous market predictor in the US has it that the direction of the market in the whole year will be the same as that for the first five days of January. Research shows that the same rule more or less works for the UK market.

Performance of market in January [1970 to 2013]

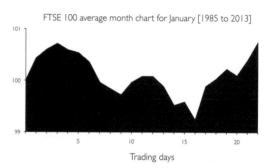

FTSE 100 average month chart for January [1985 to 2013]

Trading days

JANUARY SUMMARY			
Market performance	Average return: 0.5%	Positive: 59%	Ranking: 9th
Sector performance	*Strong* Construction & Materials, Electronic & Electrical Equipment, Equity Investment Instruments, Financial Services, General Industrials, Health Care Equipment & Services, Industrial Metals, Media, Software & Computer Services, Support Services	*Weak* Beverages, Food & Drug Retailers, Food Producers	
Share performance	*Strong* Aveva Group, Electra Private Equity, Euromoney Institutional Investor, SIG, St James's Place	*Weak* Berkeley Group Holdings (The), FirstGroup, GlaxoSmithKline, Pennon Group, Tesco	
Main features of the month	Small cap stocks often outperform large cap stocks in January (January Effect)		
	The FTSE 250 is particularly strong relative to the FTSE 100 in this month		
	FTSE 100 often underperforms the S&P500 in January		
	Week beginning 6 Jan: the weakest market week		
	First trading day average return: 0.43%; positive: 62%		
	Last trading day average return: 0.19%; positive: 62%		
Significant dates	01 Jan: LSE, NYSE, TSE, HKEX closed		
	03 Jan: US Nonfarm payroll report (anticipated)		
	09 Jan: MPC interest rate announcement at 12 noon (anticipated)		
	20 Jan: Martin Luther King Day (US) - NYSE closed		
	28 Jan: Two-day FOMC meeting starts		
	31 Jan: Chinese New Year (Year of the horse)		
	Don't forget: the last date to file your 2013 tax return online is 31 January		

Mon

30

6th strongest market week

→

FTSE 100	60	0.2	0.9
FTSE 250	68	0.3	0.6
S&P 500	64	0.2	0.7
NIKKEI	50	0.3	1.5

1960: The farthing ceases to be legal tender in the UK.

Tue

31

New Year's Eve
LSE closes early at 12h30
TSE closed

→

FTSE 100	53	0.0	1.1
FTSE 250	71	0.0	0.6
S&P 500	69	0.2	0.7
NIKKEI			

1923: The chimes of Big Ben are broadcast on BBC radio for the first time.

Wed

1

New Year's Day
LSE, NYSE, HKEX, TSE closed
New moon
40th anniversary of the start of the Three-Day Week in UK

1788: London's *Daily Universal Register* becomes *The Times* newspaper.

Thu

2

TSE closed

→

FTSE 100	59	0.4	1.2
FTSE 250	75	0.6	1.1
S&P 500	63	0.3	1.4
NIKKEI			

1959: Luna 1, the first spacecraft to reach the vicinity of the Moon and to orbit the Sun, is launched by the Soviet Union.

Fri

3

TSE closed
Nonfarm payroll report (anticipated)

→

FTSE 100	57	0.3	1.1
FTSE 250	69	0.4	1.0
S&P 500	49	0.2	1.2
NIKKEI			

2007: Land Securities Group closes at all-time high of 20.7956.

Sat 4

Sun 5

COMPANY NEWS

Interims
Finals

"A man always has two reasons for what he does – a good one, and the real one."
J. P. Morgan

STRONG/WEAK SHARES BY MONTH

In Week 22 we look at FTSE 350 shares that have been strong/weak in the month of June over the last ten years. Such analysis can be done for every month and the results of this are shown in the table below. The obvious hedge strategy would be to short the weak shares against a long position in the strong shares for each month.

	Strong	Weak
Jan	Aveva Group Electra Private Equity Euromoney Institutional Investor SIG St James's Place	Berkeley Group Holdings (The) FirstGroup GlaxoSmithKline Pennon Group Tesco
Feb	BG Group Bunzl Croda International Fidessa Group Savills	AstraZeneca Vodafone Group
Mar	Aggreko Cobham IMI Intertek Group Restaurant Group (The)	Aviva HSBC Holdings Renishaw Royal Bank of Scotland Group (The) RSA Insurance Group
Apr	Diploma Menzies (John) Royal Dutch Shell Severn Trent Xaar	Balfour Beatty Centamin Shire UNITE Group
May	3i Group Babcock International Group Cranswick Homeserve Severn Trent	Petra Diamonds Ltd Sainsbury (J) Stagecoach Group Taylor Wimpey Workspace Group
Jun	BT Group Halma Synergy Health Ted Baker	Barclays Rotork United Utilities Group Vesuvius
Jul	Brown (N) Group Dairy Crest Group Greene King Pace Wetherspoon (J D)	Man Group Petra Diamonds Ltd
Aug	Bunzl Centrica Fisher (James) & Sons Keller Group Tesco	Investec Pennon Group Rio Tinto
Sep	Aberdeen Asset Management Ashtead Group Carnival Diploma JPMorgan Indian Investment Trust	Carpetright Compass Group Pace Premier Farnell SVG Capital
Oct	Brewin Dolphin Holdings Diageo easyJet Restaurant Group (The) Tate & Lyle	Dialight Grainger Worldwide Healthcare Trust
Nov	Babcock International Group Compass Group Premier Farnell Shire Tate & Lyle	AstraZeneca Greggs Herald Investment Trust Rentokil Initial Tullett Prebon
Dec	Alliance Trust Balfour Beatty JPMorgan Emerging Markets Inv Trust William Hill Witan Investment Trust	Amlin Centamin Rank Group (The)

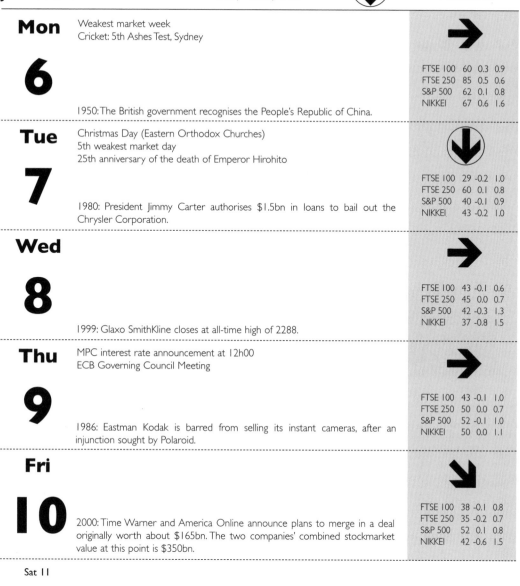
Mon

6

Weakest market week
Cricket: 5th Ashes Test, Sydney

1950: The British government recognises the People's Republic of China.

FTSE 100	60	0.3	0.9
FTSE 250	85	0.5	0.6
S&P 500	62	0.1	0.8
NIKKEI	67	0.6	1.6

Tue

7

Christmas Day (Eastern Orthodox Churches)
5th weakest market day
25th anniversary of the death of Emperor Hirohito

1980: President Jimmy Carter authorises $1.5bn in loans to bail out the Chrysler Corporation.

FTSE 100	29	-0.2	1.0
FTSE 250	60	0.1	0.8
S&P 500	40	-0.1	0.9
NIKKEI	43	-0.2	1.0

Wed

8

1999: Glaxo SmithKline closes at all-time high of 2288.

FTSE 100	43	-0.1	0.6
FTSE 250	45	0.0	0.7
S&P 500	42	-0.3	1.3
NIKKEI	37	-0.8	1.5

Thu

9

MPC interest rate announcement at 12h00
ECB Governing Council Meeting

1986: Eastman Kodak is barred from selling its instant cameras, after an injunction sought by Polaroid.

FTSE 100	43	-0.1	1.0
FTSE 250	50	0.0	0.7
S&P 500	52	-0.1	1.0
NIKKEI	50	0.0	1.1

Fri

10

2000: Time Warner and America Online announce plans to merge in a deal originally worth about $165bn. The two companies' combined stockmarket value at this point is $350bn.

FTSE 100	38	-0.1	0.8
FTSE 250	35	-0.2	0.7
S&P 500	52	0.1	0.8
NIKKEI	42	-0.6	1.5

Sat 11

Sun 12

COMPANY NEWS

Interims
Finals

"Forecasts may tell you a great deal about the forecaster; they tell you nothing about the future."
Warren Buffett

AVERAGE MARKET BEHAVIOUR

The average month

If we take the returns for the FTSE 100 on the first trading day of January over a period of years, and calculate the average of those returns, it will give us a figure for the average performance of the index on the first trading day of January.

For example, if we take the index returns on the first trading of January for the 29 years since 1985 we can calculate the average return to be 0.43%. With this we can say that on average the FTSE 100 increased 0.43% on the first trading day of January over the period 1985 to 2013. We can repeat this process for the second trading day of January, and the third, etc. until we have a set of average returns for all the trading days of January.

With this set of returns we can plot an average index for the market in January (we will set the index to start at 100). For example, the average return for the market on the first trading day is 0.43%, and so the average index would close at 100.43 on the first trading day of January.

The following chart plots the average index for the month of January from 1985 to 2013.

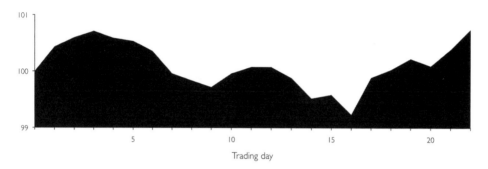

From the chart we can see that, on average, the market in January rises for the first couple of days (a continuation of the preceding end-of-year market ebullience), but then the market turns and falls for the following three weeks (15 trading days), until it reverses again and then rises strongly in the final week.

[Note: Average index charts for all the months can be seen on each respective month summary page in the Diary.]

The average year

By concatenating the average index data for each month, we can create an average index chart for the whole year (shown below).

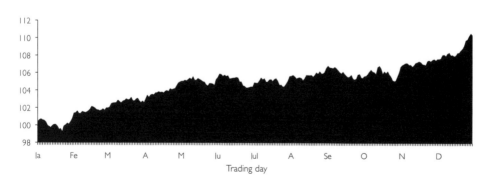

In the above chart we can see that, on average, the year starts with the three weak weeks (we saw this in the preceding average chart for January). After that the market is strong until May. From May to October the market is fairly flat, and then rises strongly in the final two months of the year.

This annual market behaviour profile concurs with what we already knew about the market, but it is illustrated simply and efficiently in this one chart.

48, -0.3, 2.6

Mon

Coming of Age Day (Japan) – TSE closed
Tennis: Australian Open, Melbourne (until 26 January)

13

FTSE 100	35	-0.2	0.9
FTSE 250	50	-0.1	0.8
S&P 500	44	0.0	0.6
NIKKEI			

2012: France loses its AAA credit rating from Standard & Poor's.

Tue

14

FTSE 100	57	-0.1	1.5
FTSE 250	50	0.0	1.0
S&P 500	71	0.2	0.9
NIKKEI	72	0.7	1.0

2013: The HMV Group confirms that its shares are being suspended from the London Stock Exchange with immediate effect as it files for administration.

Wed

Beige Book published

15

FTSE 100	62	0.2	1.3
FTSE 250	47	-0.1	1.1
S&P 500	65	0.2	0.9
NIKKEI	56	-0.6	2.0

1943: The Pentagon – the world's largest office building – is dedicated in Virginia, USA.

Thu

Full moon

16

FTSE 100	57	0.2	0.9
FTSE 250	60	0.0	0.7
S&P 500	57	0.1	0.7
NIKKEI	47	0.1	2.2

2006: Carnival closes at all-time high of 33.97.

Fri

17

FTSE 100	57	0.2	0.9
FTSE 250	65	0.4	0.6
S&P 500	58	0.1	1.0
NIKKEI	55	0.2	1.5

1917: The United States pays Denmark $25m for the Virgin Islands.

Sat 18

Sun 19

COMPANY NEWS

Interims IG Group Holdings
Finals

"I try not to borrow. First you borrow, then you beg."
Ernest Hemingway

THE JANUARY EFFECT(S)

It's January, so let's talk about the January Effect.

But which January Effect would that be?

There are three different uses of the term floating around:

1. Small-caps outperform large caps in January

The most common use of the term *January Effect* describes the tendency of small-cap stocks to outperform large-cap stocks in January.

In 1976 an academic paper found that equally weighted indices of all the stocks on the NYSE had significantly higher returns in January than in the other 11 months during 1904 to 1974. This indicated that small capitalisation stocks outperformed larger stocks in January. Over the following years many further papers were written confirming this finding. In 2006 a paper tested this effect on data from 1802 and found the effect was consistent up to the present time.

The UK market experiences the same January Effect as seen in the US market. The small cap outperformance in January is significantly strong: the FTSE Small Cap Index has outperformed the FTSE 100 by an average 2.7 percentage points in January since 1995. And the Small Cap Index has underperformed the FTSE 100 in just three Januaries in the past 19. The following chart shows the average FTSE Small Cap Index outperformance of the FTSE 100 for each month since 1994.

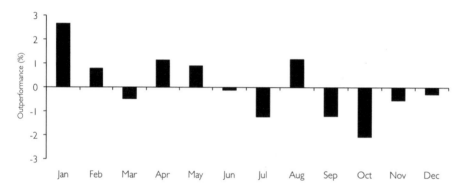

2. January predicts the market for the rest of the year

Historically, the returns in January have signalled the returns for the rest of the year. If January market returns are positive, then returns for the whole year have tended to be positive (and vice versa).

This is sometimes called the *January Predictor* or *January Barometer* and was first mentioned by Yale Hirsch of the *Stock Trader's Almanac* in 1972. A variant of this effect has it that returns for the whole year can be predicted by the direction of the market in just the first five days of the year.

Academic research has largely found that January returns can predict the rest of the year, but there is some doubt as to whether the effect can be exploited.

And Dan Greenhaus of BTIG points out that January is not necessarily any better a predictor of full year performance than any other month. According to him:

> When February is down, the 12 month return inclusive of that February is 2.0%. When February is up, the S&P 500 returns 12.53%.

This is similar for the other months.

3. The market tends to rise in January

In 1942 Sidney B. Wachtel wrote a paper – 'Certain Observations on Seasonal Movements in Stock Prices' – in which he proposed that stocks rose in January as investors began buying again after the year-end tax-induced sell-off.

Looking at the returns for the FTSE 100 since 1984, it is true that they tend to be positive – but not strongly so. The index has risen in 59% of all Januaries since 1984 with an average increase of 0.5% – which ranks it only ninth of the 12 months.

JANUARY

55, 0.0, 1.8 Week 4

Mon 20

Martin Luther King Jr. Day (US) – NYSE closed
6th weakest market day

FTSE 100	30	-0.5	0.8
FTSE 250	35	-0.3	0.6
S&P 500			
NIKKEI	43	-0.5	1.3

2009: Barack Obama is inaugurated as the first black President of the US.

Tue 21

→

FTSE 100	43	-0.5	1.3
FTSE 250	35	-0.4	1.0
S&P 500	48	0.0	1.0
NIKKEI	38	-0.3	1.4

2002: The Canadian Dollar sets all-time low against the US Dollar (US$0.6179).

Wed 22

World Economic Forum Annual Meeting, Davos, Switzerland (until 25 January)
MPC meeting minutes published
ECB Governing Council Meeting

→

FTSE 100	48	0.0	1.3
FTSE 250	45	0.1	1.1
S&P 500	53	-0.1	0.9
NIKKEI	38	-0.3	2.0

1984: The Apple Macintosh, the first consumer computer to popularise the mouse and graphical user interface, is introduced during Super Bowl XVIII with its famous '1984' television commercial.

Thu 23

↘

FTSE 100	38	-0.3	0.9
FTSE 250	21	-0.3	0.6
S&P 500	65	0.2	0.7
NIKKEI	36	-0.4	1.8

1986: The Rock and Roll Hall of Fame inducts its first members: Little Richard, Chuck Berry, James Brown, Ray Charles, Fats Domino, the Everly Brothers, Buddy Holly, Jerry Lee Lewis and Elvis Presley.

Fri 24

→

FTSE 100	62	0.5	1.2
FTSE 250	60	0.3	0.6
S&P 500	61	0.0	1.0
NIKKEI	64	0.0	1.6

2001: HSBC closes at all-time high of 951.6.

Sat 25   Burns Night

Sun 26   75th anniversary of the capture of Barcelona by Franco.

COMPANY NEWS

Interims City of London Investment Trust
Finals Bankers Investment Trust, Chemring Group, Unilever

"Personal finances are like people's personal health, crucial and tragic to the sufferer but tedious to the listener."
Thomas Keneally

FEBRUARY MARKET

Market performance this month

The performance of the market in this month has improved in recent years. Five years ago it ranked 9th of all months, whereas today it is 3rd. The market has risen in February in 59% of all years, with an average return of 1.0%; in fact the market has only fallen five times in February in the last 20 years.

FTSE 100	59	1.0	4.1
FTSE 250	75	2.4	4.0
S&P 500	55	-0.1	3.5
NIKKEI	60	0.8	4.8

The average chart shows that on average the market rises for the first two-and-a-half weeks and then drifts lower for the rest of the month. The first trading day (FTD) of February is the strongest FTD of all months in the year.

This is the busiest month for FTSE 100 results announcements – 34 companies announce their prelims in February (as do 53 FTSE 250 companies).

Along with January, February is the best month for mid-cap stocks relative to the large caps. On average the FTSE 250 outperforms the FTSE 100 by 1.3 percentage points in this month.

This month is one of the four months in the year that the FTSE 100 has historically outperformed the S&P 500, on average by 0.6 percentage points in February.

Performance of market in February [1970 to 2013]

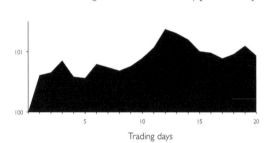

FTSE 100 average month chart for February [1985 to 2013]

Trading days

FEBRUARY SUMMARY			
Market performance	Average return: 1.0%	Positive: 59%	Ranking: 3rd
Sector performance	Strong Chemicals, Construction & Materials, General Retailers, Household Goods, Mining, Oil Equipment, Services & Distribution	Weak Electronic & Electrical Equipment, Financial Services, Fixed Line Telecommunications, Mobile Telecommunications, Technology Hardware & Equipment	
Share performance	Strong BG Group, Bunzl, Croda International, Fidessa Group, Savills	Weak AstraZeneca, Vodafone Group	
Main features of the month	Strong month for gold price The FTSE 250 is particularly strong relative to the FTSE 100 in this month FTSE 100 often outperforms the S&P 500 in this month GBPUSD historically weak this month Busiest month for FTSE 100 preliminary results announcements First trading day average return: 0.61%; positive: 57% (year's strongest) Last trading day average return: -0.07%; positive: 45%		
Significant dates	06 Feb: MPC interest rate announcement at 12 noon (anticipated) 07 Feb: US Nonfarm payroll report (anticipated) 12 Feb: MSCI quarterly index review 17 Feb: President's Day (US) – NYSE closed		

Mon	7th strongest market week	FTSE 100	50	0.2	1.3
27		FTSE 250	55	0.2	1.0
		S&P 500	53	0.2	0.8
		NIKKEI	52	0.2	1.5
	2010: The Apple iPad is announced.				

Mon

27

7th strongest market week

FTSE 100 50 0.2 1.3
FTSE 250 55 0.2 1.0
S&P 500 53 0.2 0.8
NIKKEI 52 0.2 1.5

2010: The Apple iPad is announced.

Tue

28

Two-day FOMC meeting starts

FTSE 100 57 0.1 1.1
FTSE 250 45 0.2 0.9
S&P 500 60 0.2 1.1
NIKKEI 52 0.2 1.5

1813: Jane Austen's *Pride and Prejudice* is published.

Wed

29

FTSE 100 43 -0.2 1.0
FTSE 250 55 0.0 1.0
S&P 500 56 0.1 1.0
NIKKEI 57 0.2 1.4

1985: Oxford University snubs Prime Minister Margaret Thatcher by refusing her an honorary degree.

Thu

30

New moon

FTSE 100 57 0.3 1.1
FTSE 250 60 0.1 0.7
S&P 500 54 0.0 0.9
NIKKEI 55 0.0 1.5

1934: In the US the Gold Reserve Act is passed, which pegs the value of the dollar to gold.

Fri

31

Chinese New Year (Year of the Horse) – HKSE closed
Last day to file 2013 Tax Returns online without incurring penalties.

FTSE 100 62 0.2 0.8
FTSE 250 60 0.1 0.6
S&P 500 63 0.3 0.8
NIKKEI 73 0.7 1.8

1990: The first McDonald's in the Soviet Union opens in Moscow.

Sat 1   Rugby: Six Nations Championship (until 15 March)

Sun 2   American Football: Super Bowl XLVIII, MetLife Stadium, New Jersey

COMPANY NEWS

Interims British Sky Broadcasting Group, Diageo, PZ Cussons, Rank Group, Renishaw
Finals Aberforth Smaller Companies Trust, AstraZeneca, Royal Dutch Shell

"Thy shalt not worship thy investment advisor, for if she were so smart she would be retired by now."
Steven J. Lee

FIRST TRADING DAYS OF THE MONTH

Does the market display any abnormal effect on the first trading day of each month?

FTSE 100 daily data was analysed from 1984 to discover if the UK equity market had a tendency to significantly increase or decrease on the first trading day (FTD) of each month. The results are shown in the table below.

	Number of days analysed	Positive	Positive (%)	Avg (%)
All days	7418	3878	52.3	0.03
First trading day of each month (from 1984)	352	214	60.8	0.24
First trading day of each month (from 2000)	164	107	65.2	0.33

Analysis

Of the 352 months since 1984, the market has risen 214 times (60.8%) on the FTD of each month, with an average rise of 0.24%. This is significantly greater than the average for all days, where the market has risen 52.3% of the time with an average return of 0.03%.

The effect seems to be, if anything, stronger in recent years. Since 2000, the market has increased 65.2% on months' FTDs with an average rise of 0.33% (10 times greater than the average return for all days in the period).

The table below breaks down the performance of the market on the first trading days by month since 1984. For example, on average the return on the FTD of April has been 0.5%.

	Jan	Feb	Mar	Apr	May	Jun	Jul	Aug	Sep	Oct	Nov	Dec
Positive (%)	64.3	60.7	60.7	72.4	55.2	55.2	72.4	65.5	65.5	62.1	65.5	48.3
Average (%)	0.4	0.6	0.0	0.5	0.1	0.2	0.5	0.1	0.2	0.2	0.2	0.0

The strongest FTDs are for the months of February, April and July. The average return on the FTD of July has been 0.5% (16 times greater than the average return for all days of the month), with a positive return for 72.4% of all July FTDs.

The weakest month FTD is December – this is the only month when the market has fallen more often than risen on the first trading day. This is an unexpected result since December as a whole is one of the stronger months for the market.

A summary of the first trading day effect (by month) is shown in the chart below.

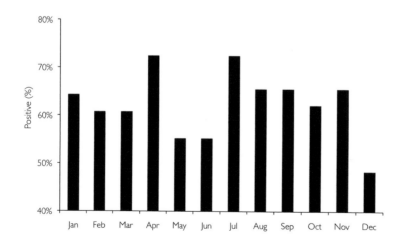

Note: see also Last trading days of the month, Week 44.

Mon **3**	HKSE closed 1000th anniversary of Cnut being declared King of England. 1690: The colony of Massachusetts issues the first paper money in America.	→ FTSE 100 50 0.3 1.2 FTSE 250 60 0.3 0.7 S&P 500 64 0.2 0.7 NIKKEI 38 0.0 0.9
Tue **4**	10th anniversary of the launch of Facebook. 1971: British car maker Rolls-Royce declares itself bankrupt.	→ FTSE 100 43 -0.3 1.1 FTSE 250 50 0.1 1.0 S&P 500 42 -0.2 1.1 NIKKEI 48 0.2 1.1
Wed **5**	 1997: Morgan Stanley and Dean Witter investment banks announce a $10bn merger.	→ FTSE 100 48 -0.1 1.2 FTSE 250 60 -0.1 1.0 S&P 500 44 -0.1 0.9 NIKKEI 29 -0.6 1.2
Thu **6**	MPC interest rate announcement at 12h00 ECB Governing Council Meeting 2013: The Royal Bank of Scotland is fined £390m by UK and US authorities for its part in the Libor rate-fixing scandal.	→ FTSE 100 62 0.0 0.9 FTSE 250 60 0.2 0.7 S&P 500 54 0.1 0.8 NIKKEI 64 0.1 1.5
Fri **7**	Winter Olympics, Sochi, Russia (until 23 February) Nonfarm payroll report (anticipated) 50th anniversary of the start of the first Beatles tour of the US 1992: The European Union is formed.	→ FTSE 100 52 0.0 1.1 FTSE 250 55 0.1 0.8 S&P 500 48 0.0 0.6 NIKKEI 55 0.1 0.8

Sat 8

Sun 9

COMPANY NEWS

Interims Hargreaves Lansdown

Finals ARM Holdings, Beazley, BG Group, BP, Countrywide, esure Group, GlaxoSmithKline, Ocado Group, Randgold Resources Ltd, Smith & Nephew, St Modwen Properties

"It had not exactly been gold... but more like the fairy dream that the gold is there, at the end of the rainbow, and will continue to be there forever – provided, naturally, that you don't go and look. This is known as finance."
Terry Pratchett

COMPARATIVE PERFORMANCE OF THE FTSE 100 AND FTSE 250

The table below shows the monthly outperformance of the FTSE 100 over the mid-cap FTSE 250. For example, in January 1986, the FTSE 100 increased 1.6%, while the FTSE 250 increased 2.6%. The outperformance of the former over the latter was therefore -1.0. The cells are highlighted if the number is negative (i.e. the FTSE 250 outperformed the FTSE 100).

	Jan	Feb	Mar	Apr	May	Jun	Jul	Aug	Sep	Oct	Nov	Dec
1986	-1.0	-1.1	0.4	-4.0	-0.1	-1.5	-1.0	2.3	-0.8	-0.3	-2.3	1.5
1987	-1.8	2.6	-2.1	1.3	1.3	-4.8	-2.7	-0.1	-1.3	2.6	1.0	-4.1
1988	-2.0	-1.0	-0.3	-0.5	-1.4	-0.6	-1.3	0.9	0.5	-2.0	0.3	2.0
1989	1.3	-3.6	1.5	2.8	-1.3	2.6	0.1	3.2	-2.1	2.2	2.6	1.8
1990	-1.0	1.4	0.7	-0.3	2.8	-0.8	0.3	4.8	1.9	-1.7	2.9	-1.2
1991	2.7	-4.8	-1.4	1.6	2.2	0.0	2.0	-1.9	-1.9	0.4	0.4	4.0
1992	-1.6	-2.3	-0.2	-3.9	-0.4	1.4	4.8	1.1	1.0	-1.1	-0.1	-6.1
1993	-4.6	-0.6	-2.0	-3.1	-0.1	-0.1	-1.3	-0.3	0.2	1.6	1.1	-0.9
1994	-5.6	-1.6	-2.0	0.5	0.8	2.5	-1.0	0.6	1.5	1.7	0.0	-0.6
1995	1.3	0.2	2.8	-0.3	-0.3	1.5	-2.0	-1.9	0.0	2.0	2.2	-0.9
1996	-0.7	-3.0	-3.4	-2.0	-0.9	2.5	2.6	0.1	2.8	-0.1	1.8	0.1
1997	1.5	-0.5	1.8	4.5	4.2	1.1	5.2	-4.3	3.9	-3.8	-0.5	3.5
1998	4.7	-1.3	-3.4	-1.6	-6.2	6.1	0.5	2.6	1.5	1.5	3.7	3.4
1999	-3.3	0.3	-2.4	-2.8	-1.4	-2.4	-3.3	-0.6	2.0	4.9	-4.7	1.0
2000	-5.5	-4.9	4.6	1.1	0.0	-6.7	-1.9	0.7	-0.3	3.0	-1.4	-0.7
2001	-1.7	-4.7	3.5	0.8	-5.4	1.5	1.4	-3.9	8.1	-2.0	-5.8	-1.3
2002	0.5	-1.0	-2.5	-1.2	-0.3	0.7	4.2	-2.0	-0.2	5.5	0.0	-0.3
2003	-2.5	1.9	0.8	-2.2	-6.6	-3.5	-4.2	-4.9	0.7	-0.1	1.5	1.5
2004	-5.7	-1.8	-2.2	3.1	1.2	-3.0	2.9	0.0	-0.5	0.3	-2.3	-3.1
2005	-2.5	1.2	0.2	3.7	-2.3	-0.6	0.1	-1.6	0.8	0.1	-6.0	-2.0
2006	-1.8	-2.5	-1.3	0.7	0.9	0.6	2.3	-3.0	-3.2	-0.9	-4.2	-1.9
2007	0.4	-0.4	-3.3	0.2	1.1	4.6	-2.1	-0.6	5.0	-1.8	3.6	1.2
2008	-1.7	-1.8	-2.6	5.7	0.2	1.9	-0.6	-1.8	2.9	9.6	1.0	-1.0
2009	-4.7	-4.5	-2.9	-10.0	3.5	-1.7	0.6	-3.7	0.9	1.1	2.5	-0.1
2010	-3.4	2.0	-2.7	-4.2	0.5	-2.4	0.7	0.6	-1.0	-0.7	-0.4	-2.2
2011	0.1	0.9	-1.2	-0.9	-1.7	0.3	1.0	1.6	1.8	1.4	0.9	3.3
2012	-4.6	-3.0	-2.5	0.5	0.3	1.2	-0.7	-1.1	-2.3	-1.0	0.6	-2.3
2013	1.1	-3.8	-0.8	0.1	-0.5	-1.7	-1.3					

The average outperformance of the FTSE 100 over the FTSE 250 for each month since 1986 is shown in the following chart.

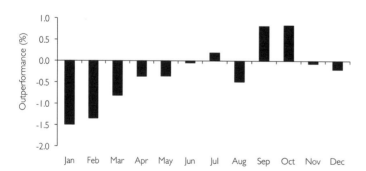

1. The FTSE 250 tends to outperform the FTSE 100 in the first three months of the year and in August; it is particularly relatively strong in January and February.

2. The FTSE 100 is strong relative to the FTSE 250 in September and October.

3. In recent years (since 2000) the above characteristics have if anything been even stronger, suggesting a certain degree of persistency.

Mon

10

1996: The IBM supercomputer, Deep Blue, defeats Garry Kasparov at chess for the first time.

FTSE 100	35	-0.3	0.8
FTSE 250	40	-0.3	0.8
S&P 500	50	0.0	1.0
NIKKEI	57	0.1	0.8

Tue

11

National Foundation Day (Japan) – TSE closed

1990: Nelson Mandela is released from Victor Verster Prison outside Cape Town, South Africa, after serving 27 years as a political prisoner.

FTSE 100	62	0.4	1.0
FTSE 250	80	0.3	0.7
S&P 500	53	0.0	0.9
NIKKEI			

Wed

12

MPC Inflation Report published
MSCI Quarterly Index Review (announcement date)

2002: Body Shop shares fall 10% on the announcement that its founder and co-chairman, Anita Roddick, is to step down, and that the company is pulling out of takeover talks.

FTSE 100	38	-0.1	1.2
FTSE 250	55	0.1	0.9
S&P 500	54	0.1	0.8
NIKKEI	76	0.4	1.4

Thu

13

100th anniversary of the founding of the American Society of Composers, Authors and Publishers (ASCAP), established to protect the copyrighted musical compositions of its members

1663: Galileo Galilei arrives in Rome for his trial before the Inquisition.

FTSE 100	67	0.2	0.6
FTSE 250	70	0.1	0.5
S&P 500	56	0.2	0.7
NIKKEI	45	-0.2	1.0

Fri

14

St Valentine's Day
Full moon

2013: The Food Safety Authority of Ireland reveals the results of a targeted study that has found undeclared horse DNA in frozen beefburgers on sale in Tesco, Iceland, Aldi and Lidl.

FTSE 100	43	0.0	0.7
FTSE 250	60	0.2	0.6
S&P 500	43	0.0	0.7
NIKKEI	73	0.3	1.4

Sat 15   450th anniversary of the birth of Galileo Galilei, Italian astronomer and physicist.

Sun 16

COMPANY NEWS

Interims Dunelm Group
Finals African Barrick Gold Ltd, AMEC, Barclays, Catlin Group Ltd, Fidessa Group, Morgan Advance Material, Reckitt Benckiser Group, Rio Tinto, Rolls-Royce Group, Shire, SVG Capital, Telecity Group, Tullow Oil

"Money, if it does not bring you happiness, will at least help you be miserable in comfort."
Helen Gurley Brown

FRANCE

This week sees the 200th anniversary of the Great Stock Exchange Fraud of 1814. Briefly, a uniformed man arrived in Dover on the morning of 21 February with news that Napoleon Bonaparte had been killed and the Bourbon Dynasty was restored to the kingdom of France. The news spread quickly and when it reached London the value of government securities rocketed. However, by the afternoon it was realised this was a hoax and prices of the securities fell back to their original levels. Another run-of-the-mill day in the stock market.

An interesting side story is that the chief perpetrators of the hoax were sentenced to twelve months prison, a fine of £1000, and an hour in the public pillory. One of those charged was the naval hero Lord Cochrane and such was the popular outcry at his sentence that subsequently the punishment of the public pillory was officially discontinued in Britain. (Although no doubt some would like it reinstated for dodgy financiers.)

On the topic of beating the French, the following chart shows the average monthly outperformance of the FTSE 100 over the CAC 40 (in sterling terms) from 1990 to 2013. For example, on average the CAC 40 (£) outperformed the FTSE 100 by 1.6 percentage points in January over the period.

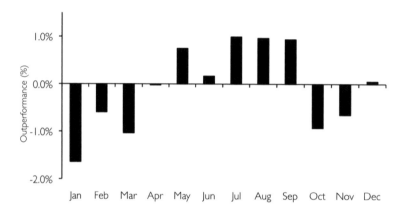

The FTSE 100 has historically been strong relative to the CAC 40 (£) in the months of May and August; while it has been weak in January, March and November (this behaviour is also reflected in recent years, since 2003).

The chart below shows the performance of the FTSE 100 and the CAC 40 (again in sterling terms) since 1990.

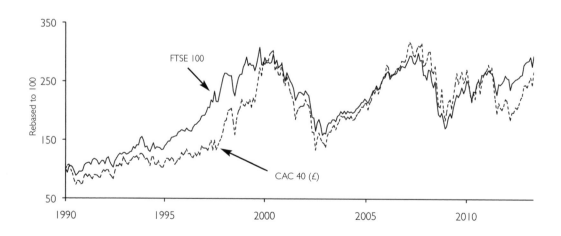

It is rather remarkable quite how closely the two markets have tracked each other – especially during the period 2000 to 2011.

52, 0.0, 2.3 **Week 8**

Mon	Presidents' Day (US) – NYSE closed 6th strongest market day

17

FTSE 100	75	0.4	0.9
FTSE 250	80	0.3	1.0
S&P 500			
NIKKEI	76	0.5	1.1

2003: The London Congestion Charge scheme begins.

Tue	450th anniversary of the death of Michelangelo

18

FTSE 100	40	0.0	0.7
FTSE 250	65	0.3	0.7
S&P 500	53	0.1	0.9
NIKKEI	50	0.1	1.3

1979: Snow falls in the Sahara Desert in southern Algeria for the only time in recorded history.

Wed	MPC meeting minutes published ECB Governing Council Meeting

19

FTSE 100	48	0.0	1.1
FTSE 250	55	0.0	0.7
S&P 500	49	-0.1	0.9
NIKKEI	52	-0.1	0.9

1987: Apple registers the Apple.com domain name, making it one of the first hundred companies to register a .com address on the nascent internet.

Thu	

20

FTSE 100	43	-0.3	1.1
FTSE 250	45	-0.2	0.9
S&P 500	53	0.0	0.9
NIKKEI	41	-0.2	1.2

1811: Austria declares itself bankrupt.

Fri	20th anniversary of the LSE flotation of Herald Investment Trust

21

FTSE 100	43	-0.1	0.8
FTSE 250	35	-0.2	0.6
S&P 500	32	-0.2	0.7
NIKKEI	41	0.2	1.8

1814: The Great Stock Exchange Fraud takes place in London.

Sat 22

Sun 23

COMPANY NEWS

Interims Ashmore Group, BHP Billiton, Galliford Try, Go-Ahead Group, Murray Income Trust
Finals Anglo American, AZ Electronic Materials SA, BAE Systems, BlackRock World Mining Trust, CSR, Drax Group, Essentra, Herald Investment Trust, Informa, InterContinental Hotels Group, Ladbrokes, Lancashire Holdings Ltd, Mondi, Rathbone Brothers, Rexam, RSA Insurance Group, Spectris, Temple Bar Investment Trust, Travis Perkins

"Finance is the art of passing currency from hand to hand until it finally disappears."
Robert Sarnoff

SECTOR MONTHLY SEASONALITY

The following chart plots the average outperformance of the FTSE 350 Software & Computer Services sector over the FTSE 100 by month since 1999. For example, since 1999 on average the sector has outperformed the FTSE 100 Index by 4.4 percentage points in January.

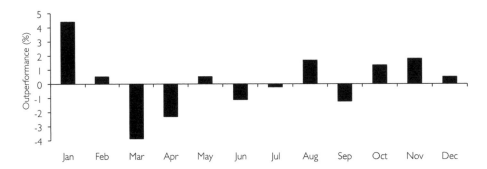

From the above chart we can see that since 1999 the sector has been especially strong in January and weak in March.

By similarly analysing all FTSE 350 sectors we can draw up a calendar (below) of all the sectors and their respective strongest and weakest months.

	Strong	Weak
January	Construction & Materials, Electronic & Electrical Equipment, Financial Services, General Industrials, Media, Software & Computer Services, Support Services, Equity Investment Instruments, Industrial Metals & Mining, Industrial Transportation, Automobiles & Parts, Health Care Equipment & Services	Food & Drug Retailers, Food Producers, Beverages
February	General Retailers, Chemicals, Mining, Construction & Materials, Household Goods, Oil Equipment, Services & Distribution, Automobiles & Parts, Tobacco	Electronic & Electrical Equipment, Financial Services, Fixed Line Telecommunications, Technology Hardware & Equipment, Mobile Telecommunications
March	Industrial Engineering, Aerospace & Defense, General Retailers, Financial Services, General Industrials, Oil & Gas Producers, Oil Equipment, Services & Distribution	Gas, Water & Multiutilities, Nonlife Insurance, Health Care Equipment & Services
April	Industrial Engineering, Electronic & Electrical Equipment, Personal Goods	Mining, Household Goods, Software & Computer Services, Mobile Telecommunications
May	Aerospace & Defense, Gas, Water & Multiutilities, Food Producers, Equity Investment Instruments, Tobacco, Electricity	General Industrials, Life Insurance
June	Pharmaceuticals & Biotechnology, Oil & Gas Producers, Beverages	
July	Chemicals, Personal Goods, Real Estate Investment Trusts, Technology Hardware & Equipment	Gas, Water & Multiutilities, Support Services, Beverages, Industrial Transportation
August	Gas, Water & Multiutilities, Food & Drug Retailers, Household Goods, Software & Computer Services, Health Care Equipment & Services	Chemicals
September	Pharmaceuticals & Biotechnology, Food & Drug Retailers, Electricity, Mobile Telecommunications	Industrial Engineering, Aerospace & Defense, General Retailers, Chemicals, Electronic & Electrical Equipment, Media, Real Estate Investment Trusts, Technology Hardware & Equipment, Industrial Metals & Mining, Automobiles & Parts
October		Pharmaceuticals & Biotechnology, Construction & Materials, Food & Drug Retailers, Household Goods, Life Insurance, Equity Investment Instruments, Industrial Transportation, Automobiles & Parts, Health Care Equipment & Services, Electricity
November	Mining, Electronic & Electrical Equipment, Fixed Line Telecommunications, Food Producers, Life Insurance, Media, Technology Hardware & Equipment, Travel & Leisure, Beverages	Aerospace & Defense, General Industrials, Oil & Gas Producers, Real Estate Investment Trusts, Banks
December	Construction & Materials, Life Insurance, Support Services, Travel & Leisure, Mobile Telecommunications	General Retailers, Pharmaceuticals & Biotechnology, Banks

Mon

24

2011: The final launch of Space Shuttle Discovery (OV-103) takes place at Cape Canaveral, Florida.

FTSE 100	40	-0.1	0.9
FTSE 250	55	0.0	0.6
S&P 500	53	0.1	1.1
NIKKEI	50	-0.4	1.2

Tue

25

1913: The Sixteenth Amendment, which effectively paves the path for the United States' adoption of an income tax, is ratified.

FTSE 100	71	0.4	1.1
FTSE 250	70	0.5	1.0
S&P 500	51	0.0	0.9
NIKKEI	86	0.7	1.2

Wed

26

1936: Adolf Hitler opens the first Volkswagen plant in eastern Germany.

FTSE 100	57	0.2	0.9
FTSE 250	60	0.2	0.7
S&P 500	60	0.1	0.8
NIKKEI	48	-0.2	1.3

Thu

27

425: The University of Constantinople is founded by Emperor Theodosius II at the urging of his wife Aelia Eudocia.

FTSE 100	48	-0.1	0.9
FTSE 250	70	0.0	1.1
S&P 500	48	-0.2	0.9
NIKKEI	55	0.2	1.6

Fri

28

2013: Benedict XVI resigns as Pope, the first to do so since Gregory XII in 1415, and the first to do so voluntarily since Celestine V in 1294.

FTSE 100	48	-0.2	1.1
FTSE 250	60	0.1	0.7
S&P 500	57	0.0	0.6
NIKKEI	64	0.1	1.3

Sat 1   St David's Day, New moon

Sun 2   10th anniversary of the LSE flotation of CSR

COMPANY NEWS

Interims Barratt Developments, Dechra Pharmaceuticals, Genesis Emerging Markets Fund Ltd, Genus, Hays, JPMorgan Emerging Markets Investment Trust, Kier Group, Petra Diamonds Ltd, Redrow

Finals Bodycote, Bovis Homes Group, British American Tobacco, Bunzl, Capita Group, Capital & Counties Properties, Carillion, Centrica, COLT Group SA, CRH, Croda International, Derwent London, Devro, Dialight, Direct Line Insurance Group, Domino's Pizza UK & IRL, Elementis, Fidelity European Values, GKN, Henderson Group, Hiscox Ltd, Howden Joinery Group, International Consolidated Airlines Group SA, Interserve, Intu Properties, ITV, Jupiter Fund Management, Man Group, Millennium & Copthorne Hotels, Murray International Trust, National Express Group, NMC Health, Pearson, Persimmon, Petrofac Ltd, Provident Financial, Reed Elsevier, Restaurant Group, RIT Capital Partners, Royal Bank of Scotland Group, RPS Group, Segro, Senior, Spirent Communications, St James's Place, Weir Group

"Money is not the most important thing in the world. Love is. Fortunately, I love money."
Jackie Mason

MARCH MARKET

Market performance this month

March is a middling month for the market, ranking 7th of all months in performance. Since 1984 the market has risen in 59% of years with an average return of 0.7% in the month.

The general trend for the market in March is to rise for the first three weeks and then fall back in the final week – the last week of March has historically been one of the weakest weeks in the whole year.

FTSE 100	59	0.7	3.4
FTSE 250	61	1.4	4.0
S&P 500	66	1.2	3.4
NIKKEI	60	1.7	6.8

March marks the end of the 3-month period when mid-cap stocks strongly outperform large caps: on average the FTSE 250 has outperformed the FTSE 100 by 0.8 percentage points this month.

This is another busy month of company announcements: the busiest for FTSE 250 companies in the year with 74 companies announcing their prelims this month (along with 29 FTSE 100 companies).

Events to watch out for this month include the FTSE 100 review on the 12th and triple witching on the 21st.

Performance of market in March [1970 to 2013]

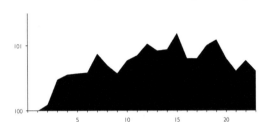

FTSE 100 average month chart for March [1985 to 2013]

Trading days

MARCH SUMMARY			
Market performance	Average return: 0.7%	Positive: 59%	Ranking: 7th
Sector performance	*Strong* Aerospace & Defense, Financial Services, General Industrials, General Retailers, Industrial Engineering, Oil & Gas Producers, Oil Equipment, Services & Distribution	*Weak* Gas, Water & Multiutilities, Health Care Equipment & Services, Nonlife Insurance	
Share performance	*Strong* Aggreko, Cobham, IMI, Intertek Group, Restaurant Group (The)	*Weak* Aviva, HSBC Holdings, RSA Insurance Group, Renishaw, Royal Bank of Scotland Group (The)	
Main features of the month	The FTSE 250 is particularly strong relative to the FTSE 100 in this month Weak month for gold price Busiest month for FTSE 250 preliminary results announcements First trading day average return: 0.00%; positive: 57% (2nd weakest in year) Last trading day average return: 0.12%; positive: 52%		
Significant dates	06 Mar: MPC interest rate announcement at 12 noon (anticipated) 07 Mar: US Nonfarm payroll report (anticipated) 12 Mar: FTSE 100 Index review announced 19 Mar: Chancellor's Budget (anticipated) 20 Mar: Two-day FOMC meeting starts 21 Mar: Triple Witching		

Mon

3

MSCI Quarterly Index Review (effective date)

1865: The founding member of the HSBC Group, Hongkong and Shanghai Banking Corporation, opens for business.

FTSE 100	55	0.1	1.0
FTSE 250	65	0.2	0.5
S&P 500	69	0.1	0.7
NIKKEI	40	-0.3	1.4

Tue

4

Shrove Tuesday (Pancake Day)

1797: In the first ever peaceful transfer of power between elected leaders in modern times, John Adams is sworn in as President of the United States, succeeding George Washington.

FTSE 100	57	0.4	1.2
FTSE 250	80	0.5	1.0
S&P 500	53	0.2	0.9
NIKKEI	76	0.5	1.4

Wed

5

Ash Wednesday (Lent begins)
Beige Book published

1980: The Hunt brothers' attempt to corner the silver market comes to a disastrous end when they receive a $135m margin call from their broker which they can't pay, triggering an avalanche of sell orders and a collapse in the value of their 4000 'long' contracts.

FTSE 100	52	0.1	1.3
FTSE 250	60	0.0	1.1
S&P 500	59	0.1	1.0
NIKKEI	50	0.2	1.4

Thu

6

MPC interest rate announcement at 12h00
ECB Governing Council Meeting

2000: Vodafone closes at all-time high of 399.

FTSE 100	52	0.2	1.0
FTSE 250	65	0.1	1.1
S&P 500	48	0.0	0.9
NIKKEI	59	0.3	1.4

Fri

7

Winter Paralympics, Sochi, Russia (until 16 March)
Nonfarm payroll report (anticipated)

1966: The first North Sea gas lands in the UK.

FTSE 100	48	-0.2	0.8
FTSE 250	60	-0.1	0.9
S&P 500	46	-0.2	0.7
NIKKEI	45	-0.4	1.3

Sat 8

Sun 9   50th anniversary of the first Ford Mustang rolling off the assembly line.

COMPANY NEWS

Interims Regus

Finals Admiral Group, Aggreko, Amlin, Aviva, Balfour Beatty, BBA Aviation, Berendsen, Cobham, Dignity, Fisher (James) & Sons, Foreign & Colonial Investment Trust, Glencore Xstrata, Hammerson, HSBC Holdings, Hunting, IMI, Inmarsat, International Personal Finance, Intertek Group, IP Group, Jardine Lloyd Thompson Group, John Wood Group, Keller Group, Laird, Law Debenture Corporation, Legal & General Group, Lloyds Banking Group, Meggitt, Melrose Industries, Menzies (John), Michael Page International, Moneysupermarket.com Group, Old Mutual, Ophir Energy, Pace, Perform Group, Regus, Rightmove, Rotork, Schroders, Serco Group, SIG, Spirax-Sarco Engineering, Standard Chartered, Standard Life, Taylor Wimpey, Tullett Prebon, UBM, Ultra Electronics Holdings, UNITE Group, William Hill, WPP Group

"It doesn't matter if you're black or white... the only colour that really matters is green."
Family Guy

FTSE 100 REVIEWS – COMPANIES JOINING THE INDEX

The charts below show the share price of 9 companies that have joined the FTSE 100 in the past year. The time period for each chart is 6 months, starting from 3 months before the company joined the index. Therefore it is possible to see the share price behaviour in the 3 months leading up to joining, and the 3 months after.

The dotted line on each chart marks the point at which the company joined the index.

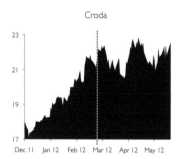

Croda

Aberdeen Asset Management

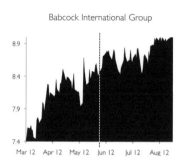

Babcock International Group

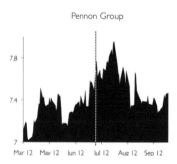

Pennon Group

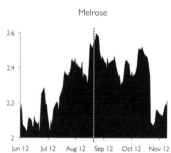

Melrose

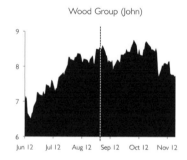

Wood Group (John)

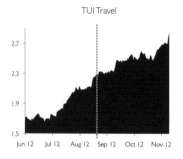

TUI Travel

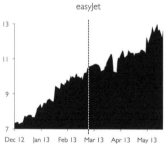

easyJet

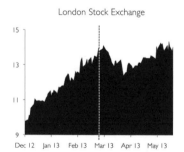

London Stock Exchange

Observation

It can be seen that, in most cases, the share price rises immediately before the company joins the FTSE 100, while immediately afterwards the price is usually flat or falls back again.

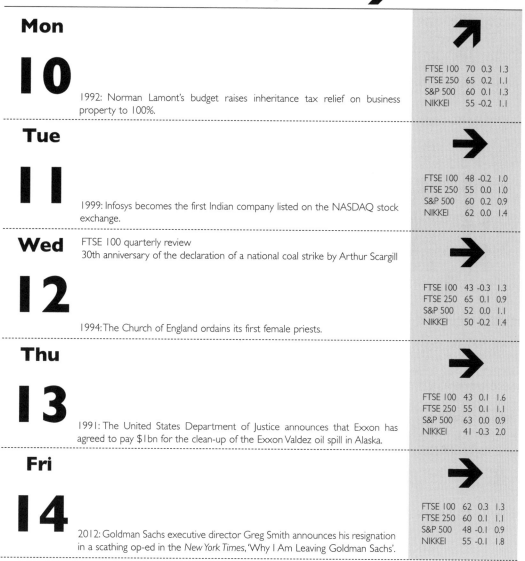

Mon

10

1992: Norman Lamont's budget raises inheritance tax relief on business property to 100%.

FTSE 100	70	0.3	1.3
FTSE 250	65	0.2	1.1
S&P 500	60	0.1	1.3
NIKKEI	55	-0.2	1.1

Tue

11

1999: Infosys becomes the first Indian company listed on the NASDAQ stock exchange.

FTSE 100	48	-0.2	1.0
FTSE 250	55	0.0	1.0
S&P 500	60	0.2	0.9
NIKKEI	62	0.0	1.4

Wed

FTSE 100 quarterly review
30th anniversary of the declaration of a national coal strike by Arthur Scargill

12

1994: The Church of England ordains its first female priests.

FTSE 100	43	-0.3	1.3
FTSE 250	65	0.1	0.9
S&P 500	52	0.0	1.1
NIKKEI	50	-0.2	1.4

Thu

13

1991: The United States Department of Justice announces that Exxon has agreed to pay $1bn for the clean-up of the Exxon Valdez oil spill in Alaska.

FTSE 100	43	0.1	1.6
FTSE 250	55	0.1	1.1
S&P 500	63	0.0	0.9
NIKKEI	41	-0.3	2.0

Fri

14

2012: Goldman Sachs executive director Greg Smith announces his resignation in a scathing op-ed in the *New York Times*, 'Why I Am Leaving Goldman Sachs'.

FTSE 100	62	0.3	1.3
FTSE 250	60	0.1	1.1
S&P 500	48	-0.1	0.9
NIKKEI	55	-0.1	1.8

Sat 15

Sun 16   Full moon, Formula 1: Australian Grand Prix, Albert Park Melbourne Circuit

COMPANY NEWS

Interims Close Brothers Group
Finals 888 Holdings, Alliance Trust, Antofagasta, Computacenter, F&C Asset Management, Ferrexpo, Fresnillo, G4S, Hansteen Holdings, Hikma Pharmaceuticals, Hochschild Mining, Inchcape, Kenmare Resources, Morrison (Wm) Supermarkets, Playtech, Prudential, Salamander Energy, Savills, SOCO International, Witan Investment Trust

"If you would know the value of money, go and try to borrow some."
Benjamin Franklin

GOLD

46 years ago this week (on 17 March 1968) the system that fixed the price of gold at USD35.00 collapsed and the price of gold was allowed to fluctuate.

The chart on the left below shows the average price returns for gold by month since 1986. The chart on the right shows the proportion of months that have seen positive returns for the same period, 1986 to 2013.

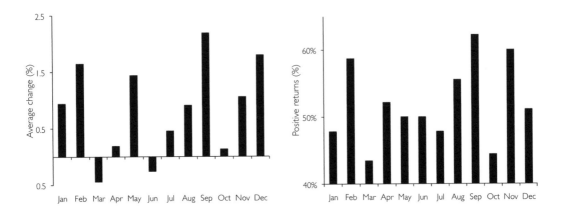

It can be seen that gold has been historically strong in February, September and November, and weak in March and October. This profile of behaviour would seem to have some persistency as the same pattern can be seen for the periods 1990 to 2013 and 2000 to 2013.

Gold and equities

The following chart shows the ratio of the FTSE All-Share Index to gold (priced in sterling) since 1968. (One can regard the chart as the UK equity market priced in gold.)

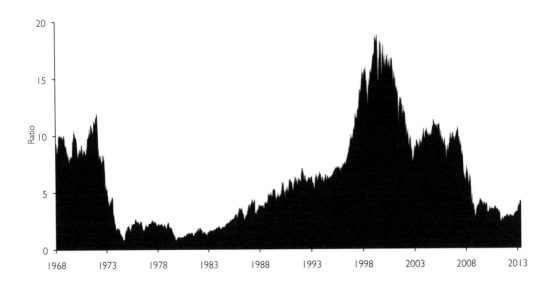

The ratio peaked at 18.8 in July 1999 and then fell to a low of 2.3 in September 2011. Since 1968 the ratio average is 6.3.

Mon
17
St Patrick's Day
9th weakest market week

2008: J.P. Morgan buys Bear Stearns for just $240m – a $17.75bn discount on its value a year earlier – as the Wall Street bank comes close to imploding.

FTSE 100	55	0.0	1.4
FTSE 250	65	0.1	1.1
S&P 500	62	0.2	1.1
NIKKEI	65	0.3	1.5

Tue
18
Two-day FOMC meeting starts
800th anniversary of Jacques de Molay, the last Grand Master of the Knights Templar, being burnt at the stake

1990: In the largest art theft in US history, 12 paintings, collectively worth around $300m, are stolen from the Isabella Stewart Gardner Museum in Boston, Massachusetts.

FTSE 100	48	0.1	1.1
FTSE 250	50	0.2	0.9
S&P 500	56	0.2	0.9
NIKKEI	62	0.2	1.7

Wed
19
MPC meeting minutes published
ECB Governing Council Meeting

2008: Rio Tinto closes at all-time high of 5847.17.

FTSE 100	62	0.1	0.8
FTSE 250	55	0.2	0.8
S&P 500	43	-0.1	0.8
NIKKEI	59	0.5	1.7

Thu
20
Spring Equinox, also known as Ostara
ECB General Council Meeting

2000: Several 'new economy' stocks join the FTSE 100 – the biggest shake-up ever for the index. The new stocks are: Baltimore, C&W Comms, Capita, Celltech, EMAP, Freeserve, Kingston Comms, Nycomed Amersham, Psion and Thus.

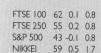

FTSE 100	48	0.1	1.0
FTSE 250	55	-0.1	0.8
S&P 500	48	0.0	0.8
NIKKEI	58	0.0	1.5

Fri
21
Triple Witching
Vernal Equinox (Japan) – TSE closed

1924: Mass Investors Trust becomes the first mutual fund set up in the US.

FTSE 100	45	0.0	1.0
FTSE 250	58	0.1	0.8
S&P 500	38	-0.1	0.9
NIKKEI			

Sat 22

Sun 23 Formula 1: Malaysian Grand Prix, Sepang International Circuit

COMPANY NEWS

Interims Smiths Group, Wetherspoon (J D)
Finals Bank of Georgia Holdings, Barr (A G), BH Global Ltd, BH Macro Ltd, Bwin.Party Digital Entertainment, Cairn Energy, Eurasian Natural Resources Corporation, Greggs, John Laing Infrastructure Fund Ltd, JPMorgan American Investment Trust, Mercantile Investment Trust, Next, Premier Farnell, Premier Oil, Rentokil Initial, Synthomer, Ted Baker, UK Commercial Property Trust Ltd, Vesuvius, Xaar

"The only place where success comes before work is in the dictionary."
Vidal Sassoon

EXXON V SHELL

It was 25 years ago this week that the Exxon Valdez ran aground in Prince William Sound in Alaska. The subsequent oil spill was one of the worst in US history. The tanker ran through several names after this incident (the name Exxon Valdez having become rather tainted) including Exxon Mediterranean, SeaRiver Mediterranean, Dong Fang Ocean and finally Oriental Nicety. In August 2012, the Oriental Nicety was beached (deliberately this time) on the Gujarat coast in advance of being dismantled.

Let's take this opportunity to look at Exxon Mobil shares and see if they have any correlation with those of Royal Dutch Shell shares (at the time of writing these are the two largest capitalised stocks in their respective markets).

The following scatter chart plots monthly returns of Exxon [XOM] shares against monthly returns of Royal Dutch Shell [RDSB] shares for the period 2000 to 2013. As Exxon shares are listed on the NYSE and are priced in US dollars the returns used here are the US dollar returns of Exxon converted into sterling.

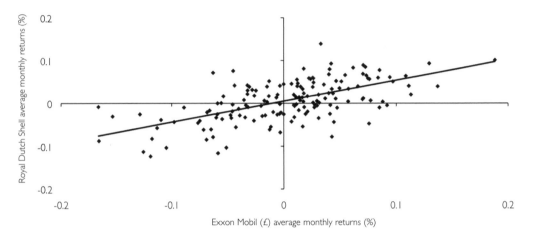

Looking at the scatter chart one can see that while the correlation is not as high as it might be, there is still some rough correlation there.

Now, to look at the comparative performance by month of these two companies.

The chart below shows the average monthly outperformance of Exxon shares (in sterling terms) over Shell shares. For example, since 2000 Exxon shares have outperformed Shell shares by an average of 2.4 percentage points in January.

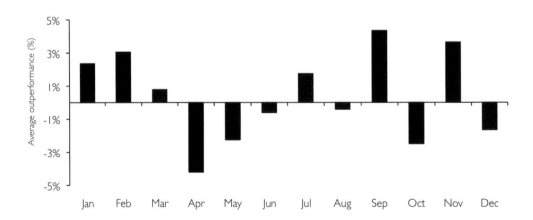

The chart shows that in recent years Exxon shares have outperformed Shell shares in January, February, September and November. Conversely, Shell shares have been the stronger in April and October.

Mon

10th weakest market week

24

FTSE 100	50	-0.2	1.4
FTSE 250	56	0.0	1.0
S&P 500	48	-0.2	1.1
NIKKEI	40	-0.1	1.6

1989: The Exxon Valdez oil tanker runs aground in Prince William Sound, Alaska.

Tue

200th anniversary of the establishment of De Nederlandsche Bank

25

FTSE 100	45	0.2	1.1
FTSE 250	42	0.1	1.1
S&P 500	41	0.1	0.8
NIKKEI	67	0.5	1.3

1085: William the Conqueror orders the first Domesday Survey of England.

Wed

26

FTSE 100	57	0.2	0.9
FTSE 250	45	0.1	0.5
S&P 500	57	0.1	0.8
NIKKEI	67	0.7	1.7

2007: Hammerson closes at all-time high of 11.8551.

Thu

Comet Holmes reaches perihelion

27

FTSE 100	50	0.0	1.0
FTSE 250	58	0.1	0.8
S&P 500	40	-0.1	0.9
NIKKEI	59	0.4	1.4

1871: The first international rugby match takes place between Scotland and England in Edinburgh at Raeburn Place. Scotland wins the match with two tries and one conversion, against England's one try.

Fri

28

FTSE 100	39	-0.3	0.7
FTSE 250	53	0.0	0.5
S&P 500	49	-0.1	0.8
NIKKEI	57	0.3	1.3

1979: The Three Mile Island partial nuclear meltdown occurs in Dauphin County, Pennsylvania.

Sat 29

Sun 30 Mother's Day, New moon, Start of BST (clocks go forward)

COMPANY NEWS

Interims Bellway, Wolseley

Finals Afren, Alent, Centamin, EnQuest, International Public Partnership Ltd, Kazakhmys, Kentz Corporation Ltd, Kingfisher, Merchants Trust, Phoenix Group Holdings, Resolution Ltd

"Money was never a big motivation for me, except as a way to keep score. The real excitement is playing the game."
Donald Trump

APRIL MARKET

Market performance this month

April is one of the most interesting months for the stock market. Five years ago April was the strongest month for the market in the year, but it is now ranked 2nd. On average the market rises 1.8% in this month and the probability of a positive return in the month is 69% based on its recent track record. From 1971 the market rose in April every year for 15 years – a recent record for any month – although the number of years with negative returns in the month has been increasing lately.

FTSE 100	69	1.8	3.6
FTSE 250	68	2.2	5.2
S&P 500	69	1.	3.8
NIKKEI	60	1.7	5.9

The market often gets off to a strong start in the month – the first trading day of April is the second strongest first trading day of all months in the year. The market tends to be fairly flat for the middle two weeks and then rises strongly in the final week.

From a seasonality viewpoint, the great significance of April is that it is the last month in the strong part of the six-month cycle.

Academic studies have shown that markets tend to be strong on the day immediately before a holiday and the day following a holiday. This effect is strongest around Easter – which occurs on the 20th this year.

Performance of market in April [1970 to 2013]

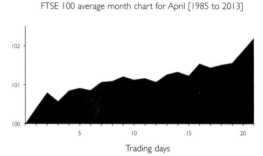

FTSE 100 average month chart for April [1985 to 2013]

Trading days

APRIL SUMMARY			
Market performance	Average return: 1.8%	Positive: 69%	Ranking: 2nd
Sector performance	Strong Electronic & Electrical Equipment, Industrial Engineering, Personal Goods		Weak Household Goods, Mining, Mobile Telecommunications, Software & Computer Services
Share performance	Strong Diploma, Menzies (John), Royal Dutch Shell, Severn Trent, Xaar		Weak Balfour Beatty, Centamin, Shire, UNITE Group
Main features of the month	2nd strongest month in the year Market abnormally strong on day before and day after Easter holiday GBPUSD historically strong this month First trading day average return: 0.50%; positive: 70% (2nd strongest in year) Last trading day average return: 0.17%; positive: 53% 8 Apr: 3rd weakest market day of the year 14 Apr: 4th weakest market day of the year		
Significant dates	04 Apr: US Nonfarm payroll report (anticipated) 10 Apr: MPC interest rate announcement at 12 noon (anticipated) 19 Apr: Good Friday – LSE, NYSE, HKSE closed 21 Apr: Easter Monday – LSE HKSE closed 29 Apr: Two-day FOMC meetings starts		

Mon

31

8th strongest market week

1980: The Chicago, Rock Island and Pacific railroad operates its final train after being ordered to liquidate its assets because of bankruptcy and debts.

FTSE 100	44	0.1	1.4
FTSE 250	33	-0.1	0.9
S&P 500	40	0.0	0.7
NIKKEI	35	-0.6	1.6

Tue

1

7th strongest market day
50th anniversary of the LSE flotation of Elementis

1933: English cricketer Wally Hammond sets a record for the highest individual Test innings of 336 not out, during a Test match against New Zealand.

FTSE 100	75	0.5	1.2
FTSE 250	67	0.4	1.4
S&P 500	69	0.3	0.9
NIKKEI	57	0.2	1.7

Wed

2

2002: Caffè Nero agrees to buy the Aroma coffee house chain from McDonalds for £2.15m. The 31-site Aroma chain made an operating loss of £3.7m in 2001.

FTSE 100	68	0.7	1.2
FTSE 250	89	0.6	1.0
S&P 500	52	0.1	1.0
NIKKEI	59	0.1	2.3

Thu

3

ECB Governing Council Meeting

1954: Oxford wins the 100th Boat Race.

FTSE 100	41	-0.3	1.1
FTSE 250	50	-0.1	1.0
S&P 500	51	0.0	1.0
NIKKEI	68	0.5	1.7

Fri

4

Nonfarm payroll report (anticipated)

1975: Microsoft is founded as a partnership between Bill Gates and Paul Allen.

FTSE 100	50	0.0	0.9
FTSE 250	56	-0.2	0.9
S&P 500	53	-0.1	0.6
NIKKEI	45	0.0	1.1

Sat 5   Horseracing: Grand National, Aintree Racecourse

Sun 6   Rowing: Oxford and Cambridge Boat Race

COMPANY NEWS

Interims

Finals

"Those who cast the votes decide nothing. Those who count the votes decide everything."
Joseph Stalin

MARKET BEHAVIOUR – BY DAY

The two tables below list the historic 10 best and worst days for the market since 1984.

For example, historically the very best day of the whole year has been 27 December; the market has risen on this day in 85% of all years. And on this day the market has risen by an average of 0.4.%. The second strongest day of the year is 24 December.

Considering a combination of the average change on days and their standard deviation the strongest day of the year could be considered to be 23 December.

A small observation to make is that all the ten strongest days occur in the first or last week of months.

On the reverse side, the worst day of the year is 30 May – the market has only risen on this day in 22% of previous years and has fallen by an average of 0.4% on this day.

The performance figures below are ranked by the Positive (%) column – the percentage of years that the market has a positive return on the day.

10 strongest days in the year

Day	Positive (%)	Avg Chng (%)	StdDev
27 Dec	85	0.4	1.2
24 Dec	81	0.2	0.6
26 Jan	80	0.7	1.1
23 Dec	80	0.4	0.6
02 May	76	0.5	0.9
27 Sep	76	0.7	1.1
02 Aug	76	0.6	1.1
01 Oct	76	0.4	1.5
31 Oct	76	0.4	1.1
05 Oct	76	0.3	1.7

10 weakest days in the year

Day	Positive (%)	Avg Chng (%)	StdDev
30 May	22	-0.4	1.3
08 Jul	25	-0.2	0.9
08 Apr	26	-0.3	0.7
14 Apr	28	-0.3	0.9
10 Aug	29	-0.6	1.3
07 Jan	29	-0.2	1.0
20 Jan	30	-0.5	0.8
04 Aug	30	-0.4	0.9
09 Sep	30	-0.3	0.8
11 Sep	30	-0.1	0.9

Note: The above best days for the market are marked on the diary pages with a square around the arrow icon and the worst days are marked on the diary pages with a circle around the arrow icon.

Analysis of all days

Average Positive (%) [StdDev]	52.4 [11.0]
Average Change (%) [StdDev]	0.03 [0.25]

Since 1984 the market has risen on 52% of all days with an average daily return of 0.03%.

The standard deviation is 11 for the average Positive (%) value, which means that:

• days that have a Positive (%) value over 63 (the average plus one standard deviation) can be considered **strong** days, and

• days that have a Positive (%) value under 41 (the average minus one standard deviation) can be considered **weak** days.

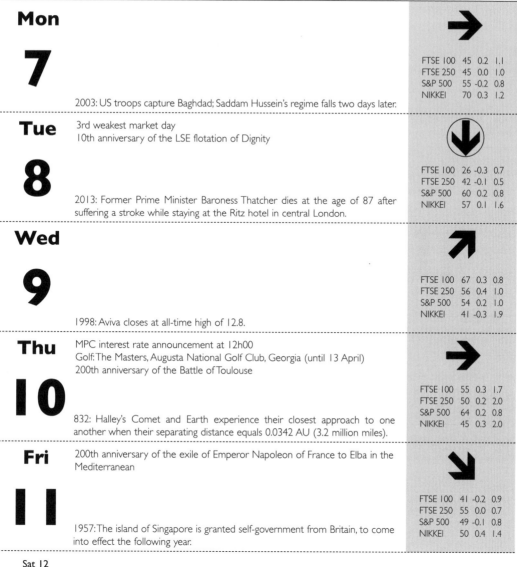

Mon
7

FTSE 100   45   0.2   1.1
FTSE 250   45   0.0   1.0
S&P 500   55   -0.2   0.8
NIKKEI   70   0.3   1.2

2003: US troops capture Baghdad; Saddam Hussein's regime falls two days later.

Tue
8

3rd weakest market day
10th anniversary of the LSE flotation of Dignity

FTSE 100   26   -0.3   0.7
FTSE 250   42   -0.1   0.5
S&P 500   60   0.2   0.8
NIKKEI   57   0.1   1.6

2013: Former Prime Minister Baroness Thatcher dies at the age of 87 after suffering a stroke while staying at the Ritz hotel in central London.

Wed
9

FTSE 100   67   0.3   0.8
FTSE 250   56   0.4   1.0
S&P 500   54   0.2   1.0
NIKKEI   41   -0.3   1.9

1998: Aviva closes at all-time high of 12.8.

Thu
10

MPC interest rate announcement at 12h00
Golf: The Masters, Augusta National Golf Club, Georgia (until 13 April)
200th anniversary of the Battle of Toulouse

FTSE 100   55   0.3   1.7
FTSE 250   50   0.2   2.0
S&P 500   64   0.2   0.8
NIKKEI   45   0.3   2.0

832: Halley's Comet and Earth experience their closest approach to one another when their separating distance equals 0.0342 AU (3.2 million miles).

Fri
11

200th anniversary of the exile of Emperor Napoleon of France to Elba in the Mediterranean

FTSE 100   41   -0.2   0.9
FTSE 250   55   0.0   0.7
S&P 500   49   -0.1   0.8
NIKKEI   50   0.4   1.4

1957: The island of Singapore is granted self-government from Britain, to come into effect the following year.

Sat 12

Sun 13   Palm Sunday (Christian), Formula 1: Chinese Grand Prix, Shanghai Circuit

COMPANY NEWS

Interims WH Smith
Finals Evraz, Polymetal International

"Anyone who lives within their means suffers from a lack of imagination."
Oscar Wilde

HOLIDAYS AND THE MARKET

In 1990 an academic paper[1] was published with the finding that the trading day prior to holidays in the US market had an average return 14 times greater than the average for the other days in the year. This, and other papers, found that the day immediately before holidays had the highest returns (in the period around holidays), with the third day before the holidays having the next highest return and the day following the holiday having negative returns.

Does such a holiday effect exist in the UK market?

The following charts show the results of research on the daily returns of the FTSE 100 around holidays. The four trading days immediately prior to holidays, H(-4) to H(-1), and the three trading days after holidays, H(+1) to H(+3) were analysed. A holiday was defined as a 3-day (or longer) period with no trading. The bars in the chart show the average return on the seven days around holidays. The chart on the left is for the period 1984 to 2013, the chart on the right for the period 2000 to 2013.

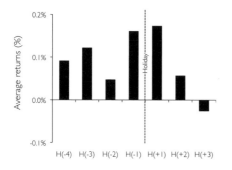
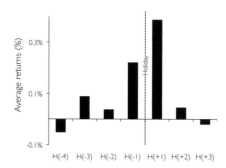

From the chart on the left we can see that, as with the US studies, H(-3) and H(-1) were strong during the holiday periods. Although, unlike the US studies, the day after a holiday, H(+1), was also found to be strong – this day has an average return of 0.17% (six times greater than the average return for all days in the year).

Looking at the chart on the right it can be seen that the UK holiday effect has changed slightly in recent years. In the last ten years or so the market has still been significantly strong on the days immediately before and after holidays but weak on the fourth day before and third day after holidays.

As Easter is upon us, let's look specifically at the market around the Easter holiday.

Easter

As above, the following charts analyse the market behaviour around holidays, but this time the data is restricted to just Easter holidays.

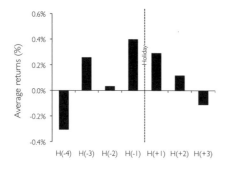
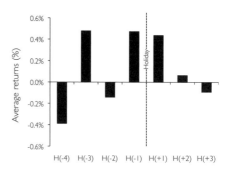

Looking at the chart on the left, the general profile of behaviour around Easter can be seen to be similar to that for all holidays. The main differences are that H(-4) is significantly weak, and the average returns for the two days immediately before and after Easter are significantly higher than for all holidays. For example, the average return for H(+1) is 0.4% (13 times greater than the average return for all days in the year).

The chart on the right shows that the behaviour of the market around Easter has not changed significantly in recent years.

[1] Ariel, R. A. 'High stock returns before holidays: existence and evidence on possible causes', *Journal of Finance* (1990).

Mon

14

4th weakest market day

FTSE 100	28	-0.3	09
FTSE 250	44	0.0	0.9
S&P 500	58	-0.1	1.5
NIKKEI	45	-0.2	1.2

1998: Lloyds Bank closes at all-time high of 533.26.

Tue

15

Passover (until 23 April)
Full moon
Total lunar eclipse (visible from North America, South America and Australia)
25th anniversary of the Hillsborough disaster

FTSE 100	62	0.3	0.9
FTSE 250	70	0.2	0.8
S&P 500	70	0.2	0.7
NIKKEI	52	0.1	1.2

2013: Two bombs explode at the Boston Marathon in Massachusetts, killing three people and injuring 264.

Wed

16

Beige Book published
ECB Governing Council Meeting
50th anniversary of the release of *The Rolling Stones*, the band's debut album

FTSE 100	55	0.1	1.2
FTSE 250	61	0.4	0.8
S&P 500	58	0.2	1.0
NIKKEI	59	-0.3	1.4

2001: The Labour government overtakes Unilever and Proctor & Gamble to become the biggest advertiser in the country.

Thu

17

FTSE 100	56	0.0	1.1
FTSE 250	50	-0.1	1.2
S&P 500	63	0.3	1.0
NIKKEI	50	-0.2	1.9

1973: George Lucas begins writing the treatment for *The Star Wars*.

Fri

18

Good Friday
LSE, NYSE, HKSE closed

FTSE 100			
FTSE 250			
S&P 500			
NIKKEI	59	0.3	1.7

1980: The Republic of Zimbabwe (formerly Rhodesia) comes into being, with Canaan Banana as the country's first President. The Zimbabwe dollar replaces the Rhodesian dollar as the official currency.

Sat 19

Sun 20   Easter Sunday, Formula 1: Bahrain Grand Prix, Bahrain International Circuit

COMPANY NEWS

Interims Debenhams
Finals NB Global Floating Rate Income Fund Ltd, Tesco

"Money frees you from doing things you dislike. Since I dislike doing nearly everything, money is handy."
Groucho Marx

SIX-MONTH EFFECT

The six-month effect is the strongest – and strangest – seasonality effect in the market. We begin by splitting the year into two six-month periods:

1 *winter period*: 1 November to 30 April

2 *summer period*: 1 May to 31 October

The chart to the right compares the performance since 1982 of the FTSE All-Share Index for the two periods; each bar represents the outperformance of the winter period over the following summer period. For example, from 1 November 2011 to 30 April 2012 the index rose 4.3%, while during the following period 1 May 2012 to 31 October 2012 the index increased 1.3%. The difference in performance was therefore 3.0 percentage points, and that is the figure plotted on the chart for 2012.

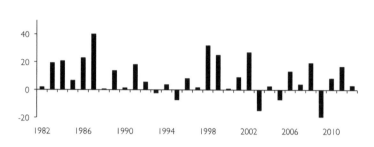

The chart shows a quite remarkable thing, namely that the market seems to perform much better in the six-month winter period than the summer period:

- in the 31 years since 1982, the winter period has outperformed the summer period 26 times
- the average annual outperformance since 1982 has been 9%!

The behaviour is extraordinary and should not exist in a modern, efficient(ish) market. But the UK stock market is not the only market to display such an effect.

The six-month effect is global

An academic paper[1] published in 2012 gives the results of a study that crunched the numbers on all available data for 108 stock markets to see how widespread the six-month effect (aka Sell in May or Halloween Effect) might be.

The authors found evidence for the effect in 81 out 108 countries, and of it being statistically significant in 35 countries.

The strongest six month effects were found among Western European countries for the past 50 years. They also found that the effect had been strengthening in recent years.

The chart to the right is from the paper and shows average returns for November to April periods (back row) compared to average returns for May to October periods for developed markets.

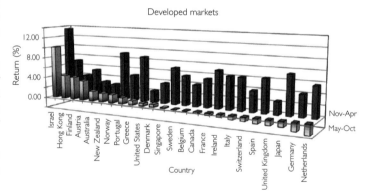

The first mention of the market adage "Sell in May" the authors found was in the *Financial Times* of 10 May 1935:

> A shrewd North Country correspondent who likes a stock exchange flutter now and again writes me that he and his friends are at present drawing in their horns on the strength of the old adage "Sell in May and go away."

A "stock exchange flutter" – does anyone say this any more?

---

[1] Jacobsen, Ben and Zhang, Cherry Yi, 'The Halloween Indicator: Everywhere and All the Time' (October 1, 2012).

Mon

Easter Monday
LSE, HKSE closed

21

FTSE 100			
FTSE 250			
S&P 500	55	0.3	0.8
NIKKEI	45	-0.1	1.4

2006: BP closes at all-time high of 712.

Tue

→

22

FTSE 100	45	0.1	0.8
FTSE 250	68	0.2	0.7
S&P 500	41	0.0	1.1
NIKKEI	52	0.0	1.0

1864: The US Congress passes the Coinage Act which mandates that the inscription "In God We Trust" be on all coins.

Wed

St George's Day
MPC meeting minutes published
450th anniversary of the birth of William Shakespeare

↘

23

FTSE 100	41	-0.1	1.0
FTSE 250	65	0.2	0.9
S&P 500	46	-0.1	0.7
NIKKEI	55	0.4	0.9

1983: Pound coins are issued for the first time.

Thu

→

24

FTSE 100	52	0.1	1.1
FTSE 250	47	0.1	0.9
S&P 500	46	-0.1	0.8
NIKKEI	36	-0.1	1.1

1800: The United States Library of Congress is established when President John Adams signs legislation to appropriate $5000 to purchase "such books as may be necessary for the use of Congress".

Fri

→

25

FTSE 100	62	0.1	0.5
FTSE 250	53	0.0	0.5
S&P 500	57	0.1	0.9
NIKKEI	59	0.1	1.0

1886: Sigmund Freud opens his practice at Rathausstrasse 7, Vienna.

Sat 26

Sun 27

COMPANY NEWS

Interims Associated British Foods, Fenner
Finals Brown (N) Group, Bumi, F&C Commercial Property Trust Ltd

"If you think nobody cares if you're alive, try missing a couple of car payments."
Earl Wilson

MAY MARKET

Market performance this month

One of the most famous sayings in the stock market is "Sell in May", so it is no surprise that May is one of the weakest months of the year for shares. There are only three months where, since 1970, the market has an average return of below zero – May is one of them (the others are June and September). On average the market falls -0.2% in the month and the probability of a positive return in the month is below 50%, at 47%.

FTSE 100	47	-0.2	4.5
FTSE 250	57	0.4	4.4
S&P 500	65	0.2	3.7
NIKKEI	50	-0.1	6.1

May is the start of the weaker half of the year (historically the market over November to April greatly outperforms the period May to October). Some short-term investors, therefore, tend to reduce exposure to the stock market from May.

On average, in May the market trades fairly flat for the first two weeks of the month and then prices drift lower in the second half (as can be seen below in the chart on the right).

Strong sectors relative to the general market in May tend to be Aerospace & Defense, Electricity and Food Producers, while the weaker sectors are General Industrials and Life Insurance.

Internationally, May is the weakest month of the year for the FTSE 100 relative to the S&P 500; on average the UK index underperforms the US by 1.3 percentage points in May.

Performance of market in May [1970 to 2013]

FTSE 100 average month chart for May [1985 to 2013]

Trading days

MAY SUMMARY

Market performance	Average return: **-0.2%**		Positive: **47%**	Ranking: **10th**
Sector performance	*Strong* Aerospace & Defense, Electricity, Equity Investment Instruments, Food Producers, Gas, Water & Multiutilities		*Weak* General Industrials, Life Insurance	
Share performance	*Strong* 3i Group, Babcock International Group, Cranswick, Homeserve, Severn Trent		*Weak* Petra Diamonds Ltd, Sainsbury (J), Stagecoach Group, Taylor Wimpey, Workspace Group	
Main features of the month	FTSE 100 often underperforms the S&P 500 in this month First trading day average return: 0.08%; positive: 53% Last trading day average return: 0.04%; positive: 50% 2 May: 3rd strongest market day of the year 26 May: start of 5th weakest market week 30 May: weakest market day of the year			
Significant dates	02 May: US Nonfarm payroll report (anticipated) 05 May: Early May bank holiday – LSE closed 08 May: MPC interest rate announcement at 12 noon (anticipated) 14 May: MSCI quarterly index review (anticipated) 26 May: Spring bank holiday – LSE closed			

Mon

28

2003: The SEC exacts financial penalties from ten investment-banking firms, centering on their actions during the internet boom and bust. The total bill for the firms was $1.4bn.

FTSE 100	50	0.1	1.1
FTSE 250	55	0.0	0.8
S&P 500	56	0.0	0.7
NIKKEI	45	-0.3	1.1

Tue

29

Showa Day (Japan) – TSE closed
New moon
Annular solar eclipse (visible in Australia and southern Asia)
Two-day FOMC meeting starts

1770: James Cook arrives at and names Botany Bay, Australia.

FTSE 100	50	0.3	0.8
FTSE 250	63	0.6	1.9
S&P 500	51	0.2	0.9
NIKKEI			

Wed

30

1803: The USA buys the Louisiana territory from Napoleon for $15m, borrowing some of the money for the purchase from Britain.

FTSE 100	55	0.1	0.7
FTSE 250	60	-0.1	1.8
S&P 500	50	0.0	0.8
NIKKEI	47	0.6	1.7

Thu

1

May Day
International Workers' Day
Labour Day (HK) – HKSE closed
20th anniversary of the death of Ayrton Senna

1994: Ayrton Senna is killed in a crash at the Imola circuit during the San Marino Grand Prix.

FTSE 100	53	0.1	0.8
FTSE 250	53	0.1	0.5
S&P 500	57	0.3	0.7
NIKKEI	64	0.4	1.2

Fri

2

3rd strongest market day
Nonfarm payroll report (anticipated)

2012: A pastel version of Edvard Munch's *The Scream* sells for $120m in a New York City auction, setting a new world record for an auctioned work of art.

FTSE 100	76	0.5	0.9
FTSE 250	67	0.5	0.7
S&P 500	67	0.2	0.7
NIKKEI	62	0.5	0.8

Sat 3   Constitution Memorial Day (Japan)

Sun 4   Greenery Day (Japan)

COMPANY NEWS

Interims Aberdeen Asset Management, Edinburgh Dragon Trust, Imperial Tobacco Group
Finals Bluecrest Allblue Fund Ltd, Home Retail Group, Scottish Mortgage Investment Trust, Whitbread

"Wall Street is the only place that people ride to in a Rolls-Royce to get advice from those who take the subway."
Warren Buffett

MONTHLY SHARE MOMENTUM

Do shares exhibit a momentum effect from one month to the next?

If we selected the 10 best performing shares in one month and created an equally-weighted portfolio of those shares to hold for the following month, would that portfolio outperform the market index?

Or, more interestingly, if we did this systematically for a year (i.e. our portfolio each month is comprised of the 10 best performing shares in the previous month), would that portfolio outperform the market index?

In last year's edition of the *Almanac* we applied this analysis to the companies in the FTSE 100; this year we will apply it to FTSE 350 companies. So, the 10-share portfolio for each month will comprise the 10 best performing shares in the FTSE 350 in the previous month.

The chart below shows the result of operating such a momentum portfolio in 2012. Each bar represents the outperformance of the portfolio over the FTSE 350. For example, in January 2012 the 10-share portfolio would have increased 7.2% against a FTSE 350 increase of 2.5%, giving an outperformance of 4.7 percentage points.

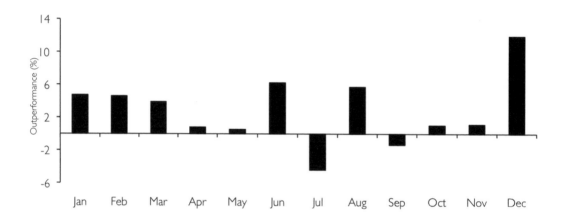

As can be seen, the momentum portfolio would only have underperformed the Index in two months. The momentum portfolio would have outperformed the FTSE 350 by an average of 2.9 percentage points each month.

The following chart shows the value of such a momentum portfolio for the year 2012; for comparison the FTSE 350 is also included. Values were rebased to 100.

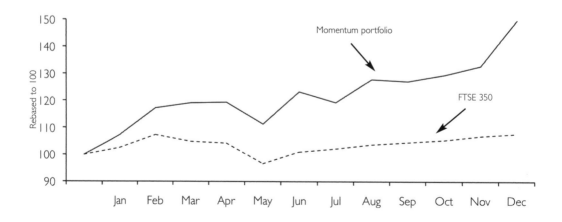

By the end of the year the momentum portfolio would have increased 49.7%, compared to an increase of 7.7% in the FTSE 350.

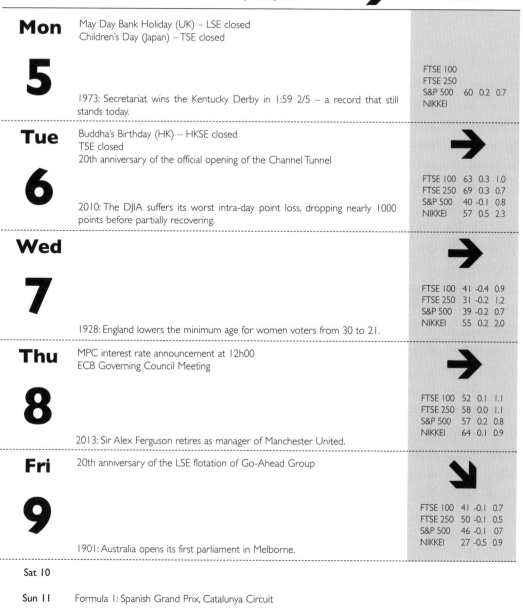

Mon

5

May Day Bank Holiday (UK) – LSE closed
Children's Day (Japan) – TSE closed

1973: Secretariat wins the Kentucky Derby in 1:59 2/5 – a record that still stands today.

FTSE 100			
FTSE 250			
S&P 500	60	0.2	0.7
NIKKEI			

Tue

6

Buddha's Birthday (HK) – HKSE closed
TSE closed
20th anniversary of the official opening of the Channel Tunnel

2010: The DJIA suffers its worst intra-day point loss, dropping nearly 1000 points before partially recovering.

→

FTSE 100	63	0.3	1.0
FTSE 250	69	0.3	0.7
S&P 500	40	-0.1	0.8
NIKKEI	57	0.5	2.3

Wed

7

1928: England lowers the minimum age for women voters from 30 to 21.

→

FTSE 100	41	-0.4	0.9
FTSE 250	31	-0.2	1.2
S&P 500	39	-0.2	0.7
NIKKEI	55	0.2	2.0

Thu

8

MPC interest rate announcement at 12h00
ECB Governing Council Meeting

2013: Sir Alex Ferguson retires as manager of Manchester United.

→

FTSE 100	52	0.1	1.1
FTSE 250	58	0.0	1.1
S&P 500	57	0.2	0.8
NIKKEI	64	0.1	0.9

Fri

9

20th anniversary of the LSE flotation of Go-Ahead Group

1901: Australia opens its first parliament in Melborne.

↘

FTSE 100	41	-0.1	0.7
FTSE 250	50	-0.1	0.5
S&P 500	46	-0.1	07
NIKKEI	27	-0.5	0.9

Sat 10

Sun 11   Formula 1: Spanish Grand Prix, Catalunya Circuit

COMPANY NEWS

Interims Sage Group, United Drug
Finals 3i Infrastructure Ltd, Experian, Sainsbury (J)

"One of the funny things about the stock market is that every time one person buys, another sells, and both think they are astute."
William Feather

MONTHLY SHARE BOUNCEBACKS

Last week we looked at a portfolio that is rebalanced each month to hold the 10 best performing shares from the previous month. Here we will look at a similar portfolio, but this time the portfolio is rebalanced each month to hold the 10 worst performing shares in the previous month.

The objective is to see if shares have a tendency to rebound after a difficult month. We will call this the Monthly Bounceback Portfolio.

The following chart shows the result of operating such a bounceback portfolio in 2012. Each bar represents the outperformance of the portfolio over the FTSE 350. For example, in February 2012 the 10-share portfolio would have increased 7.8% against a FTSE 350 increase of 4.7%, giving an outperformance of 3.1 percentage points.

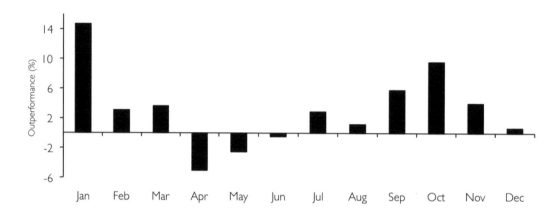

This time the portfolio would have underperformed the FTSE 350 in three months (with the momentum portfolio it underperformed in only two months). But the average monthly outperformance of the bounceback portfolio over the index would have been 3.1 (greater than that for momentum portfolio).

The following chart shows the value of the bounceback portfolio for the year 2012; for comparison the FTSE 350 is also included. Values were rebased to start at 100.

By the end of the year the bounceback portfolio would have increased 52.6%, compared to an increase of 7.7% in the FTSE 350.

So, this is interesting. Not only does the bounceback portfolio easily beat the FTSE 350, it also beats the momentum portfolio (which would have increased 49.7% in the year).

It would seem that it may be possible to beat the index by picking either the 10 best or 10 worst performing shares from the previous month – although the reasons for outperformance in the two respective cases are very different.

Mon
12
1935: Bill Wilson and Dr. Bob Smith (founders of Alcoholics Anonymous) meet for the first time in Akron, Ohio, at the home of Henrietta Siberling.

FTSE 100	55	0.0	0.9
FTSE 250	60	0.1	1.0
S&P 500	58	0.2	0.7
NIKKEI	45	0.1	1.3

Tue
13
1967: An octagonal boxing ring – designed to prevent corner injuries – is tested for the first time.

FTSE 100	57	0.2	0.9
FTSE 250	60	0.0	1.0
S&P 500	49	-0.1	0.8
NIKKEI	43	-0.1	1.2

Wed
14
Full moon
MPC Inflation Report published
MSCI Semi-Annual Index Review (announcement date)

1973: Skylab, the United States' first space station, is launched.

FTSE 100	36	-0.5	1.4
FTSE 250	40	-0.3	0.8
S&P 500	43	-0.1	0.9
NIKKEI	50	-0.1	1.1

Thu
15
1911: The United States Supreme Court declares Standard Oil to be an "unreasonable" monopoly under the Sherman Antitrust Act.

FTSE 100	55	0.2	0.9
FTSE 250	55	0.0	0.8
S&P 500	54	0.0	0.9
NIKKEI	41	0.1	1.6

Fri
16
2007: Marks & Spencer closes at all-time high of 749.

FTSE 100	41	0.1	0.6
FTSE 250	45	0.1	0.7
S&P 500	46	0.0	0.8
NIKKEI	41	-0.3	1.0

Sat 17   Football: FA Cup Final, Wembley Stadium

Sun 18

COMPANY NEWS

Interims Compass Group, Diploma, easyJet, Enterprise Inns, Euromoney Institutional Investor, Grainger, Lonmin, Marston's, Thomas Cook Group, TUI Travel

Finals 3i Group, Babcock International Group, British Land Co, BT Group, DCC, ICAP, Invensys, Land Securities Group, London Stock Exchange Group, National Grid, TalkTalk Telecom Group, Vedanta Resources

"If at first you don't succeed, try, try again. Then quit. There's no point in being a damn fool about it."
W.C. Fields

QUARTERLY SECTOR STRATEGY

In the Statistics section of the *Almanac* the performance of the FTSE 350 sectors in each quarter can be found. From this data the strong and weak sectors in each quarter can be identified. The strongest/weakest sector in each quarter is shown in the table to the right.

Quarter	Strong	Weak
1st	Industrial Engineering	Pharm & Biotech
2nd	Electricity	Construction & Materials
3rd	Software & Comp Srvs	Oil & Gas Producers
4th	Beverages	Banks

This suggests a strategy which cycles a portfolio through the four strong sectors throughout the year. In other words, the portfolio is 100% invested in the Industrial Engineering sector from 31 December to 31 March, then switches into Electricity to 31 June, then switches into Software and Computing Services to 30 September, then switches into Beverages to 31 December, and then switches back into Industrial Engineering and starts the cycle again.

The chart below illustrates the performance of such a strategy for the period Q3 2003 to Q2 2013, with a comparison to the FTSE All-Share.

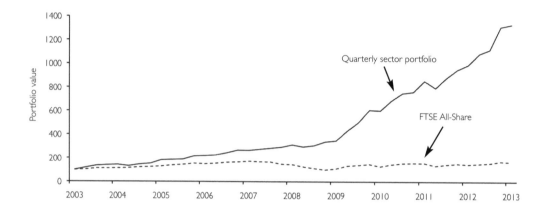

Over the ten years the strategy would have grown £1000 into £13,300, while a £1000 investment in the FTSE All-Share would have become just £1669.

Long/short strategy

A variation of the above strategy would be to add a short position in the weak sectors in each quarter. For example, in Q1 the strategy would be long the Industrial Engineering sector and short the Pharmaceuticals & Biotech sector.

The following chart shows the outperformance of the strong sector over the weak sector for each respective quarter for the period 2003 to 2013. For example, in Q2 2013 (the final quarter in the chart), the Electricity sector rose 1.5% while the Construction & Materials sector fell 5.1%, giving an outperformance of 6.6 percentage points.

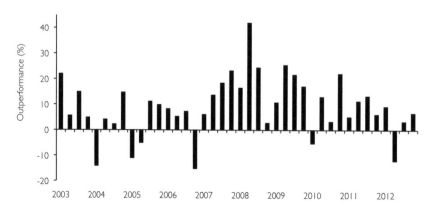

Mon

19

8th weakest market week

1999: The online toy store, eToys, goes public at $20 a share. By the end of the day it is trading near $80, making the company worth over $600m.

FTSE 100	55	-0.2	1.4
FTSE 250	65	0.0	1.2
S&P 500	53	-0.1	0.9
NIKKEI	55	0.3	1.3

Tue

20

RHS Chelsea Flower Show (until 24 May)

1609: Shakespeare's sonnets are first published in London, perhaps illicitly, by the publisher Thomas Thorpe.

FTSE 100	52	-0.1	1.0
FTSE 250	70	-0.2	1.0
S&P 500	44	-0.1	0.9
NIKKEI	48	-0.1	0.9

Wed

21

MPC meeting minutes published
ECB Governing Council Meeting

2013: Microsoft unveils the Xbox One.

FTSE 100	59	0.0	0.8
FTSE 250	65	-0.1	0.8
S&P 500	48	-0.1	0.8
NIKKEI	64	0.1	1.2

Thu

22

1987: The first ever Rugby World Cup kicks off with New Zealand playing Italy at Eden Park in Auckland. New Zeland win 70-6.

FTSE 100	55	0.0	1.0
FTSE 250	60	0.0	1.2
S&P 500	52	0.0	0.7
NIKKEI	55	-0.2	1.3

Fri

23

2003: The euro exceeds its initial trading value as it hits $1.18 for the first time since its introduction in 1999.

FTSE 100	41	-0.4	1.2
FTSE 250	45	-0.1	1.4
S&P 500	41	-0.2	0.8
NIKKEI	50	-0.3	1.9

Sat 24 Rugby: Heineken Cup Final, Football: UEFA Champions League Final, Lisbon

Sun 25 Tennis: French Open, Paris (until 8 June), Formula 1: Monaco Grand Prix

COMPANY NEWS

Interims Britvic, ITE Group, JPMorgan Indian Investment Trust, Mitchells & Butlers, Paragon Group of Companies, Schroder AsiaPacific Fund, Shaftesbury

Finals AVEVA Group, Big Yellow Group, Booker Group, BTG, Burberry Group, Cable & Wireless Communications, Cranswick, Dairy Crest Group, Electrocomponents, FirstGroup, Great Portland Estates, Halfords Group, HICL Infrastructure Company Ltd, Homeserve, Intermediate Capital Group, Investec, Marks & Spencer Group, MITIE Group, PayPoint, Pennon Group, QinetiQ Group, SABMiller, SSE, Telecom Plus, United Utilities Group, Vodafone Group

"Where facts are few, experts are many."
Donald R. Gannon

Shares that like June

The share prices of only four companies in the FTSE 350 Index have risen at least nine times in the last ten years in the month of June. The table below shows these four companies and the percentage return for the stock in the month of June for that year (for example, Synergy increased 5.4% in June 2013).

Company	TIDM	2004	2005	2006	2007	2008	2009	2010	2011	2012	2013	Avg
Synergy Health	SYR	6.0	9.7	19.2	3.6	7.3	25.1	13.1	6.0	10.6	5.4	10.6
Halma	HLMA	7.4	0.5	7.6	3.3	1.4	21.1	10.3	5.1	6.8	-2.6	6.1
Ted Baker	TED	0.5	6.8	1.2	-13.6	4.0	7.0	8.6	7.7	5.4	19.3	4.7
BT Group	BT.A	8.5	7.9	2.1	0.9	-10.0	16.1	2.4	0.3	2.5	2.4	3.3
average:		5.6	6.2	7.5	-1.5	0.7	17.3	8.6	4.8	6.3	6.1	6.2
FTSE 350:		1.2	3.1	1.8	-0.9	-7.3	-3.6	-4.9	-0.8	4.5	-5.3	-1.2
diff:		4.4	3.1	5.7	-0.6	8.0	20.9	13.5	5.6	1.8	11.4	7.4

The best performing share in June has been Synergy Health, which has an average return of 10.6% for all Junes since 2004. Synergy is also the only company in the FTSE 350 Index whose shares have risen every June for the past ten years.

The final three rows in the table are:

1. *average*: the average return for the four stocks in each year

2. *FTSE 350*: the return for the FTSE 350 Index for June of that year

3. *diff*: the difference between the *average* row and the *FTSE 350 Index* row (i.e. the outperformance of an equally-weighted portfolio of the four stocks over the index).

Shares that dislike June

The share prices of only four companies in the FTSE 350 Index have fallen nine times in the last ten years in the month of June. The table below shows these four companies and the percentage return for the stock in the month of June for that year (for example, Barclays fell 13.1% in June 2013).

Company	TIDM	2004	2005	2006	2007	2008	2009	2010	2011	2012	2013	Avg
Barclays	BARC	-1.2	6.5	-0.6	-3.6	-22.3	-4.9	-11.3	-7.3	-7.6	-13.1	-6.5
Vesuvius	VSVS	-3.0	-6.0	5.5	-1.0	-14.0	-3.3	-18.3	-2.2	-5.8	-3.4	-5.2
United Utilities Group	UU.	-4.6	-2.7	-2.9	-8.0	-8.3	-7.2	-2.6	-3.7	2.7	-9.5	-4.7
Rotork	ROR	3.5	-4.2	-2.1	-0.6	-3.3	-3.2	-6.1	-2.2	-3.0	-6.6	-2.8
average:		-1.3	-1.6	0.0	-3.3	-12.0	-4.7	-9.6	-3.9	-3.4	-8.2	-4.8
FTSE 350:		1.2	3.1	1.8	-0.9	-7.3	-3.6	-4.9	-0.8	4.5	-5.3	-1.2
diff:		-2.5	-4.7	-1.8	-2.4	-4.7	-1.1	-4.7	-3.1	-7.9	-2.9	-3.6

The worst performing share in June has been Barclays, which has an average return of -6.5% for all Junes since 2004.

Long/short strategy

An equally-weighted portfolio of the four strong June stocks would have outperformed an equally-weighted portfolio of the four weak June stocks by an average of 11.0 percentage points in each June for the past ten years.

Mon
26

Spring Bank Holiday (UK) – LSE closed
Memorial Day (US) – NYSE closed
5th weakest market week
20th anniversary of the LSE flotation of JPMorgan Indian Investment Trust

1936: The Independent Unionist MP for Shankill, Tommy Henderson, makes a speech nearly ten hours long attacking a government finance bill line by line. Mr Henderson concludes his remarks at 3.55am the following morning.

FTSE 100			
FTSE 250			
S&P 500			
NIKKEI	65	0.2	1.1

Tue
27

1932: The tallest steel arch bridge in the world, Sydney Harbour Bridge, opens. It stands at 134m high and stretches 1149m in length.

FTSE 100	41	0.0	1.1
FTSE 250	53	0.1	0.8
S&P 500	46	0.1	1.2
NIKKEI	38	-0.2	1.2

Wed
28

New moon

1959: Two monkeys become the first living creatures to survive a space flight.

FTSE 100	56	0.2	0.8
FTSE 250	53	0.2	0.7
S&P 500	56	0.0	1.4
NIKKEI	64	0.4	0.9

Thu
29

Faye's Comet reaches perihelion

2002: GUS announces it will list its Burberry brand on the LSE, valuing Burberry at between £1.2bn and £1.8bn.

FTSE 100	65	0.2	0.9
FTSE 250	69	0.2	0.7
S&P 500	53	0.2	1.2
NIKKEI	68	0.5	1.0

Fri
30

Weakest market day

1642: From this date all honours granted by Charles I are retrospectively annulled by Parliament.

FTSE 100	22	-0.4	1.3
FTSE 250	31	-0.3	1.0
S&P 500	60	0.1	1.1
NIKKEI	41	-0.3	1.3

Sat 31

Sun 1   20th anniversary of the LSE flotation of Intermediate Capital Group.

COMPANY NEWS

Interims Brewin Dolphin Holdings, British Empire Securities & General Trust, Electra Private Equity, Victrex
Finals Caledonia Investments, De La Rue, Edinburgh Investment Trust, Severn Trent, Tate & Lyle, TR Property Investment Trust

"Those who have some means think that the most important thing in the world is love. The poor know that it is money."
Gerald Brenan

JUNE MARKET

Market performance this month

This is not a good period for investors – the weak month of May is followed by the even weaker month of June. On average the market has fallen 0.8% in June and the probability of a positive return in the month is a lowly 40%. The market has only risen one June in the past seven years and the market falls in June can be quite large; the market has fallen over 3% in June in eight years since 1982.

FTSE 100	40	-0.8	3.6
FTSE 250	43	-0.7	4.7
S&P 500	50	0.0	3.5
NIKKEI	57	-0.2	5.4

In an average June the market starts strong, hitting its month high on the second or third trading day, but prices then drift down steadily for the rest of the month.

At the stock level, an interesting companies is Synergy Health; this is the only company in the FTSE 350 whose shares have risen every June for the past 10 years.

Events to watch out for this month include the FTSE 100 review on the 11th and triple witching on the 21st.

Performance of market in June [1970 to 2013]

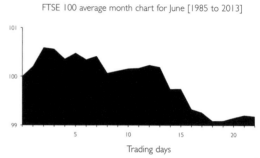

FTSE 100 average month chart for June [1985 to 2013]

Trading days

JUNE SUMMARY

Market performance	Average return: -0.8%		Positive: 40%	Ranking: 11th
Sector performance	**Strong** Beverages, Oil & Gas Producers, Pharmaceuticals & Biotechnology		**Weak**	
Share performance	**Strong** BT Group, Halma, Synergy Health, Ted Baker		**Weak** Barclays, Rotork, United Utilities Group, Vesuvius	
Main features of the month	2nd weakest month in the year			
	FTSE 100 often underperforms the S&P 500 in June			
	First trading day average return: 0.21%; positive: 53%			
	Last trading day average return: 0.18%; positive: 67% (2nd strongest in year)			
	16 Jun: start of the 2nd weakest market week in the year			
	30 Jun: start of the 5th strongest market week in the year			
Significant dates	05 Jun: MPC interest rate announcement at 12 noon (anticipated)			
	06 Jun: US Nonfarm payroll report (anticipated)			
	11 Jun: FTSE 100 Index quarterly review announcement			
	17 Jun: Two-day FOMC meeting starts			
	21 Jun: Triple Witching			

Mon 2

Tuen Ng Day (HK) – HKSE closed
MSCI Semi-Annual Index Review (effective date)

2013: Andorra agrees to introduce a tax on personal income for the first time as it faces pressure from its European neighbours to tackle tax evasion.

→

FTSE 100	50	0.2	1.0
FTSE 250	70	0.3	0.7
S&P 500	56	0.1	0.8
NIKKEI	60	0.3	1.0

Tue 3

10th anniversary of the LSE flotation of Halfords Group

1979: A blowout at the Ixtoc I oil well in the southern Gulf of Mexico causes at least 3m barrels of oil to be spilled into the water. It is the second-worst accidental oil spill ever recorded.

→

FTSE 100	60	0.1	0.8
FTSE 250	53	0.0	0.6
S&P 500	49	0.0	0.8
NIKKEI	48	-0.3	1.5

Wed 4

Beige Book published

1917: The first Pulitzer Prizes are awarded.

→

FTSE 100	55	0.1	1.0
FTSE 250	61	0.4	1.9
S&P 500	54	-0.1	1.1
NIKKEI	64	0.2	1.2

Thu 5

MPC interest rate announcement at 12h00
ECB Governing Council Meeting
25th anniversary of the Unknown Rebel halting the progress of a column of advancing tanks for over half an hour after the Tiananmen Square protests

2013: Congress abrogates the United States' use of the gold standard.

→

FTSE 100	52	0.0	1.0
FTSE 250	53	-0.4	2.1
S&P 500	61	0.1	0.9
NIKKEI	50	-0.1	1.2

Fri 6

Horseracing: The Oaks, Epsom Downs Racecourse
Nonfarm payroll report (anticipated)

1975: British voters back the UK's continued membership of the EEC by two-to-one in a nationwide referendum.

→

FTSE 100	55	0.0	1.0
FTSE 250	70	0.0	1.3
S&P 500	54	0.2	1.1
NIKKEI	32	-0.2	0.9

Sat 7   Horseracing: The Derby, Epsom Downs Racecourse

Sun 8   Pentecost, Formula 1: Canadian Grand Prix, Gilles Villeneuve

COMPANY NEWS

Interims Scottish Investment Trust
Finals Johnson Matthey, Londonmetric Property, Monks Investment Trust, Perpetual Income & Growth Investment Trust, Personal Assets Trust, RPC Group, Synergy Health, Templeton Emerging Markets Investment Trust, Worldwide Healthcare Trust

"I told the Inland Revenue I didn't owe them a penny because I lived near the seaside."
Ken Dodd

CRODA INTERNATIONAL – 50 YEARS ON THE LSE

Croda was formed in Yorkshire, England in 1925 to make lanolin. Over the years the company has expanded internationally and it now has factories in the United Kingdom, France, Spain, Italy, the Netherlands, the United States, Brazil, Singapore, India, Indonesia, Korea and Japan.

On 10 June 1964 (50 years ago this week) Croda International listed on the LSE.

Today Croda International is a speciality chemicals producer with a revenue of £1bn and a portfolio of catchily-named products, such as Priplast, Perfad, Solaveil, Incromega and NatSurf. According to its website:

> Croda has established new product naming conventions based on logical, functional categorisation of our ingredients, whilst also including additional product information in the form of user-friendly suffixes.

The following chart shows the share price of Croda from 1988.

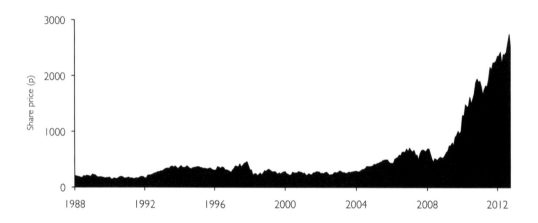

The price chart suggests that those "user-friendly suffixes" are doing well for Croda.

The following chart plots the average monthly outperformance of the shares over the FTSE 100 since 1988. For example, on average Croda International has outperformed the FTSE 100 by 4.4 percentage points in February.

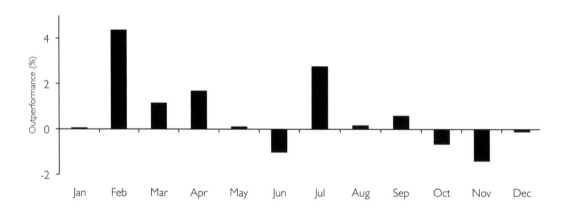

Observations

- The strongest month for Croda International shares relative to the market has been February (the shares have outperformed the market in this month in 19 of the last 25 years).
- The weakest month for Croda International relative to the market has been October (the shares have only outperformed the market in this month in 9 of the past 25 years).

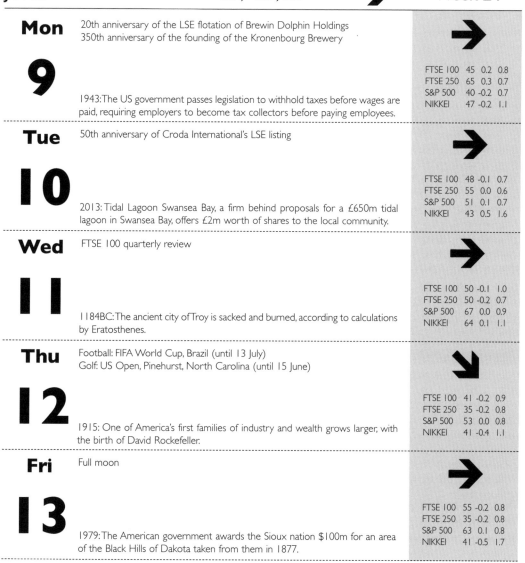

Mon

9

20th anniversary of the LSE flotation of Brewin Dolphin Holdings
350th anniversary of the founding of the Kronenbourg Brewery

1943: The US government passes legislation to withhold taxes before wages are paid, requiring employers to become tax collectors before paying employees.

➔

FTSE 100	45	0.2	0.8
FTSE 250	65	0.3	0.7
S&P 500	40	-0.2	0.7
NIKKEI	47	-0.2	1.1

Tue

10

50th anniversary of Croda International's LSE listing

2013: Tidal Lagoon Swansea Bay, a firm behind proposals for a £650m tidal lagoon in Swansea Bay, offers £2m worth of shares to the local community.

➔

FTSE 100	48	-0.1	0.7
FTSE 250	55	0.0	0.6
S&P 500	51	0.1	0.7
NIKKEI	43	0.5	1.6

Wed

11

FTSE 100 quarterly review

1184BC: The ancient city of Troy is sacked and burned, according to calculations by Eratosthenes.

➔

FTSE 100	50	-0.1	1.0
FTSE 250	50	-0.2	0.7
S&P 500	67	0.0	0.9
NIKKEI	64	0.1	1.1

Thu

12

Football: FIFA World Cup, Brazil (until 13 July)
Golf: US Open, Pinehurst, North Carolina (until 15 June)

1915: One of America's first families of industry and wealth grows larger, with the birth of David Rockefeller.

↘

FTSE 100	41	-0.2	0.9
FTSE 250	35	-0.2	0.8
S&P 500	53	0.0	0.8
NIKKEI	41	-0.4	1.1

Fri

13

Full moon

1979: The American government awards the Sioux nation $100m for an area of the Black Hills of Dakota taken from them in 1877.

➔

FTSE 100	55	-0.2	0.8
FTSE 250	35	-0.2	0.8
S&P 500	63	0.1	0.8
NIKKEI	41	-0.5	1.7

Sat 14

Sun 15   Father's Day

COMPANY NEWS

Interims
Finals Atkins (W S), Halma, KCOM Group, Oxford Instruments, Workspace Group

"The first rule in making money is not to lose it."
Steven J. Lee

SHARE PERFORMANCE IN THE SUMMER

How do shares behave in the summer?

A simple question perhaps, but first it is necessary to define "summer". When do you think summer begins and ends?

In last year's *Almanac* we took summer to be just the two-month period July to August. In this edition we'll be a bit more precise.

The summer solstice marks the date when the earth's axis is most inclined towards the sun – this results in the longest day of the year (and occurs between 20 and 22 June in the northern hemisphere). Strictly, this should mark the middle of the summer season in the astronomical calendar. However, due to seasonal lag the warmest days of the year tend to occur after this date and so in the meteorological calendar summer extends for the whole months of June, July and August. But in some countries where the temperature lag can be up to half a season (e.g. the UK), then summer is taken to start with the summer solstice and end with the autumn equinox (22 September, when the earth is tilted neither towards or away from the sun).

For the purposes of this analysis we will take the dates of summer as being 21 June to 22 September. The following analysis looked at the performance of the share prices of the companies in the FTSE 350 over summer for the ten years 2003 to 2012.

Stocks that like summer

The table below shows five companies whose share prices have risen in at least nine summers in the past ten years. For example, Centrica shares rose 3.4% in the summer of 2003 and the shares had an average summer return of 6.9% for the years 2003 to 2012. Rangold Resources is the only company in the FTSE 350 whose shares have increased every summer over the period.

Company	TIDM	2003	2004	2004	2005	2007	2008	2009	2010	2011	2012	Avg
Randgold Resources	RRS	49.4	17.5	12.7	1.6	34.8	16.5	12.4	0.9	43.7	25.4	21.5
Centrica	CAN	3.4	12.4	12.4	13.5	2.2	5.5	12.2	11.0	-10.9	7.0	6.9
SABMiller	SAB	8.2	4.4	21.7	1.3	10.9	2.4	17.8	0.1	-6.2	6.7	6.7
Bunzl	BNZL	7.8	-9.7	7.4	13.2	1.2	4.4	28.2	2.8	2.6	4.7	6.3
Tesco	TSCO	14.5	5.7	0.6	12.8	3.3	3.8	8.2	11.6	-11.8	9.8	5.9
average:		16.7	6.1	11.0	8.5	10.5	6.5	15.8	5.3	3.5	10.7	9.4
FTSE 350:		3.0	2.0	6.3	3.5	-3.3	-6.8	19.2	5.6	-11.8	4.7	2.2
diff:		13.7	4.1	4.7	5.0	13.8	13.3	-3.4	-0.3	15.3	6.0	7.2

On average over the last 10 years the market (FTSE 350) has risen 2.2% over summer, but these five stocks combined rose an average of 9.4%.

An equally-weighted portfolio of these five companies would have outperformed the FTSE 350 in eight of the past ten years; the average outperformance each year would have been 7.2% percentage points.

Stocks that don't like summer

The three stocks in the table below have all fallen in at least seven of the past 10 summers and have a negative average return for the summers in this period.

Company	TIDM	2003	2004	2005	2006	2007	2008	2009	2010	2011	2012	Avg
Cranswick	CWK	-1.2	-5.5	3.1	8.8	-14.9	-7.5	14.0	-4.0	-22.5	-0.8	-3.1
ICAP	IAP	14.3	-18.5	18.8	7.5	-0.8	-24.8	-6.8	-0.3	-0.6	-9.3	-2.1
Imperial Tobacco Group	IMT	-8.3	-0.9	2.9	9.6	-0.8	-7.5	8.8	-0.2	-0.3	-3.7	0.0
average:		1.6	-8.3	8.3	8.6	-5.5	-13.3	5.3	-1.5	-7.8	-4.6	-1.7
FTSE 350:		3.0	2.0	6.3	3.5	-3.3	-6.8	19.2	5.6	-11.8	4.7	2.2
diff:		-1.4	-10.3	2.0	5.1	-2.2	-6.5	-13.9	-7.1	4.0	-9.3	-4.0

Long-short strategy

An equally-weighted portfolio of the five strong summer stocks would have outperformed an equally-weighted portfolio of the three weak summer stocks by an average of 11.2% each summer over the 10-year period.

Mon 2nd weakest market week

16

2013: It is announced that the Co-Operative Bank will be floated on the stock exchange after it is agreed with a City regulator that the bank has a £1.5bn hole in its balance sheet.

FTSE 100	65	0.2	0.5
FTSE 250	47	0.0	0.5
S&P 500	62	0.1	0.8
NIKKEI	50	0.1	1.5

Tue Two-day FOMC meeting starts
Horseracing: Royal Ascot, Ascot Racecourse (until 21 June)
ECB Governing Council Meeting

17

1867: Joseph Lister performs the first operation under antiseptic conditions on his sister Isabella, at the Glasgow Infirmary.

FTSE 100	67	0.3	0.9
FTSE 250	60	0.1	0.8
S&P 500	51	0.1	0.8
NIKKEI	48	0.1	1.3

Wed MPC meeting minutes published
ECB General Council Meeting
30th anniversary of the Battle of Orgreave

18

1928: Aviator Amelia Earhart becomes the first woman to fly in an aircraft across the Atlantic Ocean (she is a passenger, Wilmer Stultz is the pilot and Lou Gordon is the mechanic).

FTSE 100	41	-0.3	0.7
FTSE 250	35	-0.2	0.7
S&P 500	41	-0.1	0.7
NIKKEI	41	0.1	1.4

Thu Golf: US Women's Open, Pinehurst, North Carolina (until 22 June)
25th anniversary of the LSE flotation of Templeton Emerging Markets Investments Trust

19

1997: Sir Andrew Lloyd Webber's *Cats* becomes the longest running Broadway musical upon its 6138th performance.

FTSE 100	45	-0.1	1.0
FTSE 250	50	0.0	1.2
S&P 500	53	-0.1	0.8
NIKKEI	50	-0.2	1.5

Fri Triple Witching

20

1960: Nan Winton becomes the first woman to read the national news on BBC television.

FTSE 100	36	-0.4	1.0
FTSE 250	30	-0.3	0.9
S&P 500	46	-0.1	0.8
NIKKEI	59	0.0	1.0

Sat 21 Summer Solstice, also known as Midsummer or Litha

Sun 22

COMPANY NEWS

Interims Bankers Investment Trust, Chemring Group, Crest Nicholson Holdings Ltd
Finals Ashtead Group, Berkeley Group Holdings, Fidelity China Special Situation, Imagination Technologies Group, Micro Focus International, Utilico Emerging Markets Ltd

"I'm spending a year dead for tax reasons."
Douglas Adams

FIFA WORLD CUP

Does historic behaviour of stock markets around the time of the four-yearly FIFA World Cup[1] have any interest for investors?

Hosts

The hosts for the World Cup are announced many years in advance; for example after Brazil this year the 2018 World Cup will be held in Russia, and then in 2022 it will be the turn of the soccer colossus Qatar. The World Cup is a major event, often requiring much spending to improve infrastructure, and such spending can provide a fillip to a nation's economy. If this affects prices on the stock market it is likely to happen soon after the initial announcement of a country winning the competition to host the event – long before the World Cup takes place.

However, in this analysis we will look at the performance of host country stock markets in the year of the World Cup itself. The following chart shows the performance of stock markets in six countries that have hosted the World Cup. The index data has been rebased to 100. The competition generally runs from mid-June to mid-July (as indicated by the shaded portion in the chart).

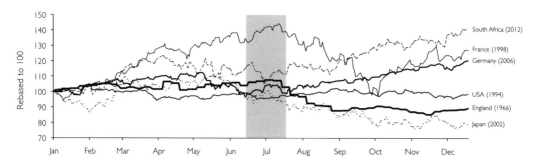

The chart suggests that the World Cup did have some effect on the stock markets. In many cases a market took a decisive turn up or down after the competition finished. In the three World Cups (presented here) before 1998 the market fell after the competition; while after the last two World Cups the markets rose. In 1998 the French were all over the place.

Let's now look at the performance of markets in nations that win the World Cup.

Winners

The following chart plots the relevant stock market index in seven countries that have won the World Cup. In each case, the period shown is 50 days before the final and 50 days after. The indices are rebased to 100 on the trading day following the final.[2]

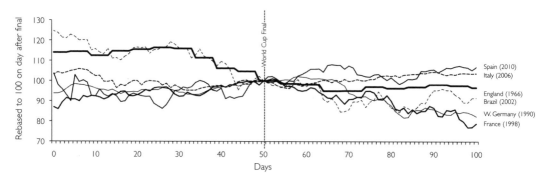

Interestingly, we see a similar pattern of behaviour to the previous chart: markets in winning nations before 2006 fell in the 50 days after the competition, whereas the markets in the two most recent winning nations (Italy in 2006 and Spain in 2010) rose after the event (albeit only marginally). But the lesson from history does seem to be that winning the World Cup is not good for the stock market.

---

[1] For the benefit of American readers, the World Cup is a soccer competition – a game where 22 men run around and then Germany wins on penalties.
[2] German market data source: Global Financial Data (www.globalfinancialdata.com).

Mon

Tennis: Wimbledon (until 6 July)

23

2006: The Court of Appeals rules that the Securities and Exchange Commission (SEC) does not have the right to regulate hedge funds – an industry with over $1.1 trillion in assets.

FTSE 100	35	-0.3	0.8
FTSE 250	30	-0.3	0.5
S&P 500	40	-0.1	0.8
NIKKEI	45	-0.1	1.2

Tue

700th anniversary of the Battle of Bannockburn

24

2002: More than 10,000 people peacefully march in Oslo, Norway, protesting against the World Bank which is holding its Annual World Bank Conference on Development Economics.

FTSE 100	38	-0.4	0.9
FTSE 250	25	-0.4	0.9
S&P 500	47	-0.1	0.8
NIKKEI	57	-0.1	1.1

Wed

25

1983: Villagers at Rottingdean, near Brighton, raise £50,000 to buy the walled garden of Rudyard Kipling's former home, to prevent it being developed for housing.

FTSE 100	59	0.1	0.8
FTSE 250	60	0.1	0.7
S&P 500	41	-0.1	0.8
NIKKEI	50	0.0	1.1

Thu

26

1963: US President John F. Kennedy gives his "Ich bin ein Berliner" speech, underlining the support of the United States for democratic West Germany.

FTSE 100	41	-0.5	1.0
FTSE 250	45	-0.3	0.9
S&P 500	42	-0.3	1.1
NIKKEI	50	-0.2	1.1

Fri

New moon

27

2007: Tony Blair steps down as Britain's Prime Minister after ten years.

FTSE 100	59	0.2	0.8
FTSE 250	55	0.0	0.6
S&P 500	53	0.0	1.1
NIKKEI	36	-0.2	1.6

Sat 28   Ramadan (Muslim, until 27 July)

Sun 29   Formula 1: British Grand Prix, Silverstone

COMPANY NEWS

Interims Carnival, Domino Printing Sciences

Finals Betfair Group, Carpetright, Dixons Retail, Essar Energy, Greene King, Smith (DS), Stagecoach Group

"In the business world, the rear-view mirror is always clearer than the windshield."
Warren Buffett

Market performance this month

After a usually disappointing May and June, shares tend to perform a bit better this month. July ranks 5th of all months for performance: on average the market increases 0.8% in July, with a probability of a positive return of 55%.

The start of the month tends to be strong: the first trading day (FTD) is one of the strongest FTDs for any month in the year and the first week of the month is among the top ten strongest weeks in the year. After that, the market has a propensity to drift lower for a couple of weeks until finishing strongly in the final week of the month.

FTSE 100	55	0.8	4.3
FTSE 250	56	0.7	5.3
S&P 500	54	1.0	4.1
NIKKEI	45	-0.4	5.1

Although this may not be an exciting month for the overall market, there can be a fair degree of divergence of performance at the sector level. Historically the sectors that have been strong in July are Chemicals, Personal Goods and Real Estate Investment Trusts while weak sectors have been Gas, Water & Multiutilities, Support Services and Beverages.

July has been the most active month for flotations; over 50 of the companies in the FTSE 350 have had their IPOs in this month. (Perhaps this is to allow company founders to go shopping for yachts in the summer months?)

Performance of market in July [1970 to 2013]

FTSE 100 average month chart for July [1985 to 2013]

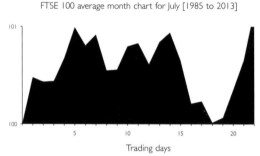

Trading days

JULY SUMMARY

Market performance	Average return: 0.8%		Positive: 55%	Ranking: 5th
Sector performance	*Strong* Chemicals, Personal Goods, Real Estate Investment Trusts, Technology Hardware & Equipment		*Weak* Beverages, Gas, Water & Multiutilities, Industrial Transportation, Support Services	
Share performance	*Strong* Brown (N) Group, Dairy Crest Group, Greene King, Pace, Wetherspoon (J D)		*Weak* Man Group, Petra Diamonds Ltd	
Main features of the month	First trading day average return: 0.48%; positive: 70% Last trading day average return: 0.16%; positive: 47% 07 Jul: start of the 3rd weakest market week in the year 08 Jul: 2nd weakest market day of the year 21 Jul: start of the 4th weakest market week in the year 28 Jul: start of the strongest market week in the year			
Significant dates	04 Jul: Independence Day (US) – NYSE closed 10 Jul: MPC interest rate announcement at 12 noon (anticipated) 29 Jul: Two-day FOMC meeting starts			

Mon
5th strongest market week

30

FTSE 100	60	0.0	0.9
FTSE 250	65	0.2	0.6
S&P 500	49	0.1	0.7
NIKKEI	60	0.3	1.2

1987: The Royal Canadian Mint introduces the $1 coin, known as the Loonie.

Tue
SAR Establishment Day (HK) – HKSE closed

1

FTSE 100	67	0.3	1.5
FTSE 250	75	0.1	1.1
S&P 500	69	0.2	0.7
NIKKEI	57	0.5	1.5

1999: The Scottish Parliament is opened by Queen Elizabeth II.

Wed
Rowing: Henley Royal Regatta (until 6 July)
50th anniversary of President Johnson signing the Civil Rights Act into law, abolishing racial segregation in the US

2

FTSE 100	55	0.0	1.1
FTSE 250	55	-0.1	1.1
S&P 500	52	0.0	1.0
NIKKEI	59	0.2	1.3

1962: The first Wal-Mart store opens for business in Rogers, Arkansas.

Thu
ECB Governing Council Meeting
25th anniversary of the LSE flotation of RSA Insurance Group

3

FTSE 100	64	0.2	1.2
FTSE 250	60	0.2	0.8
S&P 500	71	0.3	0.6
NIKKEI	59	0.1	0.9

1938: The world speed record for a steam railway locomotive of 126mph is set in England, by the Mallard.

Fri
Independence Day (US) – NYSE closed
Nonfarm payroll report (anticipated)

4

FTSE 100	55	0.4	1.0
FTSE 250	55	0.1	0.8
S&P 500			
NIKKEI	43	-0.2	0.8

1937: The Indian Independence Bill is presented before the British House of Commons, proposing the partition of the provinces of British India into two sovereign countries – India and Pakistan.

Sat 5   Cycling: Tour de France begins in Leeds, West Yorkshire

Sun 6   25th anniversary of the LSE flotation of Genesis Emerging Markets Fund Ltd.

COMPANY NEWS
Interims Anglo American, G4S, Ocado Group, St Modwen Properties
Finals Anite, Daejan Holdings

"Money is better than poverty, if only for financial reasons."
Woody Allen

BRAZIL

On Sunday this week it is the World Cup Final, the culmination of the tournament that has been taking place in Brazil since 12 June. So let's look at Brazilian shares.

Today there are quite a few Brazil-related ETFs listed on the LSE, the longest-established is the iShares MSCI Brazil [IBZL] ETF, which listed in 2005.

The following chart plots the ratio of the FTSE 100 to IBZL.

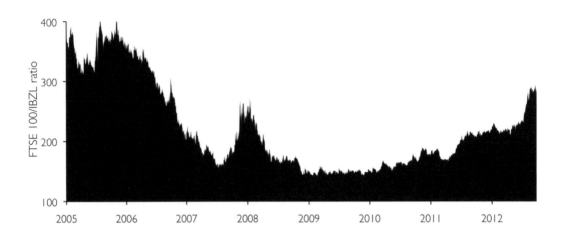

Broadly, the story has been one of relative strength of the Brazilian market over the UK market for the period 2005 to 2009, and since then a period of relative weakness.

The charts below show the monthly seasonality of the Brazilian market (as represented by the IBZL ETF). The chart on the left plots the average returns by month; the chart on the right the proportion of months with positive returns.

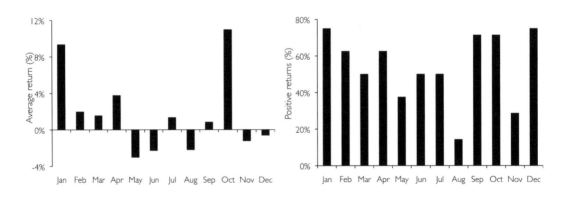

It can be seen that IBZL has been strong in January and October, and weak in May, August and November.

Brazil factette

At the final game of the 1950 FIFA World Cup the number of spectators at the Maracanã Stadium in Rio de Janeiro set the record for the world's largest attendance in an enclosed stadium – 199,854 (official stadium capacity was 78,000).

Mon

7

3rd weakest market week

1802: *The Wasp*, the first comic book, is published in Hudson, New York.

FTSE 100	60	0.4	1.0
FTSE 250	60	0.2	0.7
S&P 500	58	0.1	1.0
NIKKEI	35	0.3	1.6

Tue

8

2nd weakest market day

2011: The Space Shuttle Atlantis is launched in the final mission of the US Space Shuttle programme.

FTSE 100	25	-0.2	0.9
FTSE 250	47	-0.1	1.0
S&P 500	52	0.1	0.9
NIKKEI	50	-0.2	1.4

Wed

9

2007: CRH closes at all-time high of 23.069.

FTSE 100	57	0.1	0.8
FTSE 250	58	0.1	0.6
S&P 500	64	0.2	0.8
NIKKEI	52	0.2	1.0

Thu

10

MPC interest rate announcement at 12h00
Golf: British Women's Open, Royal Birkdale, Merseyside (until 13 July)

1997: London scientists report the findings of the DNA analysis of a Neanderthal skeleton which supports the "out of Africa theory" of human evolution, placing an African Eve at 100,000 to 200,000 years ago.

FTSE 100	38	-0.4	0.9
FTSE 250	47	-0.1	0.7
S&P 500	50	-0.2	0.9
NIKKEI	43	0.0	1.0

Fri

11

1848: Waterloo railway station opens in London.

FTSE 100	52	-0.2	1.4
FTSE 250	47	-0.3	1.1
S&P 500	56	0.1	0.8
NIKKEI	38	-0.4	1.3

Sat 12   Full moon

Sun 13   Football: FIFA World Cup Final

COMPANY NEWS

Interims Moneysupermarket.com Group
Finals Polar Capital Technology Trust, SuperGroup

"Listen to what the market is saying about others, not what others are saying about the market."
Richard Wyckoff

DAY OF THE WEEK PERFORMANCE

Is the performance of the FTSE 100 affected by the day of week?

In early 2013 the Dow Jones Industrial Average rose on 20 consecutive Tuesdays – an unprecedented streak since records began. A little earlier in the year the FTSE 100 rose for 10 consecutive Fridays. Not as remarkable as the Dow streak perhaps, but still impressive. Is this just random, or is there some significant pattern in the behaviour of the market on different days of the week?

The two charts below show the performance of the FTSE 100 on the five days of the week since the inception of the index in 1984. The chart on the left displays the percentage of days when the index rose on each of the five days; the chart on the right shows the average return for each day.

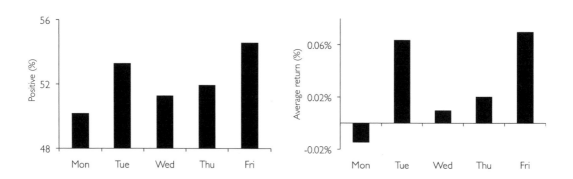

Since 1984 the strongest day of the week has been Friday; the FTSE 100 has had a positive return on 55% of all Fridays. The weakest day has been Monday; the FTSE 100 has had a positive return on 50% of Mondays. This profile is reflected in the average returns: Fridays being strongest with an average return of 0.07% and Monday being the only day of the week with a negative return.

But market behaviour changes over time. What has been the situation recently?

The two charts below are similar to those above except they are for the period from the beginning of 2012 to August 2013 (the time of writing).

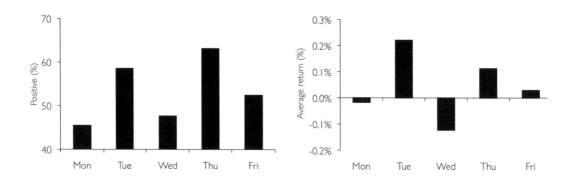

We can see that the market behaviour has changed in recent years.

Now the weakest day could be considered Wednesday, which has had an average return of -0.12% since 2012. And Tuesday and Thursday have become the strongest days: the market rises more often on Thursdays (63% of all Thursdays), but the average return is greatest on Tuesdays (+0.22%, which is five times greater than the average return on all days).

Mon Bastille Day

14

FTSE 100	60	0.3	1.0
FTSE 250	50	0.2	0.8
S&P 500	70	0.2	0.7
NIKKEI	60	0.4	1.2

1881: Billy the Kid is shot and killed by Pat Garrett outside Fort Sumner.

Tue

15

FTSE 100	45	-0.1	1.7
FTSE 250	53	-0.1	1.1
S&P 500	55	0.0	0.8
NIKKEI	60	-0.2	0.9

1799: The Rosetta Stone is found in the Egyptian village of Rosetta by French Captain Pierre-François Bouchard during Napoleon's Egyptian Campaign.

Wed Beige Book published

16

FTSE 100	48	0.1	0.8
FTSE 250	47	0.0	0.9
S&P 500	49	0.0	0.9
NIKKEI	53	-0.1	1.1

1987: British Caledonian (BCal) and British Airways (BA) announce they are to merge to compete against US airlines.

Thu Golf: British Open, Royal Liverpool Golf Course, Cheshire (until 20 July)
ECB Governing Council Meeting

17

FTSE 100	62	0.3	1.3
FTSE 250	63	0.1	1.0
S&P 500	59	0.1	0.8
NIKKEI	60	-0.1	1.2

1841: The first edition of the English magazine *Punch* is published in London.

Fri 20th anniversary of the LSE flotation of 3i Group

18

FTSE 100	38	-0.2	1.1
FTSE 250	42	0.0	1.0
S&P 500	33	-0.2	0.8
NIKKEI	26	-0.6	1.1

1968: NM Electronics is incorporated – later to be renamed Intel.

Sat 19

Sun 20

COMPANY NEWS

Interims Aberforth Smaller Companies Trust, Rio Tinto
Finals Sports Direct International

"If no one ever took risks, Michelangelo would have painted the Sistine floor."
Neil Simon

DAY OF THE WEEK STRATEGY

Last week we saw the performance characteristics of the market on the five days of the week. To recap, since 2012 the FTSE 100 has had negative average returns on Monday and Wednesday and positive average returns on Tuesday, Thursday and Friday.

This suggests a strategy of going short the market for Monday (i.e. shorting at the close the previous Friday), switching to long on Tuesday, back to short on Wednesday, and then long on Thursday and Friday (and back to short at the close of Friday).

The following chart shows the result of implementing this strategy every week from January 2012 to August 2013 (the time of writing). A spread cost of 1 point on each transaction is included in the performance figures. For comparison, a simple long-only FTSE 100 portfolio is also shown. The portfolios are rebased to start at 100.

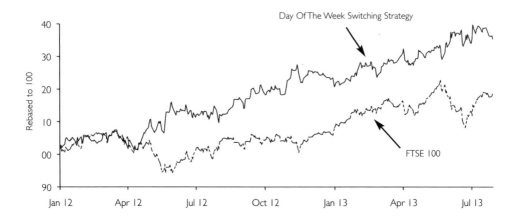

At the end of the period the FTSE 100 portfolio would have increased 19%, while the Day Of The Week Switching Strategy would have increased 35%.

Strategy variant

Looking again at the analysis on the previous page, the strength of the market on Tuesday (as measured by the average return) stands out. This suggests a variant of the above strategy whereby the unit trade size is doubled on Tuesdays.

The chart below replicates that above and adds this new 2xTuesday strategy variant. Again, a spread cost of 1 point per trade is included.

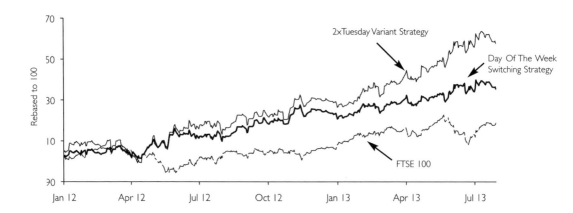

At the end of the period, the 2xTuesday portfolio would have increased 58%. Of course, further variants of the strategy are possible. For example, unit trade size on Wednesday (going short) could also be doubled.

Mon

21

Marine Day (Japan) – TSE closed
4th weakest market week

2005: China announces it is dropping its peg to the US dollar in favour of a floating rate based on a basket of foreign currencies.

FTSE 100	45	-0.1	0.9
FTSE 250	45	0.0	0.8
S&P 500	41	-0.2	0.7
NIKKEI			

Tue

22

Horseracing: Glorious Goodwood, Chichester (until 26 July)

1933: Wiley Post becomes the first person to fly solo around the world, travelling 15,596 miles in 7 days, 18 hours and 45 minutes.

FTSE 100	45	-0.5	1.5
FTSE 250	37	-0.2	0.9
S&P 500	45	-0.1	0.9
NIKKEI	25	-0.6	1.4

Wed

23

MPC meeting minutes published
Commonwealth Games, Glasgow (until 3 August)

1995: The National Trust appeals to Japan to help limit the overwhelming numbers of Japanese tourists visiting Beatrix Potter's cottage in the Lake District.

FTSE 100	57	0.0	1.1
FTSE 250	53	0.0	1.1
S&P 500	49	-0.1	0.9
NIKKEI	48	-0.1	1.6

Thu

24

2000: BP reverts to its old name (after two years as BP Amoco) and unveils a green brand image in an attempt to win over environmentally aware consumers.

FTSE 100	43	-0.4	1.1
FTSE 250	42	-0.4	1.1
S&P 500	43	0.0	1.2
NIKKEI	67	0.3	1.8

Fri

25

200th anniversary of George Stephenson successfully testing his first locomotive

2010: WikiLeaks publishes classified documents about the war in Afghanistan in one of the largest leaks in US military history.

FTSE 100	43	0.1	1.2
FTSE 250	42	-0.2	0.7
S&P 500	56	0.1	0.8
NIKKEI	48	-0.2	1.0

Sat 26   New moon

Sun 27

COMPANY NEWS

Interims ARM Holdings, Beazley, BG Group, Bodycote, British American Tobacco, Capita Group, Centrica, COLT Group SA, Croda International, CSR, Dialight, Fidelity European Values, GlaxoSmithKline, Herald Investment Trust, Howden Joinery Group, Informa, International Personal Finance, Intu Properties, ITV, Laird, Lancashire Holdings Ltd, Law Debenture Corporation, Man Group, Morgan Advance Material, National Express Group, Pace, Pearson, Provident Financial, Rathbone Brothers, Reed Elsevier, Rolls-Royce Group, Shire, St James's Place, Temple Bar Investment Trust, Travis Perkins, Unilever
Finals British Sky Broadcasting Group, IG Group Holdings, PZ Cussons, Renishaw

"A bank is a place that will lend you money if you can prove that you don't need it."
Bob Hope

AUGUST MARKET

Market performance this month

Not surprisingly perhaps, during the low-volume summer doldrums the performance of shares in August is very similar to that in July. Five years ago August was ranked the 5th best month in the year, but now it has slipped to 8th position. The average return in the month is 0.6%, while the probability of a positive return in August is 59%. There have been some nasty surprises in this August: most recently with large falls in 1998 and 2011.

FTSE 100	59	0.6	4.8
FTSE 250	70	0.6	5.5
S&P 500	56	0.0	4.6
NIKKEI	48	-0.6	7.2

In an average month for August the market tends to drift lower for the first couple of weeks and then increase for the final two weeks of the month. The final trading day of the month has historically been strong.

An interesting characteristic of August is that it is the strongest month for the FTSE 100 relative to the S&P 500 – the former has outperformed the latter by an average of 0.7 percentage points this month. In the 29 years since the inception of the FTSE 100, it has outperformed the US index in 18 years.

Finally, August is the busiest month for interim results announcements for both FTSE 100 and FTSE 250 companies.

Performance of market in August [1970 to 2013]

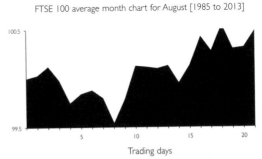
FTSE 100 average month chart for August [1985 to 2013]

Trading days

AUGUST SUMMARY

Market performance	Average return: 0.6%		Positive: 59%	Ranking: 8th
Sector performance	*Strong* Food & Drug Retailers, Gas, Water & Multiutilities, Health Care Equipment & Services, Household Goods, Software & Computer Services		*Weak* Chemicals	
Share performance	*Strong* Bunzl, Centrica, Fisher (James) & Sons, Keller Group, Tesco		*Weak* Investec, Pennon Group, Rio Tinto	
Main features of the month	Busiest month for FTSE 100 and FTSE 250 interim results announcements FTSE 100 often outperforms the S&P 500 in this month GBPUSD historically weak this month First trading day average return: 0.06%; positive: 63% Last trading day average return: 0.14%; positive: 62% 18 Aug: start of the 2nd strongest market week			
Significant dates	01 Aug: US Nonfarm payroll report (anticipated) 07 Aug: MPC interest rate announcement at 12 noon (anticipated) 13 Aug: MSCI quarterly index review announcement 25 Aug: Summer bank holiday – LSE closed			

Mon
28

Eid-Al-Fitr (end of Ramadan)
Strongest market week
8th strongest market day

FTSE 100	75	0.2	0.6
FTSE 250	60	-0.1	0.7
S&P 500	53	-0.2	0.9
NIKKEI	70	0.4	1.1

1858: Fingerprints are first used as a means of identification by William Herschel, who later established a fingerprint register.

Tue
29

9th strongest market day
Two-day FOMC meeting starts

FTSE 100	75	0.5	1.4
FTSE 250	68	0.3	0.7
S&P 500	52	0.1	1.2
NIKKEI	45	-0.1	1.2

1981: A worldwide television audience of over 700m people watch the wedding of Charles, Prince of Wales, and Lady Diana Spencer.

Wed
30

FTSE 100	57	0.3	0.9
FTSE 250	74	0.5	0.8
S&P 500	69	0.3	0.6
NIKKEI	52	0.1	1.6

2006: The world's longest running music show, Top of the Pops, is broadcast for the last time on BBC Two.

Thu
31

FTSE 100	43	0.2	1.0
FTSE 250	53	0.2	0.7
S&P 500	66	0.1	0.8
NIKKEI	57	0.4	1.1

1790: The first US patent is issued to Samuel Hopkins for a potash process.

Fri
1

Lammas
Nonfarm payroll report (anticipated)
Rubgy: Women's Rugby World Cup, France (until 14 August)
20th anniversary of the LSE flotation of Associated British Foods

FTSE 100	57	-0.2	1.4
FTSE 250	47	-0.1	0.6
S&P 500	47	0.0	0.9
NIKKEI	38	-0.2	1.4

1971: Astronauts uncover a rock which dates back to the origin of the Moon.

Sat 2

Sun 3

COMPANY NEWS

Interims African Barrick Gold Ltd, Aggreko, Alliance Trust, AstraZeneca, BAE Systems, Barclays, BP, Capital & Counties Properties, Devro, Dignity, Domino's Pizza UK & IRL, Drax Group, Elementis, Essentra, F&C Asset Management, Fidessa Group, Foreign & Colonial Investment Trust, Fresnillo, GKN, Hammerson, Hiscox Ltd, HSBC Holdings, Inchcape, Intertek Group, Jardine Lloyd Thompson Group, Jupiter Fund Management, Keller Group, Ladbrokes, Lloyds Banking Group, Millennium & Copthorne Hotels, Reckitt Benckiser Group, Rentokil Initial, Rexam, Rightmove, Rotork, Royal Bank of Scotland Group, Royal Dutch Shell, RPS Group, RSA Insurance Group, Segro, Senior, Smith & Nephew, Spectris, Spirent Communications, Standard Chartered, Taylor Wimpey, Telecity Group, Tullett Prebon, Tullow Oil, UBM, Ultra Electronics Holdings, Vesuvius, Weir Group, William Hill

Finals

"Inflation is taxation without legislation."
Milton Friedman

MONTHLY PERFORMANCE OF THE FTSE 100 INDEX

The table below shows the percentage performance of the FTSE 100 for every month since 1980. The months where the index fell are highlighted. By scanning the columns it is possible to get a feel for how the market moves in certain months.

Monthly percentage returns for the FTSE 100

	Jan	Feb	Mar	Apr	May	Jun	Jul	Aug	Sep	Oct	Nov	Dec
1980	9.2	4.9	-9.2	3.4	-2.3	11.2	3.7	0.7	3.2	5.9	0.6	-5.3
1981	-1.5	4.3	0.4	6.9	-5.0	1.9	0.4	5.0	-16.6	3.2	10.5	-1.1
1982	4.5	-4.9	3.5	1.1	3.4	-4.3	3.6	2.9	6.1	2.0	0.9	1.7
1983	3.1	0.6	1.8	8.1	0.2	2.8	-2.1	2.6	-2.6	-3.4	5.7	1.9
1984	6.3	-2.1	6.9	2.3	-10.3	2.0	-3.0	9.3	3.3	0.9	2.6	4.3
1985	3.9	-1.6	1.4	1.1	1.7	-5.9	2.2	6.3	-3.8	6.8	4.5	-1.8
1986	1.6	7.6	8.1	-0.5	-3.5	2.9	-5.6	6.6	-6.3	4.9	0.3	2.6
1987	7.7	9.5	0.9	2.6	7.4	3.7	3.4	-4.7	5.2	-26.0	-9.7	8.4
1988	4.6	-1.2	-1.5	3.4	-1.0	4.1	-0.2	-5.4	4.2	1.4	-3.2	0.0
1989	14.4	-2.4	3.6	2.1	-0.2	1.7	6.8	4.0	-3.7	-6.8	6.3	6.4
1990	-3.5	-3.5	-0.3	-6.4	11.5	1.3	-2.0	-7.0	-8.0	3.0	4.8	-0.3
1991	1.3	9.7	3.2	1.2	0.5	-3.4	7.2	2.2	-0.9	-2.1	-5.7	3.0
1992	3.1	-0.4	-4.8	8.8	2.0	-6.9	-4.8	-3.6	10.4	4.1	4.5	2.4
1993	-1.4	2.2	0.4	-2.3	1.0	2.1	0.9	5.9	-2.0	4.4	-0.1	7.9
1994	2.1	-4.7	-7.3	1.3	-5.0	-1.7	5.6	5.5	-6.9	2.3	-0.5	-0.5
1995	-2.4	0.6	4.3	2.5	3.2	-0.1	4.5	0.4	0.9	0.6	3.8	0.7
1996	1.9	-0.8	-0.7	3.2	-1.8	-1.0	-0.2	4.4	2.2	0.6	2.0	1.5
1997	3.8	0.8	0.1	2.9	4.2	-0.4	6.6	-1.8	8.9	-7.7	-0.2	6.3
1998	6.3	5.7	2.9	-0.1	-1.0	-0.7	0.1	-10.1	-3.5	7.4	5.6	2.4
1999	0.2	4.7	1.9	4.1	-5.0	1.5	-1.4	0.2	-3.5	3.7	5.5	5.0
2000	-9.5	-0.6	4.9	-3.3	0.5	-0.7	0.8	4.8	-5.7	2.3	-4.6	1.3
2001	1.2	-6.0	-4.8	5.9	-2.9	-2.7	-2.0	-3.3	-8.3	2.8	3.3	0.3
2002	-1.0	-1.2	3.3	-2.0	-1.6	-8.4	-8.8	-0.4	-12.0	8.5	3.2	-5.5
2003	-9.5	2.5	-1.2	8.7	3.1	-0.4	3.1	0.1	-1.7	4.8	1.3	3.1
2004	-1.9	2.3	-2.4	2.4	-1.3	0.8	-1.1	1.0	2.5	1.2	1.7	2.4
2005	0.8	2.4	-1.5	-1.9	3.4	3.0	3.3	0.3	3.4	-2.9	2.0	3.6
2006	2.5	0.5	3.0	1.0	-5.0	1.9	1.6	-0.4	0.9	2.8	-1.3	2.8
2007	-0.3	-0.5	2.2	2.2	2.7	-0.2	-3.8	-0.9	2.6	3.9	-4.3	0.4
2008	-8.9	0.1	-3.1	6.8	-0.6	-7.1	-3.8	4.2	-13.0	-10.7	-2.0	3.4
2009	-6.4	-7.7	2.5	8.1	4.1	-3.8	8.5	6.5	4.6	-1.7	2.9	4.3
2010	-4.1	3.2	6.1	-2.2	-6.6	-5.2	6.9	-0.6	6.2	2.3	-2.6	6.7
2011	-0.6	2.2	-1.4	2.7	-1.3	-0.7	-2.2	-7.2	-4.9	8.1	-0.7	1.2
2012	2.0	3.3	-1.8	-0.5	-7.3	4.7	1.2	1.4	0.5	0.7	1.5	0.5
2013	6.4	1.3	0.8	0.3	2.4	-5.6	6.5					

Observations

1. In recent years (i.e. since 2000) the index has been weak in January, May and June; and strong in April, October and December.

2. In the last 20 years it can clearly be seen that the strongest month has been December (only down four times in 30 years). However, in the '70s and '80s the strongest month was April (which increased every year from 1971 to 1985).

3. Looking across the table, it can be seen that the longest period of consecutive down months was April 2002 to September 2002. The longest periods of consecutive up months were July 1982 to June 1983 and June 2012 to May 2013 (the only times the FTSE 100 has risen 12 months without a break).

Mon

7th weakest market day

4

1914: Britain declares war on Germany as German troops invade Belgium.

FTSE 100	30	-0.4	0.9
FTSE 250	53	-0.2	1.1
S&P 500	44	-0.3	1.1
NIKKEI	25	-0.6	0.8

Tue

5

1957: *American Bandstand*, a show dedicated to the teenage "baby-boomers" that plays songs and shows popular dances of the time, debuts on the ABC television network.

FTSE 100	50	-0.2	1.3
FTSE 250	63	-0.1	1.2
S&P 500	43	-0.1	0.9
NIKKEI	35	-0.3	1.2

Wed

6

2011: A peaceful march in protest of the death of Mark Duggan in Tottenham, London, ends in a riot, sparking a wave of rioting throughout the UK over the following four nights.

FTSE 100	43	-0.2	1.4
FTSE 250	32	-0.4	1.1
S&P 500	53	0.0	1.1
NIKKEI	33	-0.2	1.5

Thu

MPC interest rate announcement at 12h00
ECB Governing Council Meeting

7

2012: Sir Elton John sues *The Times* for libel over articles that he says falsely linked him to immoral tax avoidance.

FTSE 100	67	0.3	0.9
FTSE 250	58	0.1	1.0
S&P 500	64	0.3	0.8
NIKKEI	43	-0.3	1.5

Fri

8

1969: At a zebra crossing in London, photographer Iain Macmillan takes the photo that becomes the cover of the Beatles album Abbey Road, one of the most famous album covers in recording history.

FTSE 100	62	0.1	1.3
FTSE 250	63	0.1	1.3
S&P 500	51	-0.1	1.3
NIKKEI	62	0.2	1.2

Sat 9

Sun 10 Full moon

COMPANY NEWS

Interims AMEC, Aviva, BBA Aviation, BlackRock World Mining Trust, Catlin Group Ltd, Cobham, Countrywide, esure Group, F&C Commercial Property Trust Ltd, Greggs, Henderson Group, Inmarsat, InterContinental Hotels Group, International Consolidated Airlines Group SA, Legal & General Group, Meggitt, Mondi, Old Mutual, Randgold Resources Ltd, Savills, Schroders, Standard Life

Finals

"Short the industry which the majority of Harvard Business School want to join."
Marc Faber

SEASONALITY OF GBPUSD

This Almanac normally restricts its focus to equities, but in this study we will divert briefly to look at currencies – more specifically, the GB sterling/US dollar exchange rate (GBPUSD).

After all, the fluctuations of sterling are very important to equity investors. Over half of all aggregate revenues of FTSE 100 companies originate outside of the UK, and any overseas investors in the UK equity market and UK investors in international markets will be affected by the sterling exchange rate.

Of course, for a while after World War II nobody needed to worry about currency fluctuations because currencies were tied to the US dollar under the Bretton Woods system. Exchange controls were in place and some older readers may remember being restricted to taking no more than £50 out of the UK. But on 15 August 1971 (43 years ago this week) President Nixon announced that the US was ending the convertibility of the US dollar to gold and this led to the end of the Bretton Woods system and fixed-rate currencies, such as sterling, became free-floating.

The following chart shows the fluctuations of GBPUSD since it became free-floating in 1971.

As can be seen, in the decade following 1971 sterling fell against the dollar (almost reaching parity in February 1985); but since then has been broadly trading in the range 1.4 to 2.0.

The following charts show the monthly changes in GBPUSD for the last 20 years. The chart on the left shows the average percentage change; for example, on average the rate has fallen 0.37% in January. The chart on the right shows the proportion of years the rate has risen that month; for example, GBPUSD has risen in January in 48% of years since 1993.

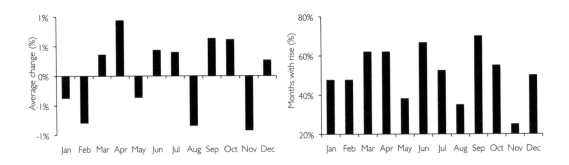

Observations

- Weak months for GBPUSD have been: February, May, August and November
- Strong months for GBPUSD have been: April and October

These same observations would seem to have some persistency as they are valid for other periods analysed: 1971 to 2013 and 2000 to 2013.

Mon

11

75th anniversary of the LSE flotation of Unilever

2003: NATO takes over command of the peacekeeping force in Afghanistan, marking its first major operation outside Europe in its 54-year history.

➔

FTSE 100	45	0.0	1.3
FTSE 250	50	0.1	1.2
S&P 500	53	0.2	1.1
NIKKEI	65	0.0	1.5

Tue

12

30BC: Cleopatra VII Philopator, the last ruler of the Egyptian Ptolemaic dynasty, commits suicide, allegedly by means of an asp bite.

↗

FTSE 100	70	0.4	1.1
FTSE 250	72	0.3	0.8
S&P 500	45	0.0	0.7
NIKKEI	40	-0.1	1.1

Wed

13

MPC Inflation Report published
MSCI Quarterly Index Review (announcement date)

1961: Berliners wake to a divided city as troops in East Germany seal off the border between East and West Berlin, shutting off the escape route for thousands of refugees from the East.

➔

FTSE 100	57	0.2	1.1
FTSE 250	58	0.2	1.0
S&P 500	51	0.0	0.8
NIKKEI	48	-0.3	1.4

Thu

14

25th anniversary of the LSE flotation of Babcock International Group

1975: *The Rocky Horror Picture Show*, the longest-running release in film history, opens at the USA Theatre in Westwood, Los Angeles, California.

↗

FTSE 100	71	0.3	1.0
FTSE 250	79	0.2	0.7
S&P 500	55	0.0	1.0
NIKKEI	71	0.7	1.2

Fri

15

75th anniversary of the Hollywood premier of *The Wizard of Oz*, starring Judy Garland

1914: The Panama Canal opens.

➔

FTSE 100	57	0.0	1.2
FTSE 250	79	0.3	0.7
S&P 500	56	0.1	0.8
NIKKEI	57	0.5	1.6

Sat 16

Sun 17

COMPANY NEWS

Interims Balfour Beatty, Bank of Georgia Holdings, Centamin, CRH, EnQuest, Eurasian Natural Resources Corporation, Hikma Pharmaceuticals, Interserve, JPMorgan American Investment Trust, Menzies (John), Michael Page International, NB Global Floating Rate Income Fund Ltd, Petrofac Ltd, Prudential, Resolution Ltd, SVG Capital, Witan Investment Trust, Xaar

Finals

"Statistics are like a bikini. What they reveal is suggestive, but what they conceal is vital."
Aaron Levenstein

MARKET BEHAVIOUR – BY WEEK

The two tables below list the historic 10 best and worst weeks for the market since 1984.

The strongest week of the whole year – when the market has historically increased the most – is the 53rd week, the last week of the year. In this week the market has risen in 80% of years. The second best week is the 31st week.

The week with the worst record is the 2nd week. In only one year in four has the market increased in this week. This is perhaps not surprising: the market is correcting after the historically strong final and first weeks of the year.

The performance figures below are ranked by the Positive (%) column – the percentage of years that the market has historically risen in the week.

10 strongest weeks in the year

Week	Positive (%)	Avg Chng (%)	StdDev
53	80	-0.6	2.1
31	79	0.6	2.6
52	76	1.0	1.5
51	76	0.8	1.6
34	76	0.4	1.9
27	70	1.0	2.0
1	69	1.2	2.6
5	66	0.9	2.0
40	66	0.8	2.5
14	66	0.7	2.1

10 weakest weeks in the year

Week	Positive (%)	Avg Chng (%)	StdDev
2	28	-0.5	1.8
25	33	-0.9	1.8
28	38	-0.6	2.4
30	38	-0.4	2.3
22	40	0.3	1.9
37	41	-0.5	2.3
38	41	-0.3	2.9
21	43	-0.3	2.0
43	45	-0.8	4.1
36	45	-0.5	2.3

Note: The ten best weeks for the market are marked on the diary pages with a square around the arrow icon and the ten worst weeks for the market are marked with a circle around the arrow icon.

Analysis of all weeks

Average Positive (%) [StdDev]	55.2 [11.7]
Average Change (%) [StdDev]	0.13 [0.49]

Since 1984 the market has risen in 55% of weeks with an average weekly return of 0.13%.

The standard deviation is 12 for the average Positive (%) value, which means that:

- weeks that have a Positive (%) value over 67 (the average plus one standard deviation) can be considered **strong** weeks, and
- weeks that have a Positive (%) value under 43 (the average minus one standard deviation) can be considered **weak** weeks.

Mon

2nd strongest market week

18

→

2005: A power blackout affecting almost 100 million people hits the Indonesian island of Java. It is the largest and most widespread power outage in history.

FTSE 100	55	0.0	1.5
FTSE 250	60	-0.2	1.3
S&P 500	44	-0.2	1.0
NIKKEI	60	0.0	1.3

Tue

19

→

1848: The *New York Herald* breaks the news to the East Coast of the US of the gold rush in California (the rush began in January).

FTSE 100	45	-0.3	1.3
FTSE 250	63	-0.2	1.1
S&P 500	45	-0.2	1.0
NIKKEI	45	-0.2	2.0

Wed

MPC meeting minutes published

20

→

1858: Charles Darwin first publishes his theory of evolution through natural selection in *The Journal of the Proceedings of the Linnean Society of London*.

FTSE 100	52	0.1	0.7
FTSE 250	53	0.0	0.7
S&P 500	58	0.3	0.9
NIKKEI	67	0.5	1.4

Thu

21

↗

2012: Abu Dhabi Investment Authority is chosen as the preferred bidder for 42 UK-based Marriott hotels after making an offer of £620m.

FTSE 100	67	0.2	1.2
FTSE 250	68	0.2	1.0
S&P 500	48	0.0	1.0
NIKKEI	52	0.2	1.6

Fri

22

→

1992: Hurricane Andrew strikes Florida, causing in excess of $25bn in damage and killing more than 20 people.

FTSE 100	52	0.2	1.0
FTSE 250	53	0.3	1.0
S&P 500	60	0.0	0.7
NIKKEI	50	0.0	1.6

Sat 23

Sun 24

COMPANY NEWS

Interims Afren, Amlin, AZ Electronic Materials SA, Berendsen, BH Global Ltd, BH Macro Ltd, Bovis Homes Group, Cairn Energy, Carillion, Derwent London, Ferrexpo, Fisher (James) & Sons, Glencore Xstrata, Hochschild Mining, IMI, IP Group, John Wood Group, Kazakhmys, Kenmare Resources, Murray International Trust, NMC Health, Persimmon, Phoenix Group Holdings, Premier Oil, SIG, SOCO International, Spirax-Sarco Engineering, UK Commercial Property Trust Ltd

Finals BHP Billiton, Diageo, Rank Group

"Whoever said money can't buy happiness didn't know where to shop."
Gertrude Stein

The table below shows the monthly outperformance of the FTSE 100 Index over the S&P 500 Index since 1984. For example, in January 1984, the FTSE 100 increased 6.3%, while the S&P 500 fell -0.9%; the outperformance of the former over the latter was therefore 7.2 percentage points.

The cells are highlighted if the number is negative (i.e. the S&P 500 outperformed the FTSE 100).

	Jan	Feb	Mar	Apr	May	Jun	Jul	Aug	Sep	Oct	Nov	Dec
1984	7.2	1.8	5.6	1.8	-4.4	0.3	-1.4	-1.3	3.6	0.9	4.1	2.1
1985	-3.5	-2.5	1.7	1.6	-3.7	-7.2	2.7	7.5	-0.3	2.5	-2.0	-6.3
1986	1.3	0.4	2.8	0.9	-8.5	1.5	0.3	-0.5	2.2	-0.6	-1.9	5.4
1987	-5.5	5.8	-1.7	3.8	6.8	-1.1	-1.5	-8.2	7.6	-4.3	-1.2	1.1
1988	0.5	-5.4	1.8	2.5	-1.3	-0.2	0.3	-1.5	0.2	-1.2	-1.3	-1.4
1989	7.3	0.5	1.5	-2.9	-3.7	2.5	-2.0	2.4	-3.1	-4.3	4.6	4.3
1990	3.4	-4.4	-2.8	-3.7	2.3	2.1	-1.5	2.4	-2.9	3.7	-1.2	-2.8
1991	-2.9	3.0	1.0	1.2	-3.3	1.4	2.7	0.2	1.0	-3.3	-1.3	-8.1
1992	5.1	-1.3	-2.6	6.0	1.9	-5.1	-8.8	-1.2	9.5	3.9	1.5	1.4
1993	-2.1	1.1	-1.5	0.3	-1.3	2.0	1.4	2.5	-1.0	2.5	1.2	6.9
1994	-1.1	-1.7	-2.7	0.1	-6.2	1.0	2.4	1.7	-4.2	0.3	3.4	-1.7
1995	-4.8	-3.0	1.5	-0.3	-0.4	-2.3	1.3	0.5	-3.1	1.1	-0.3	-1.1
1996	-1.4	-1.5	-1.5	1.9	-4.1	-1.2	4.4	2.6	-3.2	-2.0	-5.4	3.6
1997	-2.3	0.2	4.4	-3.0	-1.7	-4.7	-1.2	3.9	3.5	-4.2	-4.7	4.7
1998	5.3	-1.4	-2.1	-1.0	0.9	-4.6	1.2	4.5	-9.8	-0.6	-0.3	-3.2
1999	-3.9	8.0	-1.9	0.3	-2.5	-4.0	1.8	0.9	-0.6	-2.5	3.6	-0.7
2000	-4.5	1.4	-4.7	-0.2	2.7	-3.1	2.5	-1.2	-0.3	2.8	3.4	0.9
2001	-2.3	3.2	1.6	-1.8	-3.4	-0.1	-0.9	3.1	-0.1	1.0	-4.3	-0.5
2002	0.5	0.8	-0.3	4.1	-0.7	-1.2	-0.9	-0.9	-1.0	-0.1	-2.5	0.5
2003	-6.7	4.2	-2.0	0.5	-2.0	-1.5	1.5	-1.7	-0.5	-0.7	0.6	-2.0
2004	-3.7	1.1	-0.7	4.1	-2.5	-1.0	2.3	0.8	1.6	-0.2	-2.2	-0.9
2005	3.3	0.5	0.4	0.1	0.4	3.0	-0.3	1.5	2.6	-1.2	-1.5	3.7
2006	0.0	0.5	1.9	-0.2	-1.9	1.9	1.1	-2.5	-1.5	-0.3	-3.0	1.6
2007	-1.7	1.7	1.2	-2.1	-0.6	1.6	-0.6	-2.2	-1.0	2.5	0.1	1.2
2008	-2.8	3.6	-2.5	2.0	-1.6	1.5	-2.8	2.9	-3.9	6.2	5.4	2.6
2009	2.1	3.3	-6.0	-1.3	-1.2	-3.8	1.0	3.2	1.0	0.2	-2.8	2.5
2010	-0.4	0.3	0.2	-3.7	1.6	0.2	0.1	4.1	-2.6	-1.4	-2.4	0.2
2011	-2.9	-1.0	-1.3	-0.1	0.0	1.1	0.0	-1.6	2.2	-2.7	-0.2	0.4
2012	-2.4	-0.7	-4.9	0.2	-1.0	0.7	-0.1	-0.6	-1.9	2.7	1.2	-0.2
2013	1.4	0.2	-2.8	-1.5	0.3	-4.1	1.6					
average:	-0.6	0.6	-0.6	0.3	-1.3	-0.8	0.2	0.7	-0.2	0.0	-0.3	0.5

The average monthly outperformance of the FTSE 100 over the S&P 500 is shown in the following chart.

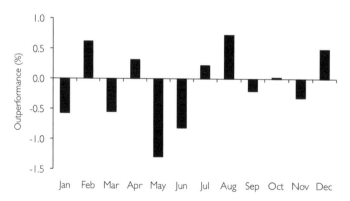

1. Although since 1984 the S&P 500 has overall greatly outperformed the FTSE 100 (+922% against +562%), there are months in the year when the FTSE 100 fairly consistently outperforms the S&P 500.

2. The five months that are relatively strong for the FTSE 100 are: February, April, July, August and December. For example, the FTSE 100 has outperformed the S&P 500 in February in 13 of the past 15 years.

3. The greatest monthly difference in performance is seen in May, when the S&P 500 on average beats the FTSE 100 by 1.3 percentage points each year.

Mon 25

Summer Bank Holiday (UK) – LSE closed
New moon
Tennis: US Open, New York (until 7 September)

1991: Linus Torvalds announces the first version of what will become Linux, a Unix-like computer operating system assembled under the model of free and open source software development and distribution.

FTSE 100			
FTSE 250			
S&P 500	47	-0.1	0.8
NIKKEI	40	-0.1	1.1

Tue 26

→

1932: The US government announces a temporary halt on home foreclosures on first mortgage homes during the depression.

FTSE 100	44	-0.1	0.8
FTSE 250	38	-0.2	0.6
S&P 500	50	0.0	0.8
NIKKEI	60	0.0	1.1

Wed 27

50th anniversary of the world premier of Walt Disney's *Mary Poppins*

→

2012: Apple asks a court to ban eight Samsung mobile phones in the US, after the South Korean company was ordered to pay $1.05bn for copying patents.

FTSE 100	56	0.2	1.1
FTSE 250	67	0.0	0.8
S&P 500	53	-0.1	1.0
NIKKEI	57	0.0	1.5

Thu 28

→

1907: Claude Ryan and Jim Casey start the American Messenger Company, later to become United Parcel Service (UPS).

FTSE 100	47	-0.3	1.4
FTSE 250	47	-0.1	1.1
S&P 500	48	-0.1	0.9
NIKKEI	48	-0.1	1.3

Fri 29

→

1898: The Goodyear tyre company is founded.

FTSE 100	47	0.0	0.8
FTSE 250	53	0.1	0.6
S&P 500	56	0.1	0.8
NIKKEI	57	0.0	1.1

Sat 30

Sun 31

COMPANY NEWS

Interims 888 Holdings, Admiral Group, Antofagasta, Bluecrest Allblue Fund Ltd, Bumi, Bunzl, Bwin.Party Digital Entertainment, Computacenter, Evraz, Hansteen Holdings, Hunting, International Public Partnership Ltd, John Laing Infrastructure Fund Ltd, Kentz Corporation Ltd, Melrose Industries, Ophir Energy, Perform Group, Playtech, Polymetal International, RIT Capital Partners, Salamander Energy, Serco Group, Synthomer, UNITE Group, WPP Group
Finals Hays

"The difference between a skinflint banker and a reckless lender is a recession."
Walter Wriston

SEPTEMBER MARKET

Market performance this month

After the summer lull, things can get exciting again for investors in September. Exciting and tricky. Since 1982 the FTSE All-Share has on average fallen 1.0% in this month – the worst average return of any month in the year. And things haven't improved recently: since 2000 the average return in September has been even worse at -1.9%.

FTSE 100	48	-1.0	5.8
FTSE 250	44	-1.9	6.8
S&P 500	44	-0.5	4.5
NIKKEI	34	-1.7	5.9

In an average month for September the market tends to gently drift lower for the first three weeks before rebounding slightly in the final week – although the final trading day (FTD) of the month has historically been one of the weakest FTDs of all months in the year.

But, however bad the month is for large caps, it is even worse for mid-cap cap stocks. On average the FTSE 100 outperforms the FTSE 250 by almost a full percentage point in September – making September the worst month for mid-cap stocks relative to the large-caps.

Events to watch out for this month include the FTSE 100 review on the 10th and triple witching on the 19th.

Performance of market in September [1970 to 2013]

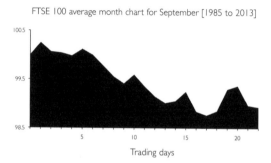
FTSE 100 average month chart for September [1985 to 2013]

Trading days

SEPTEMBER SUMMARY

Market performance	Average return: -1.0%		Positive: 48%	Ranking: 12th

Sector performance	Strong	Weak
	Electricity, Food & Drug Retailers, Mobile Telecommunications, Pharmaceuticals & Biotechnology	Aerospace & Defense, Chemicals, Electronic & Electrical Equipment, General Retailers, Media, Real Estate Investment Trusts, Technology Hardware & Equipment

Share performance	Strong	Weak
	Aberdeen Asset Management, Ashtead Group, Carnival, Diploma, JPMorgan Indian Investment Trust	Carpetright, Compass Group, Pace, Premier Farnell, SVG Capital

Main features of the month	Weakest month in the year
	The FTSE 250 is particularly weak relative to the FTSE 100 in this month
	Strong month for gold price
	First trading day average return: 0.25%; positive: 66%
	Last trading day average return: -0.05%; positive: 45% (weakest in year)

Significant dates	01 Sep: Labor Day (US) – NYSE closed
	04 Sep: MPC interest rate announcement at 12 noon (anticipated)
	05 Sep: US Nonfarm payroll report (anticipated)
	10 Sep: FTSE 100 Index quarterly review
	16 Sep: Two-day FOMC meeting starts
	19 Sep: Triple Witching

Mon

1

Labour Day (US) – NYSE closed
MSCI Quarterly Index Review (effective date)
75th anniversary of the start of World War II

1897: The Boston subway opens, becoming the first underground rapid transit system in North America.

FTSE 100	65	0.3	1.2
FTSE 250	70	0.1	1.3
S&P 500			
NIKKEI	55	0.2	1.3

Tue

2

1789: The US Treasury Department is established.

FTSE 100	50	0.0	1.0
FTSE 250	53	0.2	0.9
S&P 500	61	0.2	1.1
NIKKEI	53	-0.2	1.0

Wed

3

Beige Book published

1935: Sir Malcolm Campbell reaches a speed of 304.331 miles per hour driving on the Bonneville Salt Flats in Utah, becoming the first person to drive an automobile over 300mph.

FTSE 100	57	0.0	1.5
FTSE 250	63	0.2	1.0
S&P 500	63	0.1	1.3
NIKKEI	43	-0.2	1.7

Thu

4

MPC interest rate announcement at 12h00
ECB Governing Council Meeting

1998: Google is founded by Larry Page and Sergey Brin, two students at Stanford University.

FTSE 100	57	0.0	1.0
FTSE 250	68	0.1	0.9
S&P 500	44	-0.2	1.0
NIKKEI	33	-0.2	1.2

Fri

5

Nonfarm payroll report (anticipated)

1698: A tax on beards is imposed by the Russian Czar, Peter the Great.

FTSE 100	48	-0.4	1.1
FTSE 250	58	-0.4	1.0
S&P 500	36	-0.1	0.8
NIKKEI	48	-0.5	1.3

Sat 6

Sun 7

COMPANY NEWS

Interims Alent, Direct Line Insurance Group, Morrison (Wm) Supermarkets, Restauraunt Group
Finals Dechra Pharmaceuticals, Genus, Go-Ahead Group, Hargreaves Lansdown

"Always forgive your enemies. Nothing annoys them more."
Oscar Wilde

SIX-MONTH STRATEGY

In Week 17 we looked at the six-month effect. Let's now see how to exploit that effect in practice.

Consider two portfolios:

1. *Winter Portfolio*: this portfolio only invests in the UK stock market in the winter period (1 November to 30 April), and for the other six months of the year the portfolio is all in cash.

2. *Summer Portfolio*: does the reverse of the above portfolio – it invests in shares only in the summer period (1 May to 31 October) and is in cash for the rest of the time.

For the purposes of this simple study, we'll assume that the portfolios' investments track the FTSE All-Share Index. The chart below shows the comparative performance of the two portfolios, each starting with £100, since 1994.

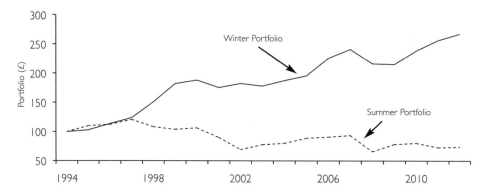

Starting with £100 in 1994 the:

- *Summer Portfolio* would be worth **£73** by 2012; but the
- *Winter Portfolio* would be worth **£267**.

This bizarre effect suggests a strategy of investing in the stock market during the period 1 November to 30 April, and then selling up and putting the cash in a deposit account or buying sterling T-bills for the other six months of the year.

The following chart compares the result of following such a Six-Month Strategy methodically since 1994 in the FTSE 100 Total Return Index to a portfolio that simply tracks the FTSE 100 Total Return Index (i.e. we are comparing the Six-Month Strategy to being fully invested in the market all year and receiving dividends).

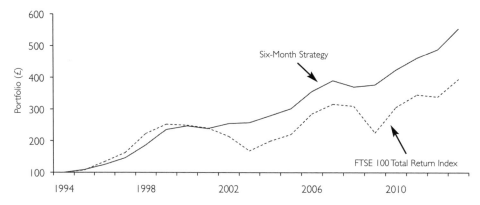

Starting in 1994 with £100 the Six-Month Strategy would have increased the portfolio to £554 by 2013; over the same period a portfolio tracking the FTSE 100 Total Return Index year round would have increased to just £395 (inc. dividends).

NB. There is evidence that the profitability of the strategy can be further enhanced by using an indicator like the MACD (as explained in the 2013 edition of the *Almanac*) to time the exact entry and exit points for the equity investment. See Week 39 for more on this.

Mon 8

6th weakest market week

1966: The first *Star Trek* series premieres on NBC.

FTSE 100	40	0.0	1.1
FTSE 250	55	0.2	1.0
S&P 500	53	0.0	1.1
NIKKEI	50	0.3	1.4

Tue 9

Day Following Mid-Autumn Festival (HK) – HKSE closed
Full moon
8th weakest market day

1995: Sony's PlayStation game console is released in the US.

FTSE 100	30	-0.3	0.8
FTSE 250	37	-0.2	0.8
S&P 500	57	-0.2	1.0
NIKKEI	45	0.1	1.2

Wed 10

FTSE 100 quarterly review

2008: The Large Hadron Collider at CERN, described as the biggest scientific experiment in history, is powered up in Geneva, Switzerland.

FTSE 100	38	-0.3	1.1
FTSE 250	47	-0.3	0.8
S&P 500	49	-0.1	0.8
NIKKEI	48	0.1	1.6

Thu 11

9th weakest market day

1997: After a nationwide referendum, Scotland votes to establish a devolved parliament within the United Kingdom.

FTSE 100	30	-0.1	0.9
FTSE 250	26	-0.3	1.0
S&P 500	53	0.0	1.1
NIKKEI	43	-0.9	1.8

Fri 12

2005: England take the Ashes from Australia for the first time since 1987.

FTSE 100	43	-0.2	1.2
FTSE 250	53	-0.2	0.9
S&P 500	52	0.0	0.9
NIKKEI	52	-0.3	1.9

Sat 13   Horseracing: St Leger's Day, Doncaster Racecourse

Sun 14

COMPANY NEWS

Interims Kingfisher, Merchants Trust, Next, Premier Farnell
Finals Ashmore Group, Barratt Developments, Dunelm Group, Kier Group, Murray Income Trust

"If it looks like a duck, sounds like a duck and walks like a duck, then it is a duck. On that basis NICs (National Insurance Contributions) are definitely tax."
John Whiting

THE SCOTTISH PORTFOLIO

In July 1698 a flotilla of five ships set sail from Leith, Scotland for Panama. Scotland had seen the colonisation successes of other European nations and wanted to get in on the action. So £400,000 was raised (about a fifth of all the wealth in Scotland at the time) for the Company of Scotland for Trading to Africa, and off they set westwards. The venture became known as the Darien Scheme.

It did not turn out well. Lack of food and water, disease, drunkenness and, finally, a Spanish siege led to the abandonment of the colony in 1700. The effect on Scotland was traumatic. Many of the nobles and landowners were financially ruined and morale damaged such that many no longer believed Scotland could be an independent major power. The failure of the Darien Scheme is thought to have been a major factor in driving Scotland to signing the 1707 Act of Union with England.

This week, 207 years later, Scotland will be voting on whether to regain independence (coincidentally, again in the wake of a financial disaster – this time the recent credit crunch).

What would an independent Scotland look like to investors?

One way of analysing this is to look at the current Scottish companies listed on the LSE. The top chart on the right plots the performance of a "Scottish" portfolio over the last ten years and also the FTSE 100 over the same period. The equally-weighted portfolio consists of the seven companies: Aberdeen Asset Management, Aggreko, Lloyds Banking Group, Royal Bank of Scotland Group, Standard Life, Weir Group, Wood Group (John). They were selected as their company addresses are in Scotland and they are in the FTSE 100.

Not too impressive – over the ten years the Scottish portfolio would have massively underperformed the FTSE 100. But…

Perhaps we should look at the portfolio without the banks; obviously the presence of RBS and Lloyds greatly affected the performance. So, the second chart on the right is as above, but this time without the bothersome banks.

Quite a different story. All five companies in the portfolio contributed to strong outperformance over the FTSE 100.

So, does this reflect the true strength of the real Scottish economy? Perhaps. But we do seem to remember that before the credit crunch apologists for Scottish independence were claiming that the Scottish financial industry – led by the banks – would be one of the economic pillars of a newly independent Scotland.

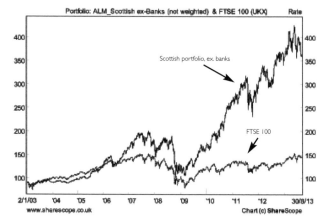

SEPTEMBER

41, -0.3, 2.9

Week 38

Mon

15

Respect for the Aged Day (Japan) – TSE closed
7th weakest market week

FTSE 100	50	-0.2	1.4
FTSE 250	60	-0.1	1.0
S&P 500	53	-0.1	1.0
NIKKEI			

2008: The investment bank Lehman Brothers files for Chapter 11 bankruptcy, having posted a $3.9bn quarterly loss a few days earlier.

Tue

16

Two-day FOMC meeting starts

FTSE 100	60	-0.1	1.2
FTSE 250	47	-0.3	1.1
S&P 500	66	0.4	0.8
NIKKEI	38	-0.9	2.2

1997: Steve Jobs returns to Apple as the interim CEO.

Wed

17

MPC meeting minutes published
ECB Governing Council Meeting
50th anniversary of James Bond's *Goldfinger* opening in the UK

FTSE 100	48	0.1	1.6
FTSE 250	42	0.0	1.4
S&P 500	51	-0.2	1.3
NIKKEI	58	0.0	1.9

2011: The Occupy Wall Street campaign begins in Zuccotti Park, New York City.

Thu

18

ECB General Council Meeting
Scottish independence referendum to be held

FTSE 100	48	-0.1	1.4
FTSE 250	47	-0.2	1.3
S&P 500	48	0.1	1.0
NIKKEI	35	-0.4	1.2

1837: Charles Lewis Tiffany and Teddy Young found their "stationery and fancy goods emporium" in New York City.

Fri

19

Triple Witching

FTSE 100	52	0.2	2.3
FTSE 250	26	0.1	2.1
S&P 500	47	0.0	1.2
NIKKEI	74	0.7	1.4

1931: The UK comes off the gold standard.

Sat 20

Sun 21

COMPANY NEWS

Interims
Finals Galliford Try, Redrow, Smiths Group, Wetherspoon (J D)

"Investors are slow to learn that security analysts do not always mean what they say."
Hersh Shefrin

5/7 MONTH STRATEGY

We have already looked at the six-month effect (the tendency for the November to April market to outperform the May to October market), and how a portfolio based on this effect can outperform an index fund (see Week 37). But it is not necessarily the case that the strong half of the year begins every year on exactly 1 November, nor that it ends exactly on 30 April. By tweaking the beginning and end dates it may be possible to enhance the (already impressive) returns of the Six-Month Strategy. An obvious rationale for this is that if investors are queuing up to buy at the end of October and sell at the end of April, it can be advantageous to get a jump on them and buy/sell a little earlier.

This idea of finessing the entry/exit dates was first proposed by Sy Harding in his 1999 book, *Riding the Bear – How to Prosper in the Coming Bear Market*. Harding's system takes the six-month seasonal trading strategy and adds a timing element using the MACD indicator.

We looked at adapting the Six-Month Strategy by incorporating an MACD timing element in the 2013 edition of the *Almanac*. In this edition we will look at another method.

Why wait a month?

If you look at the studies in Week 19 and Week 42 you can see that one of the stronger months for the market is October. This is slightly counter-intuitive as October has a reputation as a month when the market has suffered large falls (e.g. in 1987). This is true, but years when the market falls heavily in October are the exception and, certainly in recent years, October has seen strong returns for the market. Possibly one reason why October is today relatively strong is because investors anticipate the good returns towards the end of the year (and the strong six-month period itself: November to April) and look to increase their weighting in equities just before other investors pile in.

Given the strength of October, it is odd to wait until the end of that month to implement the Six-Month Strategy.

Hence the variant that is proposed here is to bring forward the date of going long the market from 1 November to 1 October. We shall call this strategy the *5/7 Month Strategy* – as it involves splitting the year into 5-month (May to September) and 7-month (October to April) periods.

The following chart shows the result of implementing the 5/7 Month Strategy, using this new date to go long. No change is made to exiting the market on 30 April. For comparison the chart also includes the portfolio returns for the standard Six-Month Strategy and the FTSE 100 Total Return Index as shown in Week 37.

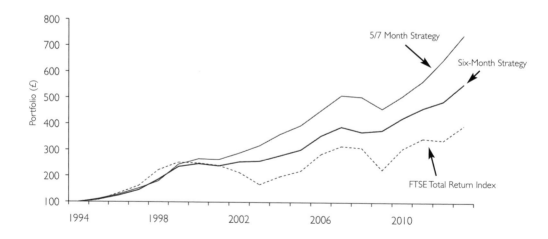

Starting in 1994 with £100 the 5/7 Month Strategy would have increased in value to £742 by 2013. Over the same period the Six-Month Strategy would have increased to £554, and the portfolio tracking the FTSE 100 Total Return Index increased to £395.

For the moment, the six-month effect would seem to have been superseded by the 5/7 month effect.

Mon
22
1955: Commercial TV begins in England.

FTSE 100	50	-0.3	1.4
FTSE 250	25	-0.5	1.0
S&P 500	47	-0.1	1.1
NIKKEI	32	-0.7	1.6

Tue
23
Autumn Equinox, also known as Mabon
TSE closed
Golf: Ryder Cup, Gleneagles Golf Course, Scotland (until 28 September)

1909: *The Phantom of the Opera* (original title: *Le Fantôme de l'Opéra*), a novel by French writer Gaston Leroux, is first published as a serialisation in *Le Gaulois*.

FTSE 100	35	-0.2	1.1
FTSE 250	37	-0.4	0.9
S&P 500	43	-0.1	1.0
NIKKEI			

Wed
24
Rosh Hashanah
New moon
10th anniversary of the LSE flotation of PayPoint

1979: Compu-Serve launches the first consumer online service, which features the first public electronic mail service.

FTSE 100	38	-0.1	1.3
FTSE 250	42	-0.2	1.1
S&P 500	42	-0.1	1.1
NIKKEI	71	0.4	1.5

Thu
25
1996: The first trading day of the newly privatised AEA Technology.

FTSE 100	48	0.0	1.1
FTSE 250	53	0.0	0.9
S&P 500	45	-0.1	0.9
NIKKEI	48	-0.4	1.3

Fri
26
Golf: Ryder Cup, Gleneagles (until 28 September)

1984: Britain and China finalise proposals to end 150 years of British rule in Hong Kong.

FTSE 100	52	0.2	1.5
FTSE 250	63	-0.1	1.0
S&P 500	56	-0.2	1.3
NIKKEI	43	-0.2	1.6

Sat 27

Sun 28   10th anniversary of the LSE flotation of Admiral Group.

COMPANY NEWS
Interims Barr (A G), Mercantile Investment Trust
Finals City of London Investment Trust, Close Brothers Group, Petra Diamonds Ltd

"Failure is only the opportunity to begin again more intelligently."
Henry Ford

OCTOBER MARKET

Market performance this month

October is a puzzling month for investors. On the one hand it has a reputation for volatility – and this is well deserved. Since 1984, seven of the 10 largest one-day falls in the market have occurred in October! The largest fall was on 20 October 1987 when the FTSE 100 fell 12.2%. Additional bad news for investors is that since 1970 the average return in the month has been just 0.3%, ranking it 9th of the 12 months. However, things have changed in recent years.

FTSE 100	76	0.7	6.8
FTSE 250	63	-0.4	8.0
S&P 500	59	0.7	5.6
NIKKEI	48	-0.9	7.3

Although the market occasionally suffers large falls in this month, for the most part the market posts a positive return. In fact, in the 20 years since 1993 the market has only fallen four times in October – this is a performance only bettered by December. In recent years the market has posted an average return of 0.7% in this month (albeit with a very high standard deviation) – ranking it 4th for monthly performance.

So, October is a volatile month but also in recent years a profitable one for investors.

In an average month for October the market tends to rise in the first two weeks, then to fall back, before a surge in prices in the last few days of the month – with the last trading day (LTD) being the strongest monthly LTD of the year.

October marks the end of the weak six-month period of the year, so many investors are looking to increase their exposure to equities towards the end of the month.

Performance of market in October [1970 to 2013]

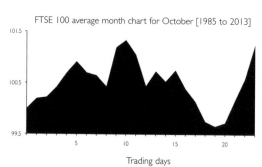

FTSE 100 average month chart for October [1985 to 2013]

Trading days

OCTOBER SUMMARY			
Market performance	Average return: 0.7%	Positive: 76%	Ranking: 4th
Sector performance	Strong	Weak	
		Automobiles & Parts, Construction & Materials, Equity Investment Instruments, Food & Drug Retailers, Health Care Equipment & Services, Household Goods, Life Insurance, Pharmaceuticals & Biotechnology	
Share performance	Strong	Weak	
	Brewin Dolphin Holdings, Diageo, easyJet, Restaurant Group (The), Tate & Lyle	Dialight, Grainger, Worldwide Healthcare Trust	
Main features of the month	The FTSE 100 is particularly strong relative to the FTSE 250 in this month		
	Weak month for gold price		
	GBPUSD historically strong this month		
	First trading day average return: 0.19%; positive: 62%		
	Last trading day average return: 0.51%; positive: 72% (year's strongest)		
	01 Oct: 4th strongest market day of the year		
	31 Oct: 5th strongest market day of the year		
Significant dates	03 Oct: US Nonfarm payroll report (anticipated)		
	09 Oct: MPC interest rate announcement at 12 noon (anticipated)		
	28 Oct: Two-day FOMC meeting starts		

Mon
29

9th strongest market week

1978: The leader of the Roman Catholic Church Pope John Paul I dies after only 33 days in office – the shortest papal reign in history.

FTSE 100	45	-0.3	1.3
FTSE 250	60	-0.3	1.4
S&P 500	44	-0.3	1.5
NIKKEI	45	0.1	0.8

Tue
30

1882: Thomas Edison's first commercial hydroelectric power plant (later known as Appleton Edison Light Company) begins operation on the Fox River in Appleton, Wisconsin, United States.

FTSE 100	45	-0.2	1.3
FTSE 250	42	-0.2	0.9
S&P 500	43	-0.1	1.3
NIKKEI	40	-0.6	1.4

Wed
1

Chinese National Day (HK) – HKSE closed
4th strongest market day

1843: The News of the World is first published in London.

FTSE 100	76	0.4	1.5
FTSE 250	68	0.1	0.8
S&P 500	58	0.3	1.3
NIKKEI	48	-0.2	1.4

Thu
2

Chung Yeung Day (HK) – HKSE closed
ECB Governing Council Meeting

1900: Keir Hardy becomes Labour's first Member of Parliament.

FTSE 100	38	-0.1	1.2
FTSE 250	68	0.0	0.9
S&P 500	68	0.2	1.0
NIKKEI	48	0.4	3.2

Fri
3

Nonfarm payroll report (anticipated)

1872: The Bloomingdale brothers open their first store at 938 Third Avenue, New York City.

FTSE 100	57	0.2	1.0
FTSE 250	47	0.0	0.7
S&P 500	44	-0.1	1.0
NIKKEI	43	-0.1	1.2

Sat 4 Yom Kippur (Jewish), Eid-Al-Adha (Muslim)

Sun 5 Horseracing: Prix de l'Arc de Triomphe, Paris

COMPANY NEWS

Interims Ted Baker, Tesco
Finals Genesis Emerging Markets Fund Ltd, Schroder AsiaPacific Fund, Wolseley

"Dogs have no money. Isn't that amazing? They're broke their entire lives. But they get through. You know why dogs have no money? ... No pockets."
Jerry Seinfeld

DAILY VOLATILITY

October has a reputation for being a volatile month for shares – is this in fact true?

Last year's *Almanac* looked at intra-day volatility; in this edition we will look at daily volatility of the stock market.

The standard way to measure volatility is to calculate the standard deviation of returns (in this case these will be daily returns). The following chart plots the standard deviation of the FTSE 100 for each trading day of the year for the period 1985 to 2013. For example, the standard deviation of the 29 daily returns on the first trading day of the year since 1985 is 1.37 and that is the first data point plotted in the chart.

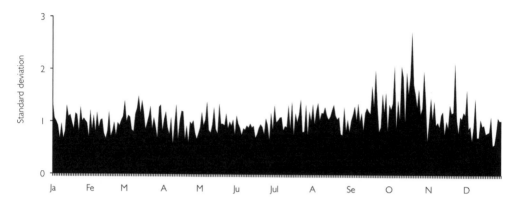

It can be seen that the volatility of daily returns is fairly even for the first eight months of the year; it then starts to increase in September and peaks in October before trailing off for the remainder of the year. So, according to this study of daily returns throughout the year, October is indeed the most volatile month.

Having looked at the daily volatility profile for the 12 months of the year, let's now look at how daily volatility has changed over the past three decades.

The chart below plots the standard deviation of daily returns of the FTSE 100 on a 50-day rolling basis for the period 1985 to 2013.

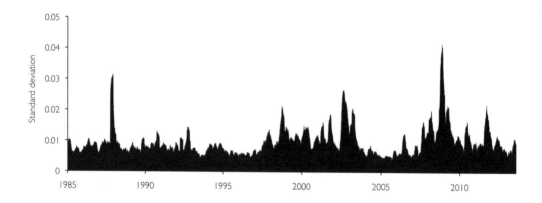

Overall it can be seen that average daily volatility levels have not changed greatly over the period. Having said that, there have obviously been periods of significantly increased volatility, notably: Black Monday in 1987; the sell-off in May 2002 (remember WorldCom?); and the credit crunch in 2008.

At the time of writing (August 2013), the 50-day rolling average daily return is 0.024% and the standard deviation is 0.97. This means that in the past 50 days, 16 days (32% of the days) have seen daily changes greater than +60 or -60 points in the FTSE 100.

Mon

6

1972: The opening day of *The Jazz Singer*, the first feature-length talking movie.

→

FTSE 100	55	0.3	2.4
FTSE 250	60	0.1	1.9
S&P 500	56	0.2	1.2
NIKKEI	65	0.1	1.5

Tue

7

20th anniversary of the LSE flotation of Man Group

1996: The American cable news network, The Fox News Channel, is launched.

→

FTSE 100	50	0.0	0.7
FTSE 250	58	0.0	0.5
S&P 500	39	-0.1	1.4
NIKKEI	50	0.0	2.0

Wed

8

Full moon
Total lunar eclipse (visible from North America, South America, eastern Asia and Australia)

1974: Franklin National Bank collapses due to fraud and mismanagement; the largest bank failure in the history of the USA to date.

→

FTSE 100	43	-0.3	1.5
FTSE 250	47	0.1	1.7
S&P 500	42	0.0	0.8
NIKKEI	44	-0.7	2.8

Thu

9

MPC interest rate announcement at 12h00

1582: Due to the implementation of the Gregorian calendar, this day does not exist in this year in Italy, Poland, Portugal and Spain.

→

FTSE 100	43	-0.2	1.2
FTSE 250	47	-0.2	0.9
S&P 500	43	-0.3	1.7
NIKKEI	37	-0.4	1.1

Fri

10

1973: Vice President of the United States, Spiro Agnew, resigns after being charged with federal income tax evasion.

→

FTSE 100	43	-0.3	2.2
FTSE 250	56	-0.3	1.6
S&P 500	44	0.1	1.3
NIKKEI	38	-1.4	3.6

Sat 11

Sun 12

COMPANY NEWS

Interims
Finals JPMorgan Emerging Markets Investment Trust, WH Smith

"If you get something for nothing, it usually turns out to be worth what it cost."
Napoleon Hill

MARKET BEHAVIOUR – BY MONTH

The table below ranks the 12 months by their historic performance since 1984.

The best month of the whole year – when the market has historically increased most often – is December. The proportion of years when the market has increased in December is 86%. On average the market increases 2.5% in this month with a low-ish standard deviation.

Surprisingly, perhaps, the fourth strongest month is October; but note the very high standard deviation indicating the volatility of the market in this month.

The month with the worst record is September. The market has only risen in September in 48% of all years and the average return for the month is -1%.

The performance figures below are ranked by the final column (Positive x Avg Change).

Ranking of monthly performance

Month	Positive (%)	Avg Chng (%)	Std Dev	Positive x Avg Chng
December	86	2.5	3.0	2.17
April	69	1.8	3.6	1.24
February	59	1.0	4.1	0.56
October	76	0.7	6.8	0.51
July	55	0.8	4.3	0.45
November	59	0.7	3.8	0.42
March	59	0.7	3.4	0.38
August	59	0.6	4.8	0.36
January	59	0.5	5.2	0.29
May	47	-0.2	4.5	-0.10
June	40	-0.8	3.6	-0.34
September	48	-1.0	5.8	-0.47

The variation in performance between the months is statistically significant.

The big change in the ranking from six years ago is the performance of January. In 2007 January was ranked fourth with an average return of 2.7%; but following a disastrous run of years from 2008 to 2011 it is now ninth with an average return of just 0.5%.

Positive returns

The chart below shows the percentage of returns that are positive for each month, for the period 1984 to 2012.

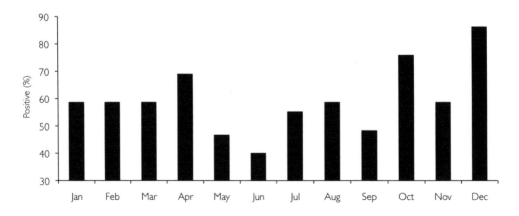

62, 0.2, 2.7 Week 42

Mon Health and Sports Day (Japan) – TSE closed

13

FTSE 100	60	0.7	2.0
FTSE 250	60	0.2	1.1
S&P 500	50	0.3	2.2
NIKKEI			

2008: The government announces that it is recapitalising HBOS, Lloyds and Royal Bank of Scotland, taking stakes in the banks at an initial cost of £37bn in a deal thrashed out over a curry that becomes known as the "Balti bail-out".

Tue 75th anniversary of the birth of Ralph Lauren, the American fashion designer

14

FTSE 100	45	0.1	1.1
FTSE 250	47	0.1	0.6
S&P 500	52	0.0	1.0
NIKKEI	53	0.8	3.4

1884: American inventor George Eastman receives a US patent on his new paper-strip photographic film.

Wed Beige Book published
ECB Governing Council Meeting

15

FTSE 100	48	-0.3	2.1
FTSE 250	47	-0.2	1.7
S&P 500	56	-0.1	1.9
NIKKEI	62	0.5	1.5

2008: The Dow Jones Industrial Average closes down 733.08 points, or 7.87%, the second worst daily percentage drop in its history.

Thu

16

FTSE 100	43	-0.8	2.0
FTSE 250	47	-0.3	2.0
S&P 500	48	-0.1	1.4
NIKKEI	57	-0.1	2.8

1814: Giant vats of beer rupture at the Meux and Company Brewery on Tottenham Court Road and flow down the street in what becomes known as the London Beer Flood.

Fri

17

FTSE 100	67	0.4	1.5
FTSE 250	53	0.2	0.8
S&P 500	42	-0.1	0.9
NIKKEI	48	0.2	1.0

1980: The Queen makes the first state visit to the Vatican by a British monarch.

Sat 18

Sun 19

COMPANY NEWS

Interims Booker Group, Brown (N) Group
Finals Bellway

"If you see the bandwagon, it's too late."
James Goldsmith

RESULTS ANNOUNCEMENTS DATES

Companies listed on the London Stock Exchange are required to release certain information to the public. Some of these statements are unpredictable one-offs, such as news of takeovers or board changes, while others follow a more regular timetable. For investors, two important announcements each year are:

1. **interim results** (known as *interims*): usually reported about eight months into a company's financial year, they relate to the un-audited headline figures for the first half of the company's year;

2. **preliminary results** (known as *prelims*): un-audited figures published prior to the full annual report at the end of the company's financial year. (Note: although these are termed "preliminary" these are very much the real, final results.)

These announcements are watched very carefully and have the potential to significantly move the share price of a company.

FTSE 100

The following chart plots the frequency distribution of the dates of these announcements for FTSE 100 companies.

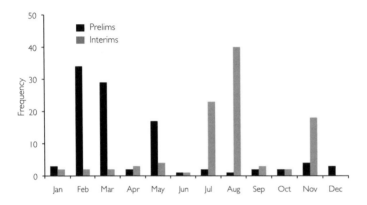

As can be seen the majority of interim results are announced in July and August, while preliminary results are clustered in February and March (63 companies announce their prelims in this two-month period).

FTSE 250

The following chart is similar to that above except this time the companies are in the FTSE 250.

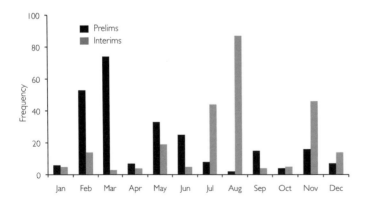

For the FTSE 250 companies, the announcements are a little more evenly distributed throughout the year, but the main months are the same as those for the FTSE 100: July/August the busiest for interims and February/March the busiest for the prelims.

Mon

20

2011: The former leader of Libya, Muammar Gaddafi, and his son Mutassim Gaddafi, are killed shortly after the Battle of Sirte.

FTSE 100	50	-0.2	3.3
FTSE 250	60	-0.4	2.7
S&P 500	62	0.4	1.3
NIKKEI	70	-0.3	3.7

Tue

21

1983: The metre is defined at the seventeenth General Conference on Weights and Measures as the distance light travels in a vacuum in 1/299,792,458 of a second.

FTSE 100	60	0.4	1.9
FTSE 250	63	0.4	1.2
S&P 500	45	0.2	1.7
NIKKEI	42	0.0	1.3

Wed

10th weakest market day
MPC meeting minutes published

22

1879: Thomas Edison tests the first practical electric incandescent light bulb (it lasts 13.5 hours before burning out).

FTSE 100	33	-0.6	1.7
FTSE 250	47	-0.6	1.5
S&P 500	33	-0.4	1.3
NIKKEI	45	0.1	3.4

Thu

Diwali (until 27 October)
New moon
Partial solar eclipse (visible in North and Central America)

23

2012: After 38 years, the world's first teletext service (BBC's Ceefax) ceases broadcast due to Northern Ireland completing the digital switchover.

FTSE 100	57	-0.1	1.4
FTSE 250	42	-0.4	1.2
S&P 500	50	-0.1	1.2
NIKKEI	48	-0.5	2.1

Fri

24

2008: "Bloody Friday" sees many of the world's stock exchanges experience the worst declines in their history, with drops of around 10% in most indices.

FTSE 100	48	-0.2	1.5
FTSE 250	42	-0.4	1.5
S&P 500	47	-0.1	1.0
NIKKEI	33	-0.5	2.2

Sat 25

Sun 26   End of BST (clocks go back)

 COMPANY NEWS

Interims Home Retail Group, Whitbread
Finals Debenhams

"Bankruptcy is a legal proceeding in which you put your money in your pants' pockets and give your coat to your creditors."
Joey Adams

LAST TRADING DAYS OF THE MONTH

Does the market display any particular behaviour on the final trading day of months?

FTSE 100 daily data was analysed from 1984 to discover if the UK equity market had a tendency to significantly increase or decrease on the last trading day (LTD) of each month. The results are shown in the table below.

	Number of days analysed	Positive	Positive (%)	Average (%)
All days	7418	3878	52.3	0.03
Last trading day of each month	352	190	54.0	0.11
Last trading day of each month (from 2000)	163	74	45.4	0.06

Analysis

Overall, since 1984, the market has a tendency to increase above the average on the LTD of each month. On average, the market has risen 0.11% on months' last trading days against 0.03% for all days in the month; and the market has had a positive return in 54% on all LTDs since 1984. However, in recent years (since 2000), the effect has somewhat reversed with the majority of last trading days seeing falls in the market (the percentage of positive last days since 2000 is 45.4%).

This behaviour is very different from that of the first trading days in the month, which strongly outperform the average for all days, and where the effect has strengthened in recent years.

The table below shows the analysis of last trading days by month from 1984. For example, on average the return on the LTD in January has been 0.2%.

	Jan	Feb	Mar	Apr	May	Jun	Jul	Aug	Sep	Oct	Nov	Dec
Positive (%)	62.1	44.8	51.7	53.3	50.0	66.7	46.7	62.1	44.8	72.4	44.8	48.3
Average (%)	0.2	-0.1	0.1	0.2	0.0	0.2	0.2	0.1	0.0	0.5	-0.1	0.0

The difference in performance between the months is quite significant. The last trading days in January, June and October are all abnormally strong – in the case of October's LTD the market rises in 75% of all LTDs of that month. By contrast, the last trading days of February, September and November are very weak.

A summary of the last trading day effect (by month) is shown in the following chart.

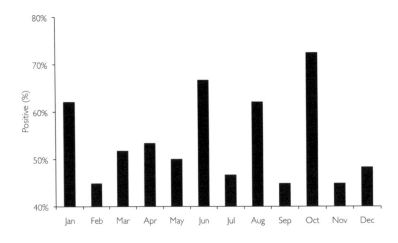

Note: see also *First trading days of the month*, Week 6.

Mon
27

1997: Exchange circuit breakers are triggered when the DJIA drops 554 points. The dip is worldwide and mostly driven by fears of a contagion from a brewing economic crisis in Asia.

→

FTSE 100	55	0.0	1.3
FTSE 250	50	-0.2	1.1
S&P 500	53	-0.1	1.5
NIKKEI	45	-0.5	1.9

Tue
28

Two-day FOMC meeting starts

1664: The Admiral's Regiment, later known as the Royal Marines, is formed.

↗

FTSE 100	65	0.1	1.3
FTSE 250	68	-0.3	1.5
S&P 500	68	0.5	1.9
NIKKEI	55	0.1	2.0

Wed
29

1945: The first ball point pen goes on sale, 57 years after it was patented.

→

FTSE 100	52	0.6	2.2
FTSE 250	58	0.5	1.4
S&P 500	59	0.3	1.3
NIKKEI	57	0.6	2.2

Thu
30

1957: Plans to reform the House of Lords are announced, including creating the first female life peerages.

↗

FTSE 100	67	0.4	1.4
FTSE 250	63	0.4	1.4
S&P 500	56	0.2	1.2
NIKKEI	29	0.3	2.6

Fri
31

Halloween
5th strongest market day

1984: Indira Gandhi, the Prime Minister of India, is killed by two assassins believed to be her own bodyguards.

↑

FTSE 100	76	0.4	1.1
FTSE 250	84	0.5	1.0
S&P 500	51	0.1	0.9
NIKKEI	62	-0.1	1.4

Sat 1   All Saints' Day (Western Christianity), Samhain

Sun 2

COMPANY NEWS

Interims BT Group, Scottish Mortgage Investment Trust
Finals Edinburgh Dragon Trust, Imperial Tobacco Group

"There's no secret about success. Did you ever know a successful man who didn't tell you about it?"
Kin Hubbard

NOVEMBER MARKET

Market performance this month

Since 1984 the FTSE 100 has risen in 59% of years in November, with an average return over the period of 0.7%. This gives it a rank of 6th place for monthly performance. Although this performance is only average, the significant feature of November is that it marks the start of the six-month strong half of the year (November to April). In other words, investors should be increasing exposure to the market this month (if they haven't already done so in October).

FTSE 100	59	0.7	3.8
FTSE 250	59	0.6	4.7
S&P 500	65	1.5	4.4
NIKKEI	59	0.5	6.5

On average the market tends to rise in the first three days of the month, then to give up those gains over the following few days, rise again and fall back, until finally increasing quite strongly over the final seven trading days of the month.

In the last 20 years the sectors that have been strong in November have been: Beverages, Electronic & Electrical Equipment, Fixed Line Telecommunications, Food Producers, Life Insurance, Media, Mining, Technology Hardware & Equipment and Travel & Leisure. The weak sectors have been: Aerospace & Defense, Banks, General Industrials, Oil & Gas Producers and Real Estate Investment Trusts.

Elsewhere, November is a strong month for gold and weak for GBPUSD.

And finally, this is a busy month for interim results: 62 companies from the FTSE 350 make their announcements this month.

Performance of market in November [1970 to 2013]

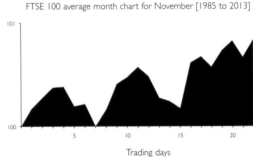

FTSE 100 average month chart for November [1985 to 2013]

Trading days

NOVEMBER SUMMARY

Market performance	Average return: 0.7%		Positive: 59%	Ranking: 6th
Sector performance	*Strong* Beverages, Electronic & Electrical Equipment, Fixed Line Telecommunications, Food Producers, Life Insurance, Media, Mining, Technology Hardware & Equipment, Travel & Leisure		*Weak* Aerospace & Defense, Banks, General Industrials, Oil & Gas Producers, Real Estate Investment Trusts	
Share performance	*Strong* Babcock International Group, Compass Group, Premier Farnell, Shire, Tate & Lyle		*Weak* AstraZeneca, Greggs, Herald Investment Trust, Rentokil Initial, Tullett Prebon	
Main features of the month	Strong month for gold price GBPUSD historically weak this month First trading day average return: 0.17%; positive: 65% Last trading day average return: -0.12%; positive: 45% (year's weakest)			
Significant dates	06 Nov: MPC interest rate announcement at 12 noon (anticipated) 07 Nov: US Nonfarm payroll report (anticipated) 12 Nov: MSCI quarterly index review announcement 27 Nov: Thanksgiving Day (US) – NYSE closed			

Mon 3

Culture Day (Japan) – TSE closed
10th strongest market week

1913: The US introduces an income tax.

→

FTSE 100	55	0.2	1.2
FTSE 250	65	0.3	1.1
S&P 500	69	0.4	1.1
NIKKEI			

Tue 4

1922: In Egypt, British archaeologist Howard Carter and his men find the entrance to Pharaoh Tutankhamun's tomb in the Valley of the Kings.

↘

FTSE 100	40	0.4	1.6
FTSE 250	53	0.4	2.0
S&P 500	54	0.2	1.0
NIKKEI	75	1.2	2.1

Wed 5

Guy Fawkes Night/Bonfire Night

1935: Parker Brothers release the board game *Monopoly*. They had initially rejected it due to its many rules and long playing time.

→

FTSE 100	62	-0.1	1.1
FTSE 250	58	-0.1	0.7
S&P 500	69	0.3	1.3
NIKKEI	43	0.2	1.6

Thu 6

Full moon
MPC interest rate announcement at 12h00
ECB Governing Council Meeting

1972: The British government imposes controversial measures, freezing pay and halting prices, to try to stymie spiralling inflation.

→

FTSE 100	62	-0.1	1.4
FTSE 250	79	0.2	1.0
S&P 500	55	-0.1	1.2
NIKKEI	52	-0.2	2.0

Fri 7

Nonfarm payroll report (anticipated)

1949: The first oil is taken in Oil Rocks, Azerbaijan, the oldest offshore oil platform.

→

FTSE 100	48	-0.2	1.0
FTSE 250	47	-0.1	0.8
S&P 500	49	-0.2	1.1
NIKKEI	14	-0.9	1.4

Sat 8

Sun 9   Remembrance Sunday, 25th anniversary of the fall of the Berlin Wall.

COMPANY NEWS

Interims 3i Infrastructure Ltd, Babcock International Group, BTG, Burberry Group, Cable & Wireless Communications, Dairy Crest Group, DCC, Electrocomponents, Experian, FirstGroup, Marks & Spencer Group, Tate & Lyle, Vedanta Resources
Finals Associated British Foods, Fenner

"It is better to spend money like there's no tomorrow than to spend tonight like there's no money."
P.J. O'Rourke

MONTHLY PERFORMANCE OF THE FTSE 250 INDEX

The table below shows the percentage performance of the FTSE 250 for every month since 1986. The months where the index fell are highlighted. By scanning the columns it is possible to get a feel for how the market moves in certain months.

Monthly percentage returns for the FTSE 250

	Jan	Feb	Mar	Apr	May	Jun	Jul	Aug	Sep	Oct	Nov	Dec
1986	2.6	8.7	7.7	3.5	-3.3	4.4	-4.6	4.3	-5.5	5.2	2.6	1.1
1987	9.5	6.8	3.0	1.4	6.2	8.4	6.0	-4.6	6.5	-28.7	-10.7	12.5
1988	6.6	-0.2	-1.2	3.9	0.4	4.7	1.1	-6.3	3.7	3.4	-3.6	-2.0
1989	13.1	1.2	2.2	-0.7	1.1	-0.9	6.7	0.8	-1.6	-9.0	3.7	4.6
1990	-2.5	-4.9	-1.1	-6.2	8.7	2.0	-2.4	-11.8	-9.9	4.7	2.0	1.0
1991	-1.5	14.5	4.6	-0.4	-1.7	-3.4	5.2	4.1	0.9	-2.5	-6.1	-1.0
1992	4.7	1.9	-4.6	12.6	2.5	-8.3	-9.7	-4.8	9.3	5.2	4.6	8.5
1993	3.2	2.8	2.4	0.8	1.1	2.2	2.2	6.2	-2.2	2.8	-1.2	8.8
1994	7.7	-3.0	-5.2	0.8	-5.7	-4.2	6.6	4.8	-8.4	0.6	-0.6	0.1
1995	-3.8	0.4	1.5	2.8	3.5	-1.7	6.5	2.3	0.9	-1.4	1.7	1.6
1996	2.6	2.2	2.7	5.2	-0.9	-3.5	-2.8	4.4	-0.6	0.7	0.1	1.4
1997	2.3	1.3	-1.7	-1.7	-0.1	-1.4	1.4	2.5	4.9	-3.9	0.3	2.8
1998	1.5	7.0	6.2	1.5	5.2	-6.7	-0.4	-12.7	-5.1	5.9	1.9	-1.0
1999	3.5	4.5	4.3	6.8	-3.6	3.9	1.9	0.8	-5.5	-1.1	10.2	4.0
2000	-4.1	4.4	0.4	-4.3	0.5	6.0	2.7	4.1	-5.4	-0.7	-3.2	2.0
2001	2.9	-1.3	-8.3	5.2	2.5	-4.1	-3.4	0.6	-16.3	4.8	9.0	1.5
2002	-1.5	-0.3	5.9	-0.8	-1.2	-9.1	-13.0	1.6	-11.8	3.0	3.2	-5.2
2003	-7.0	0.5	-1.9	10.8	9.7	3.1	7.3	5.0	-2.4	4.9	-0.2	1.6
2004	3.8	4.1	-0.2	-0.8	-2.5	3.7	-4.1	1.1	3.0	0.8	4.0	5.5
2005	3.3	1.2	-1.7	-5.6	5.7	3.6	3.2	1.9	2.6	-3.0	8.0	5.6
2006	4.3	3.0	4.3	0.3	-5.9	1.3	-0.7	2.6	4.1	3.8	2.9	4.7
2007	-0.7	-0.2	5.5	2.1	1.5	-4.8	-1.6	-0.2	-2.4	5.7	-7.9	-0.8
2008	-7.3	1.9	-0.5	1.1	-0.7	-9.0	-3.2	5.9	-15.9	-20.4	-3.0	4.4
2009	-1.7	-3.2	5.4	18.1	0.6	-2.1	7.9	10.2	3.7	-2.8	0.4	4.4
2010	-0.7	1.2	8.8	2.0	-7.0	-2.8	6.2	-1.2	7.2	3.0	-2.2	9.0
2011	-0.8	1.3	-0.3	3.6	0.4	-1.1	-3.2	-8.9	-6.7	6.7	-1.6	-2.1
2012	6.6	6.3	0.8	-1.1	-7.5	3.5	1.9	2.5	2.8	1.7	0.8	2.8
2013	5.3	5.2	1.6	0.2	2.9	-3.9	7.8					

Observations

1. The strongest months for the index have been February, April and December, with the latter being by far the strongest month. In fact, the first four months of the year together are all pretty strong. Whereas the weak months have been June and September.

2. In recent years (since 2000) the situation has not changed significantly; except that January has been very weak and August has become almost as strong as December.

3. Looking across the table, it can be seen that the longest periods of consecutive positive months were September 1992 to August 1993 and June 2012 to May 2013 (the only times the FTSE 250 has risen 12 months in a row).

The chart below shows the average monthly returns of the FTSE 250.

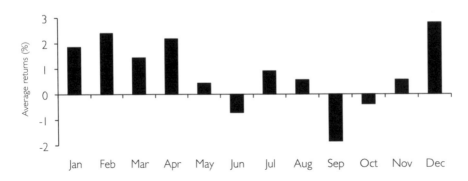

Mon

10

1871: Henry Morton Stanley locates missing explorer and missionary, Dr. David Livingstone in Ujiji, near Lake Tanganyika, famously greeting him with the words, "Dr. Livingstone, I presume?"

FTSE 100	50	0.0	0.6
FTSE 250	60	-0.2	0.8
S&P 500	58	0.0	0.8
NIKKEI	50	0.0	1.8

Tue

Armistice Day

11

1675: Gottfried Leibniz demonstrates integral calculus for the first time to find the area under the graph of $y = f(x)$.

FTSE 100	55	0.1	1.5
FTSE 250	42	0.1	1.6
S&P 500	71	0.2	1.0
NIKKEI	50	-0.5	1.5

Wed

MPC Inflation Report published
MSCI Semi-Annual Index Review (announcement date)

12

1984: Chancellor Nigel Lawson announces that pound notes will be withdrawn from circulation and replaced with coins.

FTSE 100	57	0.3	1.2
FTSE 250	58	0.1	1.2
S&P 500	52	0.0	1.3
NIKKEI	45	-0.2	1.5

Thu

13

2012: "Omnishambles", meaning a situation which is shambolic from every possible angle, is named word of the year by Oxford English Dictionary.

FTSE 100	48	-0.1	1.0
FTSE 250	26	-0.2	0.8
S&P 500	44	0.1	1.3
NIKKEI	29	0.0	2.0

Fri

14

2007: Tesco closes at all-time high of 492.

FTSE 100	52	0.2	0.8
FTSE 250	53	0.1	0.6
S&P 500	49	0.0	1.1
NIKKEI	52	0.1	1.2

Sat 15

Sun 16   100th anniversary of the Federal Reserve Bank of the United States opening.

COMPANY NEWS

Interims 3i Group, Atkins (W S), AVEVA Group, Edinburgh Investment Trust, Fidelity China Special Situation, Great Portland Estates, ICAP, Invensys, Investec, Land Securities Group, Londonmetric Property, National Grid, Oxford Instruments, Sainsbury (J), SSE, Synergy Health, TalkTalk Telecom Group, Vodafone Group, Workspace Group

Finals British Empire Securities & General Trust, Euromoney Institutional Investor, Lonmin, United Drug

"Ability is a poor man's wealth."
John Wooden

THE FTSE 100/FTSE 250 MONTHLY SWITCHING STRATEGY

Analysis of the historic data shows that although the FTSE 250 has greatly outperformed the FTSE 100 in the long-term (since 1986 the FTSE 100 has increased 369% compared with an increase of 953% for the FTSE 250) there are certain months for which the large-cap index on average outperforms the mid-cap index. We will look at a strategy that exploits this feature.

In Week 7 we saw the results of analysing the monthly comparative performances of the two indices. To recap, the chart showing the average outperformance of the FTSE 100 over the FTSE 250 by month is shown below (this time for the shorter period of 2000-2013).

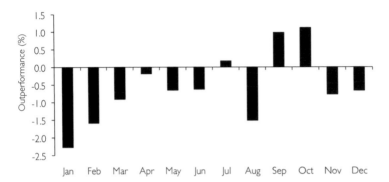

As can be seen, there are only two months, September and October, in which the FTSE 100 convincingly outperforms the FTSE 250.

The FTSE 100/FTSE 250 monthly switching strategy

The above results suggest a strategy of investing in the FTSE 250 for the year but switching into the FTSE 100 for just the two-month period September-October. In other words, the portfolio would be invested in the FTSE 250 from January to August, at the end of August it switches out of the FTSE 250 and into the FTSE 100 for two months, then back into the FTSE 250 until the end of August the following year.

The following chart shows the result of operating such a strategy every year from 1986. For comparison, the chart also includes the portfolio returns from continuous investments in the base FTSE 100 and FTSE 250.

The result: the FTSE 100 portfolio would have grown +369%, the FTSE 250 +953%, but the FTSE 100/FTSE 250 monthly switching portfolio would have increased +1618%. Switching between the indices would have incurred some transactions costs, but these would have been negligible relative to the overall returns.

The strategy also works over the shorter period from 2000 to 2013. The figures for the returns are FTSE 100: +96%, FTSE 250: +231%, Switching Strategy: +314%.

Mon 17

20th anniversary of the LSE flotation of Kenmare Resources

FTSE 100	40	-0.2	1.1
FTSE 250	45	-0.3	0.9
S&P 500	62	0.0	0.8
NIKKEI	50	0.2	2.1

1948: The House of Commons votes to nationalise the steel industry.

Tue 18

FTSE 100	60	0.1	0.8
FTSE 250	53	0.1	0.7
S&P 500	48	0.0	0.8
NIKKEI	55	0.3	1.9

1477: William Caxton produces *Dictes and Sayings of the Philosophers*, the first book printed on a printing press in England.

Wed 19

MPC meeting minutes published
ECB Governing Council Meeting

FTSE 100	33	-0.5	1.6
FTSE 250	47	-0.5	1.4
S&P 500	47	-0.4	1.3
NIKKEI	52	-0.4	1.5

1994: Britain's first National Lottery draw is shown live on BBC One.

Thu 20

FTSE 100	52	0.0	1.2
FTSE 250	53	-0.2	0.8
S&P 500	57	-0.1	1.3
NIKKEI	52	0.1	2.1

1985: Microsoft releases Windows 1.0 – its first GUI operating system.

Fri 21

FTSE 100	52	-0.1	1.3
FTSE 250	32	-0.4	1.0
S&P 500	56	0.2	1.2
NIKKEI	52	0.3	1.3

2002: NATO invites Bulgaria, Estonia, Latvia, Lithuania, Romania, Slovakia and Slovenia to become members.

Sat 22   New moon

Sun 23   Labour Thanksgiving Day (Japan)

COMPANY NEWS

Interims Big Yellow Group, British Land Co, Halfords Group, Halma, Homeserve, Intermediate Capital Group, Johnson Matthey, London Stock Exchange Group, MITIE Group, QinetiQ Group, SABMiller, Telecom Plus, TR Property Investment Trust, Utilico Emerging Markets Ltd, Worldwide Healthcare Trust

Finals Compass Group, Diploma, easyJet, Enterprise Inns, Grainger, Paragon Group of Companies

"Nothing is illegal if a hundred businessmen decide to do it."
Andrew Young

RANKING HIGH-RETURN, LOW-VOLATILITY SHARES

The chart below was created by taking the 306 FTSE 350 companies that have seven or more years of historic price data and then using regression analysis to calculate the slope of the regression line and the R-squared for each of the 306 companies' year end share prices for the last ten years.[1] These 306 pairs of statistics were then plotted on a scatter chart.

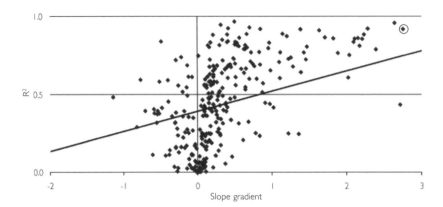

The above chart is interesting. A line of best fit has been drawn which has a positive slope, which indicates that shares with higher returns also have higher R-squareds (i.e. lower volatility around the trend line).

This is a Good Thing – this is what investors want: shares with high returns and low volatility.

Investors therefore want shares to be in the top-right quadrant of the chart above (i.e. shares with positive returns and R^2 over 0.5). An example would be Reckitt Benckiser (circled in the chart) with a slope gradient of 2.76 and R^2 of 0.92.

To identify shares in the top-right quadrant we can calculate the multiple of the slope gradient and R^2 and rank shares in descending order by this value.

The following table shows the top 20 shares in the FTSE 350 as ranked by this multiple of slope gradient and R^2. This is, in effect, a ranking of the highest-return/lowest-volatility shares for the past ten years and as such they might be regarded as the best trending shares over that period.

Company	TIDM	Slope	R2	Slope × R2
British American Tobacco	BATS	2.65	0.96	2.54
Reckitt Benckiser Group	RB.	2.76	0.92	2.53
SABMiller	SAB	2.29	0.92	2.11
Rotork	ROR	2.24	0.88	1.98
Petrofac Ltd	PFC	2.21	0.86	1.89
Intertek Group	ITRK	2.39	0.79	1.89
Aveva Group	AVV	2.16	0.86	1.86
Aggreko	AGK	2.11	0.86	1.81
Croda International	CRDA	2.18	0.81	1.77
BHP Billiton	BLT	2.10	0.84	1.75
Spirax-Sarco Engineering	SPX	1.83	0.86	1.57
Weir Group	WEIR	2.04	0.75	1.53
Tullow Oil	TLW	1.64	0.91	1.49
Shire	SHP	1.71	0.87	1.48
Rightmove	RMV	1.89	0.77	1.44
Unilever	ULVR	1.39	0.92	1.27
Next	NXT	2.02	0.61	1.23
Antofagasta	ANTO	1.47	0.81	1.19
Rio Tinto	RIO	2.72	0.43	1.18
Imperial Tobacco Group	IMT	1.43	0.77	1.10

[1] Further information on this is given in the Statistics section, pages 156-7.

Mon
24

TSE closed

1859: Charles Darwin publishes *On the Origin of Species*, the anniversary of which is sometimes called Evolution Day.

FTSE 100	55	0.6	2.3
FTSE 250	55	0.4	1.3
S&P 500	78	0.5	1.3
NIKKEI			

Tue
25

1992: The Federal Assembly of Czechoslovakia votes to split the country into the Czech Republic and Slovakia from 1 January 1993.

FTSE 100	60	0.0	1.0
FTSE 250	58	0.0	0.7
S&P 500	68	0.1	0.6
NIKKEI	70	0.4	1.9

Wed
26

1947: India's finance minister, R. K. Shanmukhan Chetty, presents the first Budget of independent India.

FTSE 100	48	-0.2	1.1
FTSE 250	58	-0.1	0.9
S&P 500	69	0.3	1.4
NIKKEI	57	0.3	1.3

Thu
27

Thanksgiving (US) – NYSE closed

2001: A hydrogen atmosphere is found on the extrasolar planet called Osiris by the Hubble Space Telescope. It is the first atmosphere ever detected on an extrasolar planet.

FTSE 100	62	0.2	0.8
FTSE 250	58	0.2	1.0
S&P 500			
NIKKEI	57	0.4	1.4

Fri
28

2006: British Land closes at all-time high of 14.268.

FTSE 100	48	0.1	1.2
FTSE 250	58	0.3	1.1
S&P 500	54	0.1	1.1
NIKKEI	50	0.0	1.5

Sat 29

Sun 30   St Andrew's Day

COMPANY NEWS

Interims Caledonia Investments, Cranswick, Daejan Holdings, De La Rue, Essar Energy, KCOM Group, PayPoint, Pennon Group, Perpetual Income & Growth Investment Trust, Personal Assets Trust, RPC Group, Severn Trent, Templeton Emerging Markets Investment Trust, United Utilities Group

Finals Aberdeen Asset Management, Britvic, Electra Private Equity, Marston's, Mitchells & Butlers, Shaftesbury, Thomas Cook Group

"Success is going from failure to failure without loss of enthusiasm."
Winston Churchill

DECEMBER MARKET

Market performance this month

December is the best month for shares. Since 1984 (when the FTSE 100 was created), the index has increased on average by 2.5% in December. In fact, in the 28 years since 1984 the market has only fallen four times in December – the last time in 2002.

FTSE 100	86	2.5	3.0
FTSE 250	78	2.8	3.9
S&P 500	76	1.7	3.2
NIKKEI	69	1.6	5.6

The market tends to increase slightly in the first two weeks of the month, but then rises strongly in the final two weeks. Indeed, this is the strongest two-week period in the whole year.

December is also one of the three best months for the performance of the FTSE 100 relative to the S&P 500: on average the former has outperformed the latter by 0.5 percentage points in December.

Events to watch out for this month include the FTSE 100 review on the 10th and triple witching on the 19th.

Performance of market in December [1970 to 2013]

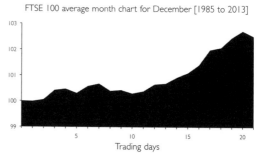

FTSE 100 average month chart for December [1985 to 2013]

DECEMBER SUMMARY

Market performance	Average return: 2.5%	Positive: 86%	Ranking: 1st
Sector performance	*Strong* Construction & Materials, Life Insurance, Support Services, Travel & Leisure	*Weak* Banks, General Retailers, Pharmaceuticals & Biotechnology	
Share performance	*Strong* Alliance Trust, Balfour Beatty, JPMorgan Emerging Markets Inv Trust, William Hill, Witan Investment Trust	*Weak* Amlin, Centamin, Rank Group (The)	
Main features of the month	Strongest month of the year		
	FTSE 100 often outperforms the S&P 500 in December		
	First trading day average return: -0.01%; positive: 48% (year's weakest)		
	Last trading day average return: 0.04%; positive: 48%		
	15 Dec: start of the 3rd strongest market week of the year		
	22 Dec: start of the 4th strongest market week of the year		
	23 Dec: 2nd strongest market day of the year		
	24 Dec: Strongest market day of the year		
Significant dates	04 Dec: MPC interest rate announcement at 12 noon (anticipated)		
	05 Dec: US Nonfarm payroll report (anticipated)		
	10 Dec: FTSE 100 Index quarterly review		
	16 Dec: Two-day FOMC meeting starts		
	19 Dec: Triple Witching		
	25 Dec: Christmas Day – LSE, NYSE, HKSE closed		
	26 Dec: Boxing Day – LSE, HKSE closed		
	31 Dec: New Year's Eve – LSE closes early at 12h30		

Mon

1

MSCI Semi-Annual Index Review (effective date)

1909: Shoppers make their first withdrawal from a new type of account introduced by the Pennsylvania Trust company, designed to help customers put aside money throughout the year for Christmas gifts.

FTSE 100	55	0.1	1.9
FTSE 250	70	0.1	1.5
S&P 500	60	0.1	1.6
NIKKEI	60	0.7	1.6

Tue

2

2001: Enron files for bankruptcy in the biggest ever US corporate failure.

FTSE 100	50	0.1	0.9
FTSE 250	74	0.3	0.8
S&P 500	48	0.1	1.0
NIKKEI	60	-0.1	1.9

Wed

3

Beige Book published

2005: XCOR Aerospace makes first manned rocket aircraft delivery of US Mail in Mojave, California.

FTSE 100	52	0.1	0.8
FTSE 250	53	-0.1	0.7
S&P 500	49	-0.1	1.1
NIKKEI	48	0.0	1.5

Thu

4

MPC interest rate announcement at 12h00
ECB Governing Council Meeting

1918: President Woodrow Wilson sails for the World War I peace talks in Versailles, becoming the first US president to travel to Europe while in office.

FTSE 100	33	-0.1	0.7
FTSE 250	53	-0.2	0.8
S&P 500	66	0.2	1.0
NIKKEI	57	-0.2	1.3

Fri

5

Nonfarm payroll report (anticipated)

1958: Britain's first motorway, the Preston By-pass, is opened by Prime Minister Macmillan.

FTSE 100	57	0.3	1.2
FTSE 250	63	0.2	1.0
S&P 500	49	0.2	1.2
NIKKEI	62	0.3	1.0

Sat 6 Full moon

Sun 7

COMPANY NEWS

Interims Anite, Greene King, HICL Infrastructure Company Ltd, Micro Focus International, Monks Investment Trust, Smith (DS), Stagecoach Group
Finals Brewin Dolphin Holdings, ITE Group, Sage Group, TUI Travel

"Relying on a 'safe, secure job' is the highest risk anyone can take."
Robert T. Kiyosaki

FTSE 100 REVIEWS – COMPANIES LEAVING THE INDEX

The charts below show the share price of 9 companies that have left the FTSE 100 in the past year. The time period for each chart is 6 months, starting from 3 months before the company leaft the index. So it is possible to see the share price behaviour in the 3 months leading up to leaving, and the 3 months after.

The dotted line on each chart marks the point at which the company left the index.

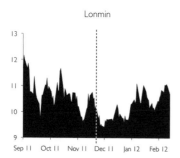

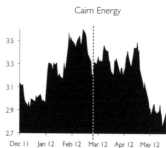

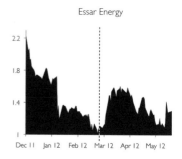

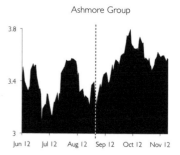

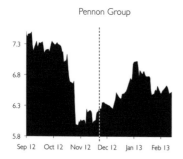

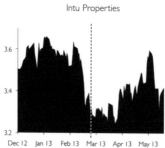

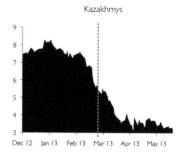

Observation

It can be seen that, in most cases, the share price falls in the period before the company leaves the FTSE 100, and then rises afterwards.

Mon

8

FTSE 100	60	0.4	1.6
FTSE 250	55	0.1	1.3
S&P 500	47	0.0	1.0
NIKKEI	40	-0.2	1.7

1980: Former Beatle John Lennon is shot dead by an unknown gunman who opens fire outside the musician's New York apartment.

Tue

9

FTSE 100	50	0.1	0.9
FTSE 250	63	0.1	1.0
S&P 500	57	0.0	0.8
NIKKEI	55	0.3	1.4

1960: The first episode of the world's longest-running television soap opera, *Coronation Street*, is broadcast in the United Kingdom.

Wed

10

FTSE 100 quarterly review

FTSE 100	38	-0.2	0.7
FTSE 250	47	0.0	0.7
S&P 500	56	0.1	0.9
NIKKEI	48	-0.1	1.3

1901: The first Nobel Prizes are awarded.

Thu

11

FTSE 100	43	-0.1	1.0
FTSE 250	53	0.1	0.8
S&P 500	45	-0.2	0.9
NIKKEI	43	-0.1	1.4

1989: The first trading day of the newly privatised United Utilities.

Fri

12

25th anniversary of the LSE flotations of Pennon Group and Severn Trent

FTSE 100	48	-0.2	0.9
FTSE 250	47	-0.3	0.9
S&P 500	53	0.0	0.7
NIKKEI	67	0.3	1.6

1901: Guglielmo Marconi successfully transmits the first transatlantic radio signal. The signal is a letter S sent in Morse code.

Sat 13

Sun 14   25th anniversary of the LSE flotation of Sage Group.

COMPANY NEWS

Interims Ashtead Group, Berkeley Group Holdings, Betfair Group, Carpetright, Imagination Technologies Group, Polar Capital Technology Trust, Sports Direct International, SuperGroup
Finals Domino Printing Sciences, Scottish Investment Trust, Victrex

"Shares prices follow the theorem: hope divided by fear minus greed."
Dominic Lawson

THE LOW-HIGH PRICE PORTFOLIO

The previous edition of the *Almanac* compared the historic performance of low-priced shares against high-priced ones. This page updates the study to include data from 2012.

To recap, an academic paper in 2008 found that in the US equity market share returns are inversely proportional to share price (i.e. the lower the share price the higher the future return). In addition, the paper found that a portfolio that was long of stocks under $5 and short of stocks over $20 and rebalanced annually generated average monthly returns of 0.53%. Lengthening the rebalancing period to two years increased the returns and reduced the costs.

To test whether this applies also to the UK market the performance of two portfolios was compared:

1. **Low-price_20**: this portfolio buys equal amounts of the 20 lowest priced shares in the FTSE All-Share at close on 31 December, holds the same portfolio for one year, and then rebalances the next 31 December.

2. **High-price_20**: as above, but this portfolio buys the 20 highest priced shares.

The following chart plots the outperformance of the Low-price_20 portfolio over High-price_20 for the period 2004 to 2012. For example, in 2004 the Low-price_20 portfolio increased 62% compared with an increase of 23% for the High-price_20 portfolio giving an outperformance of 39 percentage points.

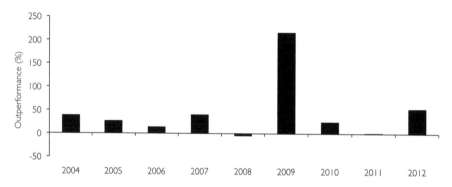

As can be seen, the Low-price_20 portfolio outperformed the High-price_20 portfolio every year except 2008. The average annual return for the Low-price_20 portfolio over the period was 50.3%, and for High-price_20 portfolio it was 4.9%, giving the former an average annual outperformance of 49.4 percentage points.

And, yes, the data for 2009 are correct – when markets rebound low-priced shares can fly.

This low/high price performance anomaly continued in 2012, with the Low-price_20 portfolio easily outperforming the High-price_20 portfolio.

Share price frequency distribution

The chart below shows the frequency distribution of share prices in the FTSE All-Share.

Share price (£)

The chart shows that, for example, there are 64 companies with share prices below £1, 120 companies with share prices £1 to £2 and 54 companies with share prices £15 to £100.

Mon

3rd strongest market week
20th anniversary of the LSE flotation of British Sky Broadcasting Group

15

1906: The London Underground's Great Northern, Piccadilly and Brompton Railway opens.

FTSE 100	50	0.0	0.7
FTSE 250	65	0.2	0.6
S&P 500	44	-0.1	0.7
NIKKEI	45	0.2	1.7

Tue

10th strongest market day
Two-day FOMC meeting starts

16

1978: Cleveland, Ohio, becomes the first post-Depression era city to default on its loans, owing $14m to local banks.

FTSE 100	75	0.6	0.8
FTSE 250	74	0.4	0.6
S&P 500	68	0.4	1.0
NIKKEI	55	0.0	0.9

Wed

Hanukkah (until 24 December)
MPC meeting minutes published
ECB Governing Council Meeting

17

1903: The Wright Brothers make the first powered heavier-than-air flight in the Wright Flyer at Kitty Hawk, North Carolina.

FTSE 100	43	-0.1	1.0
FTSE 250	42	0.0	1.0
S&P 500	51	0.1	1.0
NIKKEI	52	0.1	1.2

Thu

ECB General Council Meeting

18

1973: The Islamic Development Bank is founded.

FTSE 100	67	0.2	0.9
FTSE 250	68	0.3	0.7
S&P 500	59	0.2	1.1
NIKKEI	48	-0.1	1.0

Fri

Triple Witching

19

2012: Swiss banking giant UBS agrees to pay $1.5bn to US, UK and Swiss regulators for attempting to manipulate the Libor inter-bank lending rate.

FTSE 100	57	-0.1	0.9
FTSE 250	53	-0.1	0.7
S&P 500	42	0.0	0.7
NIKKEI	48	-0.4	1.8

Sat 20

Sun 21   Winter Solstice, also known as Yule

COMPANY NEWS

Interims Dixons Retail
Finals Carnival, Crest Nicholson Holdings Ltd

"It's not whether you are right or wrong that's important, but how much money you make when you are right and how much you lose when you're wrong."
George Soros

MONTHLY SEASONALITY WORLDWIDE

In Week 42 of this *Almanac* the results are given of analysis on the monthly seasonality of the FTSE 100. To summarise:

- the three strongest months in the year were found to be: April, October, December, and
- the three weakest months in the year were: June, May, September.

Such seasonality behaviour is not unique to the UK, most other stock markets around the world display similar behaviour – as found in an academic paper[1] published in June 2013.

The special feature of this latest study on the topic is its scope: it analyses data from 70 of the 78 operational stock markets in the world.

The paper found that across all 70 markets, on average:

- the three strongest months were: January, April, December, and
- the three weakest months were: August, September, October.

The paper doesn't make it clear, but we assume that the averages were not market-cap weighted.

The study also split the results for developed and emerging markets (shown in the following two charts).

Mean, median and standard deviation of monthly return for each month across developed stock markets

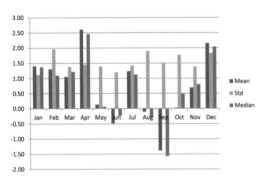

Source: Vichet Sum

Mean, median and standard deviation of monthly return for each month across emerging stock markets

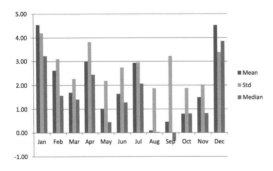

Source: Vichet Sum

The main difference between the two sets of markets is that while April was the strongest month in developed markets, it was January and December that were the strongest months for the emerging markets. In addition the developed markets were significantly weak in June and September, which was not the case in emerging markets.

---

[1] Sum, Vichet, 'Stock Market Performance: High and Low Months' (5 June 2013).

Mon

New moon
4th strongest market week

22

FTSE 100	70	0.3	0.6
FTSE 250	90	0.4	0.4
S&P 500	60	0.1	0.7
NIKKEI	60	0.1	1.4

1965: A 70mph speed limit is applied to all rural roads, including motorways, for the first time in the UK. Previously, there had been no speed limit.

Tue

Emperor's Birthday (Japan) – TSE closed
2nd strongest market day

23

FTSE 100	80	0.4	0.6
FTSE 250	89	0.4	0.4
S&P 500	48	0.0	0.8
NIKKEI			

1956: British and French troops withdraw from the Suez Canal following pressure from the USA and the UN over the Suez Crisis.

Wed

Christmas Eve
Strongest market day
100th anniversary of British and German soldiers interrupting World War I with an impromptu truce to celebrate Christmas

24

FTSE 100	81	0.2	0.6
FTSE 250	78	0.2	0.4
S&P 500	63	0.2	0.5
NIKKEI	47	-0.2	1.2

1962: The last of the men taken prisoner at the Bay of Pigs invasion of Cuba return to the US in time for Christmas.

Thu

Christmas Day
LSE, NYSE, HKSE closed

25

FTSE 100			
FTSE 250			
S&P 500			
NIKKEI	50	0.6	1.4

1990: The first successful trial run of the system which would become the World Wide Web takes place.

Fri

Boxing Day
LSE, HKSE closed

26

FTSE 100			
FTSE 250			
S&P 500	83	0.4	0.7
NIKKEI	79	0.6	1.5

1933: FM radio is patented.

Sat 27

Sun 28

COMPANY NEWS

Interims
Finals JPMorgan Indian Investment Trust

"I know at last what distinguishes man from animals; financial worries."
Romain Rolland

THE FTSE 100/S&P 500 MONTHLY SWITCHING STRATEGY

In Week 35 we saw how the FTSE 100 outperformed the S&P 500 in certain months of the year. This week we will look at a strategy that exploits this feature.

The previous figures compared the FTSE 100 and S&P 500 in their domestic currencies. We will now look at comparing the performance of the FTSE 100 with a sterling-adjusted S&P 500 (i.e. the returns a UK investor would actually get from the S&P 500 taking into account fluctuations in the GBPUSD currency rate each month).

The following table shows the original monthly comparative performance figures we saw in Week 35 and the new set of figures where the S&P 500 returns have been converted into sterling.

	Jan	Feb	Mar	Apr	May	Jun	Jul	Aug	Sep	Oct	Nov	Dec
FTSE 100 v S&P 500	-0.6	0.6	-0.6	0.3	-1.3	-0.8	0.2	0.7	-0.2	0.0	-0.3	0.5
FTSE 100 v S&P 500 (£)	-1.4	0.1	-0.2	1.1	-1.9	-0.7	1.1	0.0	-0.3	0.2	-0.6	0.8

One effect of adjusting for currency moves is to amplify the outperformance of the FTSE 100 in certain months (April, July and December). Conversely, the FTSE 100 underperformance is amplified in January, May and November. The currency-adjusted comparative performances for each month are shown in the following chart.

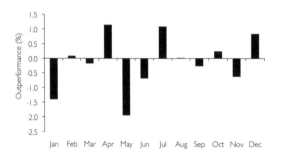

Whereas, before, the relatively strong FTSE 100 months were February, April, July, August and December, we can see that the currency-adjusted strong months are just April, July and December.

The monthly switching strategy (FSMSP)

The above results suggest a strategy of investing in the UK market (i.e. the FTSE 100) in April, July and December and in the US market (i.e. the S&P 500) for the rest of the year. In other words, the portfolio would be invested in the S&P 500 from January to March, at the end of March it switches out of the S&P 500 into the FTSE 100 for one month, then back into the S&P 500 for two months, into the FTSE 100 for July, back into the S&P 500 for four months, then back into the FTSE 100 for December, and finally back into the S&P 500 to start the next year.

The following chart shows the result of operating such a strategy every year from 1984. For comparison, the chart also includes the portfolio returns from continuous investments in the FTSE 100 and S&P 500.

The final result: the FTSE 100 portfolio would have grown 562%, the S&P 500 (£) 878%, but the FTSE 100/S&P 500 monthly switching portfolio (FSMSP) would have increased 2346%. Switching six times a year would have incurred some commission costs, but these would not have dented performance significantly. This strategy would have continued to work in the last 12 months (since the previous edition of the Almanac) with the FTSE 100, S&P 500 (£) and FSMSP returning respectively: 18%, 26% and 31%.

Mon

6th strongest market week

29

2003: The last known speaker of Akkala Sami, a Sami language that was spoken in the Kola Peninsula in Russia, dies, rendering the language extinct.

FTSE 100	75	0.4	1.2
FTSE 250	85	0.4	0.9
S&P 500	53	0.2	0.7
NIKKEI	71	0.2	0.6

Tue

30

1999: The FTSE 100 Index hits an all-time high of 6930.2.

FTSE 100	60	0.2	0.9
FTSE 250	68	0.3	0.6
S&P 500	64	0.2	0.7
NIKKEI	50	0.3	1.5

Wed

New Year's Eve
LSE closes early at 12h30
TSE closed

31

1907: For the first time, a ball drops at Times Square in New York to signal the start of the new year.

FTSE 100	53	0.0	1.1
FTSE 250	71	0.0	0.7
S&P 500	69	0.2	0.7
NIKKEI			

Thu

New Year's Day
LSE, NYSE, HKEX, TSE closed

1

1801: The legislative union of the Kingdom of Great Britain and the Kingdom of Ireland is completed to form the United Kingdom of Great Britain and Ireland.

Fri

TSE closed
Nonfarm payroll report (anticipated)

2

1893: The *Financial Times* begins to be printed on salmon pink paper to distinguish it from the similarly named *Financial News*.

FTSE 100	59	0.4	1.2
FTSE 250	75	0.6	1.1
S&P 500	63	0.3	1.4
NIKKEI			

Sat 3

Sun 4

COMPANY NEWS

Interims
Finals

"The avoidance of taxes is the only intellectual pursuit that still carries any reward."
John Maynard Keynes

2
STATISTICS

CONTENTS

MARKET INDICES

COMPARATIVE PERFORMANCE OF UK INDICES

The table below gives the year-end closing values for eight UK stock indices for the period 2003 to 2012.

Year-end closing values of UK indices

Index	EPIC	2003	2004	2005	2006	2007	2008	2009	2010	2011	2012
FTSE 100	UKX	4,476.90	4,814.30	5,618.80	6,220.80	6,456.90	4,434.17	5,412.88	5,899.94	5,572.28	5,897.81
FTSE 250	MCX	5,802.30	6,936.80	8,794.30	11,177.80	10,657.80	6,360.85	9,306.89	11,558.80	10,102.90	12,375.00
FTSE All-Share	ASX	2,207.38	2,410.75	2,847.02	3,221.42	3,286.67	2,209.29	2,760.80	3,062.85	2,857.88	3,093.41
FTSE Fledgling	NSX	2,624.20	3,170.40	3,748.80	4,389.40	4,022.30	2,321.76	4,035.39	4,789.69	4,081.64	4,751.92
FTSE Small Cap	SMX	2,475.10	2,758.10	3,305.50	3,905.60	3,420.30	1,854.20	2,780.20	3,228.60	2,748.80	3,419.07
FTSE TechMARK 100	TIX	1,015.00	1,196.43	1,431.72	1,512.38	1,641.10	1,217.00	1,704.80	2,040.00	2,064.10	2,479.80
FTSE 4Good UK 50	4UK5	3,918.64	4,199.54	4,802.23	5,267.43	5,428.60	3,787.40	4,577.90	4,852.90	4,529.80	4,864.74
FTSE AIM	AXX	835.40	1,005.60	1,046.10	1,054.00	1,049.10	394.32	653.24	933.63	693.18	707.21

The table below gives the annual percentage performance of the eight indices. The light grey cells highlight the best performing index in the year; the dark grey cells the worst performing.

Annual percentage performance of UK indices

Name	EPIC	2003	2004	2005	2006	2007	2008	2009	2010	2011	2012
FTSE 100	UKX	13.6	7.5	16.7	10.7	3.8	-31.3	22.1	9.0	-5.6	5.8
FTSE 250	MCX	34.3	19.6	26.8	27.1	-4.7	-40.3	46.3	24.2	-12.6	22.5
FTSE All-Share	AXX	16.6	9.2	18.1	13.2	2.0	-32.8	25.0	10.9	-6.7	8.2
FTSE Fledgling	ASX	56.5	20.8	18.2	17.1	-8.4	-42.3	73.8	18.7	-14.8	16.4
FTSE Small Cap	NSX	35.9	11.4	19.8	18.2	-12.4	-45.8	49.9	16.1	-14.9	24.4
FTSE TechMARK 100	SMX	56.4	17.9	19.7	5.6	8.5	-25.8	40.1	19.7	1.2	20.1
FTSE 4Good UK 50	TIX	12.6	7.2	14.4	9.7	3.1	-30.2	20.9	6.0	-6.7	7.4
FTSE AIM	4UK5	38.6	20.4	4.0	0.8	-0.5	-62.4	65.7	42.9	-25.8	2.0

The FTSE Fledgling and FTSE TechMARK 100 have been the best performing indices in the year the most number of times, while the FTSE AIM and FTSE 4Good UK 50 indices are at the bottom of the class, having been the worst performing indices in the year the most number of times.

The following chart shows the relative performance of the FTSE 100, FTSE 250, FTSE AIM and FTSE Fledgling indices.

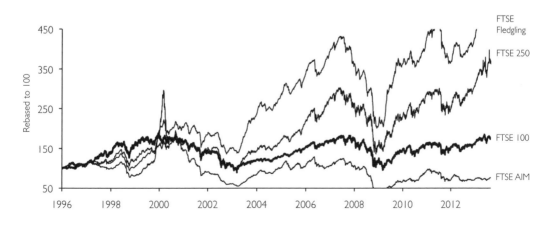

MARKET MOMENTUM (UP) ANALYSIS

The table below displays the results of analysis on market momentum – the tendency of the market to increase in one period, having also risen in the previous period(s). Notes on the analysis:

1. The index analysed was the FTSE All-Share. The number of observations to September 2013 (for each frequency) is indicated in column 0. For example, 11,284 days to September 2013 (from Jan 1969) was the sample data for the "Daily" analysis.

2. The first row ("Total") displays the number of consecutive periods that the index rose for that frequency. For example, the market rose 5967 days (out of the total 11,284); 3346 times it rose on 2 consecutive days; and 318 times it rose 6 days in a row. The second row ("% Total") expresses the first row as a percentage of the total sample. For example, the market rose 6 days in a row in 2.8% of the whole period (11,284 days).

3. The row "% 1 up" expresses the proportion of times that the market rose for n consecutive periods following the market rising for 1 period (expressed as a percentage of the number of times the market rose once). For example: after the market had risen for 1 day, the market rose for a second day in 56.1% of all cases; after the market had risen for 1 day, the market went on to rise 6 days consecutively in 5.3% of all cases.

4. The subsequent rows display the tendency of the market to rise following n consecutive increases. For example: after the market has risen 4 days consecutively, the market rose for a 5th day in 56% of all cases; after the market had risen 3 years in a row, the market rose again the following year in 72.4% of all cases.

Frequency		0	1	2	3	4	5	6
Daily	Total	11284	5967	3346	1850	1033	578	318
	% Total		52.9	29.7	16.4	9.2	5.1	2.8
	% 1 up			56.1	31.0	17.3	9.7	5.3
	% 2 up				55.3	30.9	17.3	9.5
	% 3 up					55.8	31.2	17.2
	% 4 up						56.0	30.8
	% 5 up							55.0
Weekly	Total	2539	1403	776	443	254	149	81
	% Total		55.3	30.6	17.4	10.0	5.9	3.2
	% 1 up			55.3	31.6	18.1	10.6	5.8
	% 2 up				57.1	32.7	19.2	10.4
	% 3 up					57.3	33.6	18.3
	% 4 up						58.7	31.9
	% 5 up							54.4
Monthly	Total	811	495	311	196	127	87	59
	% Total		61.0	38.3	24.2	15.7	10.7	7.3
	% 1 up			62.8	39.6	25.7	17.6	11.9
	% 2 up				63.0	40.8	28.0	19.0
	% 3 up					64.8	44.4	30.1
	% 4 up						68.5	46.5
	% 5 up							67.8
Yearly	Total	113	69	45	29	21	15	10
	% Total		61.1	39.8	25.7	18.6	13.3	8.8
	% 1 up			65.2	42.0	30.4	21.7	14.5
	% 2 up				64.4	46.7	33.3	22.2
	% 3 up					72.4	51.7	34.5
	% 4 up						71.4	47.6
	% 5 up							66.7

Observations

The market would appear to display a degree of fractal behaviour – where its properties are similar whatever time frame one looks at. Trends do seem to become more established the longer they last. For example, the probability of the market rising in a week increases the longer the period of previous consecutive up weeks, although this trend falls off after 5 consecutive up periods.

The market displays greater momentum for longer frequencies. For example, the market only rose 6 days consecutively 2.8% of the time, whereas it rose 6 years consecutively 8.8% of the time. In addition, the market rose for a 6th year (after 5 years of consecutive increases) 66.7% of the time, against just 55% for daily increases.

MARKET MOMENTUM (DOWN) ANALYSIS

The table on the previous page looked at market momentum for the market going up. The table below shows the results of analysis of market momentum when the market falls.

The structure of the table is the same as that on the previous page.

Frequency		0	1	2	3	4	5	6
Daily	Total	11284	5300	2680	1326	630	297	138
	% Total		47.0	23.8	11.8	5.6	2.6	1.2
	% 1 down			50.6	25.0	11.9	5.6	2.6
	% 2 down				49.5	23.5	11.1	5.1
	% 3 down					47.5	22.4	10.4
	% 4 down						47.1	21.9
	% 5 down							46.5
Weekly	Total	2539	1133	505	245	125	59	32
	% Total		44.6	19.9	9.6	4.9	2.3	1.3
	% 1 down			44.6	21.6	11.0	5.2	2.8
	% 2 down				48.5	24.8	11.7	6.3
	% 3 down					51.0	24.1	13.1
	% 4 down						47.2	25.6
	% 5 down							54.2
Monthly	Total	811	314	131	54	20	10	3
	% Total		38.7	16.2	6.7	2.5	1.2	0.4
	% 1 down			41.7	17.2	6.4	3.2	1.0
	% 2 down				41.2	15.3	7.6	2.3
	% 3 down					37.0	18.5	5.6
	% 4 down						50.0	15.0
	% 5 down							30.0
Yearly	Total	113	44	20	8	2	0	0
	% Total		38.9	17.7	7.1	1.8	0.0	0.0
	% 1 down			45.5	18.2	4.5	0.0	0.0
	% 2 down				40.0	10.0	0.0	0.0
	% 3 down					25.0	0.0	0.0
	% 4 down						0.0	0.0
	% 5 down							0.0

Observations

1. Since 1969, the market has fallen on 6 consecutive days on 138 occasions (the last time was November 2011 – when the market fell for 9 straight days). The most consecutive days the market has fallen is 13, which it has done once (in June 1974).

2. Since 1946 the market has only fallen for 4 consecutive months on 20 occasions (2.5%). Random chance would suggest 6.3%.

3. Since 1900, the market has never fallen for 5 consecutive years. The market has fallen for 3 consecutive years on 8 occasions, but having done so the market continued to fall for a 4th year only twice.

4. As with up markets (previous page), down markets appear to display a degree of fractal behaviour, where the properties are similar whatever time frame one looks at.

5. Down markets display far less momentum tendency than that seen for up markets. For example, if the market rises for 3 consecutive months, there's a 64.8% probability that the market will continue to rise for a 4th month as well. However, if the market falls for 3 consecutive months, there's only a 37.0% probability that the market will fall for a 4th month as well.

FTSE 100 – DAILY CHANGE MAP

If the FTSE 100 falls one day by 1.5%, is this a relatively large fall? How often does the market fall by this amount or more? The chart below aims to answer these types of questions.

The FTSE 100 daily change map

1. The chart plots the 7430 daily changes of the FTSE 100 since the index started in 1984.

2. The changes are ordered on the X-axis by size (not by date). So, all the falls in the market are on the left side of the chart, the increases in the market on the right side. The 7430 daily changes are divided into percentage deciles on the X-axis.

3. The Y-axis has been truncated at +/- 3% to enable easier reading of smaller values. Daily changes of over 3% or under -3% have occurred in less than 1% of days.

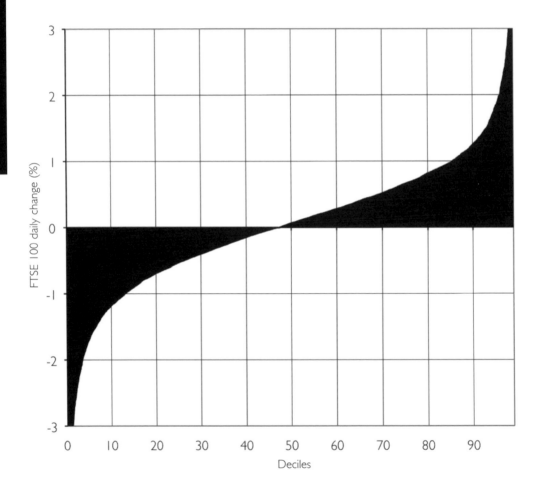

Reading the map

1. If the FTSE 100 increases one day by 1%, looking this up on the chart (on the Y-axis) gives a reading of around 86% (on the X-axis). This tells us that since 1984 the index has increased by less than 1% on 86% of all days, and increased by more than 1% on 14% of all days.

2. Looking up a daily change of -1.5%, the chart gives a value of around 5%. This means that the market has fallen 1.5% or more on 5% of all days. Or, in a year of roughly 250 trading days, we can expect the market to fall 1.5% or more on 4 days in the year.

PRICE HISTORY PROFILE OF THE FTSE ALL-SHARE INDEX

The FTSE All-Share is the aggregation of the FTSE 100, FTSE 250 and FTSE Small Cap. Effectively, it includes all those LSE listed companies with a market capitalisation above the lower limit for inclusion in the FTSE Small Cap. The FTSE All-Share is the standard benchmark for measuring the performance of the broad UK market.

Yearly data

Data starts	1899 (113 years)
Largest one year rise	136.3% (1975)
Largest one year fall	-55.3% (1974)
Average annual return (standard deviation)	5.76% (20.50)
Number of times the index has risen 5 years in a row (last time)	15 (2003-2007)
Number of times the index has risen 8 years in a row (last time)	6 (1983-1989)
Number of times the index has risen 10 years in a row (last time)	4 (1980-1989)
Most number of consecutive years risen	13 (1977-1989)
Number of times the index has fallen 3 years in a row (last time)	8 (2000-2002)
Number of times the index has fallen 4 years in a row (last time)	2 (1912-1915)
Number of times the index has fallen 5 years in a row	0

Monthly data

Data starts	1946 (811 months)
Largest one month rise	52.7% (Jan 1975)
Largest one month fall	-26.6% (Oct 1987)
Average monthly change (standard deviation)	0.67% (5.13)
Number of times the index has risen 6 months in a row (last time)	59 (Dec 12-May 13)
Number of times the index has risen 8 months in a row (last time)	21 (Oct 12-May 13)
Number of times the index has risen 10 months in a row (last time)	9 (Sep 12-May 13)
Most number of consecutive months risen (last time)	12 (Jun 12-May 13)
Number of times the index has fallen 4 months in a row (last time)	20 (Jun 11-Sep 11)
Number of times the index has fallen 6 months in a row (last time)	3 (Apr 02-Sep 02)
Number of times the index has fallen 7 months in a row	0

Daily data

Data starts	2 Jan 1969 (11,284 days)
Largest one day rise	9.4% (24 Jan 75)
Largest one day fall	-11.2% (20 Oct 87)
Average daily change (standard deviation)	0.03% (1.07)
Number of times the index has risen 5 days in a row	578
Number of times the index has risen 8 days in a row (last time)	101 (13 May 12 - 2 May 12)
Number of times the index has risen 10 days in a row (last time)	34 (9 May 12 - 2 May 12)
Most number of consecutive days risen	18 (19/12/86 - 16/01/87)
Number of times the index has fallen 5 days in a row	297
Number of times the index has fallen 8 days in a row (last time)	25 (15 Nov 11 - 24 Nov 11)
Number of times the index has fallen 10 days in a row (last time)	7 (14 Jan 03 - 27 Jan 03)
Most number of consecutive days fallen	13 (6 Jun 74 - 24 Jun 74)

STATISTICS – MARKET INDICES

INTRA-DAY VOLATILITY

Since 1985 the average daily Hi-Lo range of the FTSE 100 has been 1.25% (expressing the Hi-Lo difference as a percentage of the close). This means that when the index is at, say, 6000, the average daily difference between the high and low levels of the index is 75 points. The standard deviation of this daily range is 0.9. We could define a very volatile day as one where the day's Hi-Lo range is 2 standard deviations above the average (i.e. above 3.05%). The chart below plots the Hi-Lo range for the 288 days since 1985 when the range has been over 3.05%.

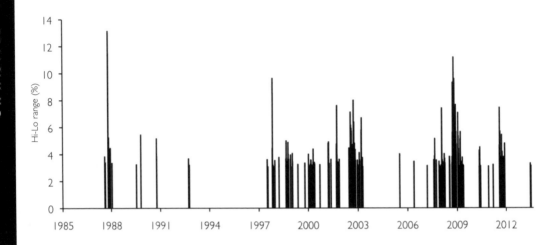

As can be seen, the intra-day volatility of the index seems to be increasing. However, the record for the greatest Hi-Lo range in a day is still 13.1%, seen on 20 October 1987.

After a greater than 2SD daily return, the average return on the following day is 0.14%, and the average return over the following 5-day period is 0.41%.

Hi-Lo-Close

The table to the right shows the frequency with which the index closes within a certain percentage of the high (or low) of the day. For example, since 1985 the FTSE 100 has closed within 10% of its daily high on 21.2% of all days, and it has closed within 1% of its low on 5.6% of all days.

	10%	5%	1%
Top (%)	21.2	15.6	10.1
Bottom (%)	14.9	9.8	5.6

It's interesting to note that for 1 in 10 days the index closes within 1% of its high for the day.

Continuing this analysis of where the index closes relative to the Hi-Lo range of the day, the table to the right shows the performance of the FTSE 100 on the following day. For example, on the days when the index closes within 10% of its low for the day, on average the index return is 0.011% the following day; and when the index closes within 1% of its high for the day, on average the index return is 0.172% the following day.

	10%	5%	1%
Top (%)	0.115	0.136	0.172
Bottom (%)	0.011	0.008	0.026

The table to the right shows the 10 largest one-day rises and falls in the FTSE 100 since its inception in 1984.

It would seem that the majority of the largest one-day moves have occurred in recent years.

Is the FTSE 100 becoming increasingly volatile on a daily basis?

Since 1984 there have been 361 very large one-day moves, where "very large move" is defined as a move of more than two standard deviations (in other words a move of more than 2.23% away from the average daily return). These very large one-day moves are plotted on the following chart (the left Y-axis gives the one-day percentage move, the right Y-axis gives the level of the FTSE 100).

Largest one-day rises		Largest one-day falls	
Date	Return (%)	Date	Return (%)
24 Nov 08	9.8	20 Oct 87	-12.2
19 Sep 08	8.8	10 Oct 08	-8.8
13 Oct 08	8.3	06 Oct 08	-7.9
29 Oct 08	8.1	15 Oct 08	-7.2
21 Oct 87	7.9	26 Oct 87	-6.2
08 Dec 08	6.2	19 Oct 87	-5.7
13 Mar 03	6.1	06 Nov 08	-5.7
10 Apr 92	5.6	22 Oct 87	-5.7
20 Oct 08	5.4	21 Jan 08	-5.5
17 Oct 08	5.2	15 Jul 02	-5.4

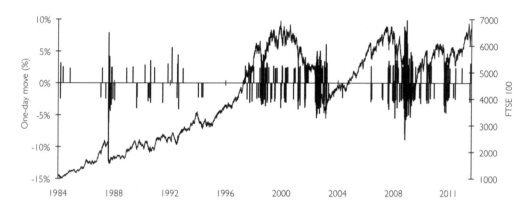

The chart does indeed show that the frequency of very large one-day moves has increased in recent years. Another observation is that there is a certain symmetry to the chart, in that large market rises often occur in an immediate response to a large fall.

After the move

The following chart shows how on average the index has performed in the days immediately following a very large move. The Y-axis is the percentage move from the close of the index on the day of the respective large rise or fall. For example, by day 5 the index has risen 0.8% above the index close on the day of the large fall.

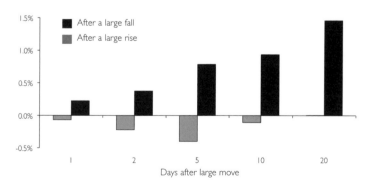

As can be seen, in the 20 days following a large fall the index has tended to rise strongly and steadily. In the 5 days following a large market rise the index tends to fall back, losing some of its one-day gain, but the index then tends to recover and after 20 days has almost regained the level reached by the very large one-day rise.

TRIPLE WITCHING

Derivatives contract expiry

Triple witching days 2014
21 March
20 June
19 September
19 December

Exchange-traded options and futures are financial contracts that expire on a certain day. On this expiry day the underlying assets (in the case we're interested in, stocks and stock indices) can experience an increased level of volatility. This can be for a couple of reasons:

1. Traders that have positions in the derivative instruments (e.g. options) may try to influence the closing price of the underlying stocks to which the settlement prices of the derivatives are related. For example, if a trader is long call (or short put) options they might try to ramp the underlying stock in the closing period of trading. Conversely, traders long of puts (or short calls) might try to sell the stock down in the closing period.

2. If traders with arbitrage positions (i.e. matched holdings in derivatives and underlying stocks) unwind their positions at contract expiry this can create buying or selling pressure on the stocks.

Triple witching

The derivatives contracts that are relevant here are: stock index futures, stock index options and stock options. The expiries of these contracts happen in a programmed calendar throughout the year. However, on four days a year these three different types of derivative all expire on the same day – the third Friday of the months of March, June, September and December. The final hour of these days has come to be known in the US as triple witching hour. And with the recent introduction of single stock futures, triple witching has become quadruple witching.

Due to the correlation of the US and UK markets, the UK would be affected by US triple witching anyway; however, the UK also has it own version of triple witching as the expiries of stock options and futures on LIFFE also coincide on the same four days as those in the US.

The chart below shows the recent average trading range (defined as the percentage range between the high and low prices on the day) for the FTSE 100 on the triple witching day, TW(0), and that for the day immediately prior to it and following it, TW(-1) and TW(+1) respectively. The dotted line shows the average trading range for all days since year 2000.

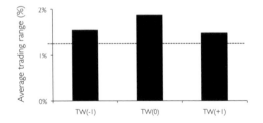

As can be seen the trading range for the three days is higher than that for normal days, with the greatest volatility seen on the triple witching day itself.

The chart below shows the average returns in the FTSE 100 on the three days around triple witching. The dotted line shows the average return for all days since the year 2000.

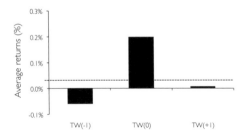

It can be seen that the average change on triple witching day is significantly above average.

TURN OF THE MONTH

This study analyses the behaviour of the market on the 10 days around each turn of the month (ToM). The days studied are the 5 last trading days of the month, from ToM(-5) to ToM(-1), the latter being the last trading day of the month, and the first 5 trading days of the following month, from ToM(+1) to ToM(+5). The index analysed is the FTSE All-Share.

From 1970

The charts below analyse the 525 ToMs since 1970. The left chart shows the percentage number of positive days and the right chart is the average return on the day. For example, on ToM(-5) the market has on average risen 49.1% of the time with an average return of -0.03%.

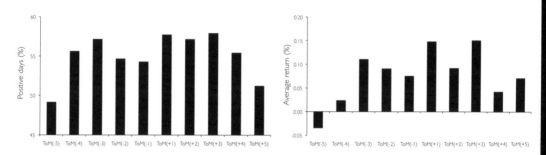

We can see that there is a definite trend for the market to be weak at the beginning of the 10-day period, to then strengthen around the turn of the month, and afterwards to weaken again.

Does this behaviour persist in more recent years?

From 2000

The charts below are the same configuration as above, except they look at a shorter time period: the 165 ToMs from the year 2000 to mid-2013.

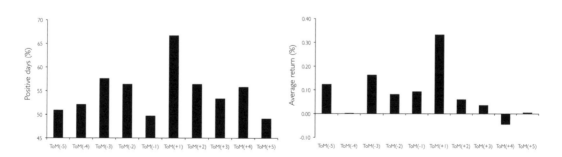

Broadly, the behaviour has been the same for the last few years as that since 1970. The main observation is that the strength of the first trading day of the month, ToM(0), has become even more pronounced. On average the market rises 67% of all ToM(0) with an average change of 0.33% (which is ten times the average change on all trading days).

TUESDAY REVERSES MONDAY

Some traders believe that Tuesday's market reverses Monday's. In other words, if the market rises on Monday it will fall the following day, and vice versa.

Is this true?

The following chart shows the change in the FTSE 100 on:

1. Tuesdays when the market has **risen** the previous day (*Monday up*), and

2. Tuesdays when market has **fallen** the previous day (*Monday down*).

The data analysed covers two periods: 1984 to 2013 and 2000 to 2013.

For example, in the period 2000 to 2013, the market fell on average 0.08% on Tuesdays following a Monday increase.

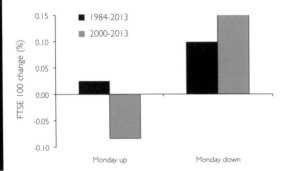

As can be seen, for the longer period of 1984 to 2013 the theory that Tuesday reverses Monday does not fully hold. For this period, when the market falls on Monday the return is positive the next day (which is fine), but when the market rises on Monday the average Tuesday returns are positive as well (i.e. no reversal).

However, since 2000 the theory appears to be working rather well. Tuesday returns have on average been the reverse of Monday. In fact, when the market is down on Monday, the average returns the following day have been five times greater than the average returns on all days since 2000.

How can this be exploited?

The following chart shows the value of three portfolios since 2000 (all starting with a value of 100):

1. **Portfolio 1**: tracks the FTSE 100.

2. **Portfolio 2**: if the market is down on Monday this portfolio goes long the market at the end of Monday and closes the position at the end of Tuesday (for four days out of five the portfolio is in cash).

3. **Portfolio 3**: similar to the above, with the addition that it also goes short the market on Tuesday if Monday was up.

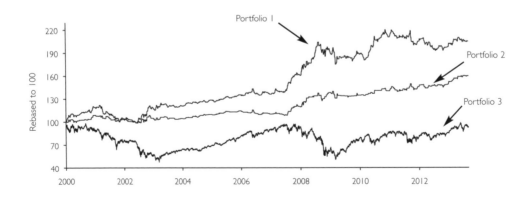

By 2013 the market portfolio (Portfolio 1) value would be 93, Portfolio 2 would be worth 160 and Portfolio 3 would be worth 205.

It's interesting to observe that both portfolios 2 and 3 performed well during the steep market fall of 2007 to 2008. The chart below looks at the effectiveness of the theory on a year-by-year basis for the period 2009 to 2012.

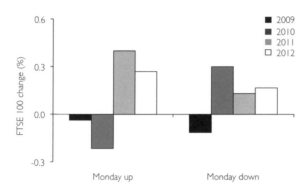

It can be seen that while the theory worked well in 2010, it did not fully do so in the other years. Albeit the Tuesday reversing a Monday fall has been reliable in the last three years.

COMPANY PROFILE OF THE FTSE 100 INDEX

Rank 2013	Rank 2012	Company	TIDM	Turnover (£m)	Profit (£m)	Profit margin (%)	Capital (£m)	Weighting (%)	Cumulative weighting (%)
1	1	Royal Dutch Shell	RDSB	287,390	30,938	7.5	133,138	7.3	7.3
2	2	HSBC Holdings	HSBA		12,703		130,405	7.1	14.4
3	3	Vodafone Group	VOD	44,445	3,255	11.3	101,816	5.6	20.0
4	4	BP	BP.	231,055	11,571	3.8	83,956	4.6	24.6
5	5	GlaxoSmithKline	GSK	26,431	6,692	27.9	79,311	4.3	29.0
6	6	British American Tobacco	BATS	15,190	5,648	33.6	63,313	3.5	32.4
7	17	Lloyds Banking Group	LLOY		-570		54,232	3.0	35.4
8	9	SABMiller	SAB	15,302	3,106	18.7	50,344	2.8	38.2
9	11	Diageo	DGE	11,433	3,123	30.6	49,930	2.7	40.9
10	7	Rio Tinto	RIO	31,355	-1,580	22.6	45,303	2.5	43.4
11		Glencore Xstrata	GLEN	131,920	662	1.3	44,408	2.4	45.8
12	8	BG Group	BG.	11,647	3,916	44.2	41,077	2.3	48.1
13	10	BHP Billiton	BLT	43,246	11,716		40,800	2.2	50.3
14	13	AstraZeneca	AZN	17,209	4,748	34.9	39,599	2.2	52.5
15	18	Barclays	BARC		246		39,436	2.2	54.6
16	12	Standard Chartered	STAN		4,230		36,832	2.0	56.6
17	16	Unilever	ULVR	41,625	5,420	13.7	32,322	1.8	58.4
18	21	Reckitt Benckiser Group	RB.	9,567	2,420	26.3	31,820	1.7	60.2
19	19	Tesco	TSCO	64,826	1,960	6.0	30,015	1.6	61.8
20	24	Prudential	PRU		3,188		29,765	1.6	63.4
21	22	National Grid	NG.	14,359	2,920	35.6	27,564	1.5	64.9
22	25	BT Group	BT.A	18,017	2,501	16.5	27,397	1.5	66.4
23	15	Anglo American	AAL	17,694	-147	19.5	22,439	1.2	67.7
24	27	Royal Bank of Scotland Group	RBS		-5,165		22,005	1.2	68.9
25	23	Imperial Tobacco Group	IMT	28,574	1,081	9.9	21,978	1.2	70.1
26	28	Rolls-Royce Group	RR.	12,161	2,705	15.4	21,153	1.2	71.2
27	26	Centrica	CNA	23,942	2,442	12.3	20,452	1.1	72.4
28	36	WPP Group	WPP	10,373	1,092	12.4	17,005	0.9	73.3
29	33	Compass Group	CPG	16,905	789	5.0	15,436	0.8	74.1
30	30	SSE	SSE	28,305	601	3.9	15,083	0.8	75.0
31	35	BAE Systems	BA.	17,834	1,369	14.6	14,291	0.8	75.7
32	40	Associated British Foods	ABF	12,252	761	7.8	14,290	0.8	76.5
33	46	ARM Holdings	ARM	577	221	36.1	13,804	0.8	77.3
34	37	Shire	SHP	2,880	561	24.6	13,752	0.8	78.0
35	34	British Sky Broadcasting Group	BSY	7,235	1,257		13,522	0.7	78.8
36	38	Aviva	AV.		246		12,103	0.7	79.4
37	39	Experian	EXPN	3,118	290	12.8	11,938	0.7	80.1
38	44	Legal & General Group	LGEN		1,210		11,820	0.6	80.7
39	42	CRH	CRH	15,133	547	5.6	10,832	0.6	81.3
40	41	Pearson	PSON	5,059	434	12.3	10,566	0.6	81.9
41	31	Tullow Oil	TLW	1,442	687	51.3	9,759	0.5	82.5
42	51	Kingfisher	KGF	10,573	691	7.0	9,693	0.5	83.0
43	47	Reed Elsevier	REL	3,235	546	19.9	9,652	0.5	83.5
44	43	Old Mutual	OML		1,395		9,372	0.5	84.0
45	45	Wolseley	WOS	13,421	198	4.5	9,273	0.5	84.5
46	29	Fresnillo	FRES	1,327	716	53.6	8,975	0.5	85.0
47	32	Antofagasta	ANTO	4,146	1,694	49.4	8,735	0.5	85.5
48	56	Marks & Spencer Group	MKS	10,027	564	7.0	8,225	0.5	86.0
49	50	Standard Life	SL.		996		8,184	0.4	86.4
50	58	Next	NXT	3,563	667	18.5	8,166	0.4	86.9
51	52	Sainsbury (J)	SBRY	23,303	788	3.4	7,529	0.4	87.3
52	62	Burberry Group	BRBY	1,999	351	22.2	7,268	0.4	87.7
53	84	ITV	ITV	2,196	348	25.5	7,129	0.4	88.1
54	54	Land Securities Group	LAND	737	533	56.2	7,083	0.4	88.4
55	55	Smith & Nephew	SN.	2,545	677	22.4	6,943	0.4	88.8

Rank 2013	Rank 2012	Company	TIDM	Turnover (£m)	Profit (£m)	Profit margin (%)	Capital (£m)	Weighting (%)	Cumulative weighting (%)
56	48	Morrison (Wm) Supermarkets	MRW	18,116	879	5.3	6,935	0.4	89.2
57	69	Schroders	SDR	1,425	360	24.9	6,760	0.4	89.6
58	63	Capita Group (The)	CPI	3,352	290	11.3	6,549	0.4	89.9
59	95	International Consolidated Airlines	IAG	14,693	-809	-1.7	6,121	0.3	90.3
60	59	Johnson Matthey	JMAT	10,729	355	3.7	6,100	0.3	90.6
61	78	GKN	GKN	6,510	588	8.6	5,780	0.3	90.9
62	61	British Land Co	BLND	329	260	76.9	5,697	0.3	91.2
63	72	Whitbread	WTB	2,030	355	18.2	5,628	0.3	91.5
64	67	Intertek Group	ITRK	2,054	257	14.7	5,474	0.3	91.8
65	70	Smiths Group	SMIN	3,030	366	17.5	5,354	0.3	92.1
66		easyJet	EZJ	3,854	317	8.6	5,254	0.3	92.4
67	60	Carnival	CCL	9,598	812	11.7	5,226	0.3	92.7
68	64	InterContinental Hotels Group	IHG	1,129	342	33.7	5,026	0.3	93.0
69	77	Weir Group	WEIR	2,538	424	16.8	5,014	0.3	93.3
70	57	Petrofac Ltd	PFC	3,891	471	12.1	4,881	0.3	93.5
71	91	Hargreaves Lansdown	HL.	292	195		4,838	0.3	93.8
72	90	IMI	IMI	2,190	317	16.1	4,757	0.3	94.0
73	89	Resolution Ltd	RSL		66		4,639	0.3	94.3
74	66	United Utilities Group	UU.	1,636	305	41.6	4,636	0.3	94.6
75	83	Aberdeen Asset Management	ADN	869	270	31.4	4,555	0.2	94.8
76	81	Bunzl	BNZL	5,359	269	6.0	4,481	0.2	95.0
77	68	RSA Insurance Group	RSA		479		4,450	0.2	95.3
78	53	Aggreko	AGK	1,583	367	24.0	4,442	0.2	95.5
79		London Stock Exchange Group	LSE	726	299	46.1	4,387	0.2	95.8
80	88	Meggitt	MGGT	1,606	292	20.6	4,363	0.2	96.0
81	86	Babcock International Group	BAB	3,029	225	8.6	4,301	0.2	96.3
82	49	Randgold Resources Ltd	RRS	811	350	43.0	4,254	0.2	96.5
83	74	Severn Trent	SVT	1,832	215	24.5	4,100	0.2	96.7
84	79	Rexam	REX	4,312	354	10.5	4,034	0.2	96.9
85		Travis Perkins	TPK	4,845	313	6.0	3,978	0.2	97.1
86		TUI Travel	TT.	14,460	201	2.5	3,973	0.2	97.4
87		Melrose Industries	MRO	1,551	92	11.6	3,961	0.2	97.6
88	80	G4S	GFS	7,501	175	6.3	3,946	0.2	97.8
89	76	Sage Group (The)	SGE	1,340	334	25.9	3,847	0.2	98.0
90	94	Tate & Lyle	TATE	3,256	309	10.7	3,638	0.2	98.2
91		William Hill	WMH	1,277	278	23.7	3,631	0.2	98.4
92	87	Croda International	CRDA	1,052	253	24.1	3,602	0.2	98.6
93	85	Hammerson	HMSO	298	94	43.6	3,537	0.2	98.8
94		Persimmon	PSN	1,721	222	12.6	3,507	0.2	99.0
95	92	Admiral Group	ADM		345		3,361	0.2	99.2
96	97	Vedanta Resources	VED	9,881	1,125	16.4	3,182	0.2	99.3
97	82	AMEC	AMEC	4,158	263	6.9	3,147	0.2	99.5
98		Wood Group (John)	WG.	4,196	207	5.5	3,058	0.2	99.7
99	65	Eurasian Natural Resources Corp	ENRC	3,888	-338	14.6	2,833	0.2	99.8
100	96	Serco Group	SRP	4,913	302	5.7	2,833	0.2	100.0

Notes to the table

1. The *Weighting* column expresses a company's market capitalisation as a percentage of the total capitalisation of all companies in the FTSE 100. The table is ranked (in descending order) by this column.

2. Figures accurate as of September 2013.

Observations

- The 5 largest companies in the FTSE 100 account for 29% of the total market capitalisation. (In 2004 the comparable figure was 36%.)

- The 13 largest companies in the index account for just over half of total capitalisation. (2004: 10)

- The 25 smallest companies in the index account for only 5% of total capitalisation. In other words, the individual movements of these 25 companies has very little impact on the level of the index.

- The aggregate capitalisation of all 100 companies in the index is £1,825bn (2012: £1,640bn; 2006: £1,397bn). When the index started in 1984 the aggregate capitalisation was £10bn.

INDEX PROFILES – COMPANY FINANCIALS

The table below presents a range of company financials characteristics for six stock market indices in the UK. For example, the average turnover for the 248 companies in the FTSE Small Cap is £199m.

	FTSE 100	FTSE 250	Small Cap	Fledgling	AIM	techMARK
Number of companies in index	100	250	248	116	1,096	65
Turnover, average (£m)	14,675	965	199	60	41	2,346
Turnover growth last five years, average (%)	76	81	47	26	160	55
Turnover to capitalisation ratio, average	0.9	0.9	1.6	4.5	2.3	0.9
Number of companies making a profit	94	181	98	39	428	52
Number of companies making a profit (%)	94	72	40	34	39	80
Profit, average (£m)	1,534.0	51.6	0.1	-4.7	-0.4	335.4
Profit growth last five years, average (%)	102	66	57	-16	116	143
Profit / turnover, average (%)	17	16	-14	-18	-695	-4
Current ratio, average	1.3	2.1	12.7	4.1	6.6	2.5
Net cash, average (£m)	5,839	208	27	8	10	404
Net cash, sum total (£m)	566,363	50,486	6,217	849	10,207	25,031
Price to net cash ratio, average	24	31	37	22	19	20
Net borrowings, average (£m)	-1,710	213	93	14	6	959
Net borrowings, sum total (£m)	-165,902	42,123	11,264	966	5,887	59,480
Net gearing, average	1	21	17	10	-28	-86
Interest cover, average	70	61			-21	0
Dividend cover, average	3	3	2	1	4	3
ROCE, average (%)	50	92	70	15	-28	29
ROCE, standard deviation	108	598	245	86	292	65

Notes and observations

1. Care should be taken with some of the figures above – especially those of indices with few companies (such as the FTSE Fledgling and techMARK) – as the averages can be significantly affected by one or two outlier numbers. In addition, the techMARK is very non-homogenous, being comprised of very large *and* very small companies.

2. Only 40% of Small Caps and 39% of AIM companies reported a profit for 2012.

3. On average, FTSE 100 companies have £5,839m net cash (2007: £1,647m), while FTSE 250 companies have net cash of £208m (2007: £114m).

Data compiled September 2013.

INDEX PROFILES – SHARE PRICES

The table below presents a range of share price related characteristics for six stock market indices in the UK. For example, the average market capitalisation of the 1,096 companies in the AIM is £64m.

	FTSE 100	FTSE 250	Small Cap	Fledgling	AIM	techMARK
Number of companies in index	100	250	248	116	1,096	65
Market capitalisation, average (£m)	18,253	1,338	228	36	64	5,190
Market capitalisation, standard deviation	24,837	795	126	25	188	16,740
Share price, average (£)	12.94	7.76	3.51	4.58	0.93	5.96
Number of companies paying a dividend	96	211	184	71	252	47
Number of companies paying a dividend (%)	96	84	74	61	23	72
Dividend yield, average (%)	2.9	2.8	3.0	4.0	3.7	2.6
Dividend yield, standard deviation	1.3	1.7	1.9	3.4	8.6	1.8
PE ratio, average	20.2	29.0	47.4	34.9	29.9	25.6
PE ratio, standard deviation	14.3	47.2	68.8	61.0	58.5	21.0
PEG, average	2.4	2.0	2.7	1.6	1.8	1.7
Correlation (FTSE 100), average	0.5	0.4	0.3	0.2	0.1	0.2
Correlation (FTSE 100), standard deviation	0.1	0.2	0.2	0.1	0.1	0.1
Beta (FTSE 100), average	1.0	0.7	0.5	0.3	0.2	0.6
Beta (FTSE 100), standard deviation	0.4	0.3	0.3	0.2	0.2	0.3

Notes and observations

1. As with the accompanying table "Index profiles – company financials", care should be taken with some of the figures above – especially those of indices with few companies (such as the FTSE Fledgling and techMARK) – as the averages can be significantly affected by one or two outlier numbers. In addition, the techMARK is very non-homogenous, as it is comprised of very large *and* very small companies.

2. Just 23% of AIM companies pay a dividend. The figures for all the indices have changed very little from 2007. (NB. The average dividend yield is an average for the companies that pay a dividend, which is not all the companies in the index.)

3. The average PE for the FTSE 100 companies is 20.2 with the PE values fairly tightly clustered around this average level, but the PEs for companies in the other indices have a very wide range around the average (i.e. a high standard deviation).

4. Correlation is calculated relative to the FTSE 100. (Note: the averages calculated here are equally weighted, not market capitalisation weighted.)

5. Beta is calculated relative to the FTSE 100.

Data compiled September 2013.

FTSE 100 INDEX QUARTERLY REVIEWS

To keep the FTSE 100 in accordance with its purpose, the constituents of the index are periodically reviewed. The reviews take place on the Wednesday after the first Friday of the month in March, June, September and December. If any changes are to be made (i.e. companies ejected or introduced) these are announced sometime after the market has closed on the day of the review.

The review dates for 2014 are: 12 March, 11 June, 10 September and 10 December.

Since the index's inception in 1984, the company that has danced in and out of the index the most is Tate & Lyle, which has been added 6 times (and ejected 5 times).

Below is a table of companies entering and exiting the FTSE 100 since January 2008 as a result of the FTSE quarterly reviews.

Company	In	Out
3i Group	Jun 09	Mar 09, Sep 11
Aberdeen Asset Management	Mar 12	
African Barrick Gold	Jun 10	Mar 11
Aggreko	Dec 09	
Alliance & Leicester		Jun 08
Alliance Trust		Mar 11
Amlin	Dec 08	Jun 09
Ashmore Group	Sep 11	Sep 12
Autonomy Corporation	Sep 08	
Babcock International Group	Jun 12	
Balfour Beatty		Sep 09
Bunzl	Apr 08, Sep 11	Mar 11
Cable and Wireless Worldwide		Sep 10
Cairn Energy		Mar 12
Carphone Warehouse Group		Sep 08
Cobham	Mar 08	Dec 10
Coca-Cola HBC AG	Sep 13	
CRH	Dec 11	
Croda International	Mar 12	
Drax Group	Jun 08	Jun 09
easyJet	Mar 13	
Enterprise Inns		Sep 08
Essar Energy	Jun 10	Mar 12
Eurasian Natural Resources	Mar 08	Sep 13
Evraz	Dec 11	
Ferrexpo	Jun 08	Sep 08
First Group		Mar 09
Foreign & Col Inv Trust	Mar 09	Sep 09
Fresnillo	Sep 08, Mar 09	Dec 08
Glencore	May 11	
Hargreaves Lansdown	Mar 11	
Home Retail Group	Dec 08	Jun 08, Sep 10
ICAP		Sep 12
IMI	Dec 10	
Inmarsat	Sep 08	Dec 11
International Power		Jun 12
Intertek Group	Mar 09	
Intu Properties		Mar 13
Invensys	Jun 08	May 11
Investec	Mar 10	Dec 11
ITV	Mar 11	Sep 08
Kazakhmys		Mar 13

Company	In	Out
London Stock Exchange Group	Jun 09, Mar 13	Mar 09, Jun 10
Lonmin	Mar 09	Dec 08, Dec 11
Man Group		Jun 12
Melrose	Sep 12	
Mondi	Sep 13	
Pennon Group	Jun 12	Sep 09, Dec 12
Persimmon		Jun 08
Petrofac	Jun 08, Mar 09	Dec 08
Polymetal International	Dec 11	
Randgold Resources	Dec 08	
Rentokil Initial	Sep 09	Mar 08, Dec 09
Resolution	Sep 10	Apr 08, Mar 10
Scottish & Newcastle		Apr 08
Segro	Sep 09	Sep 10
Sports Direct International	Sep 13	
Serco Group	Dec 08	Sep 13
Stagecoach Group	Sep 08	Dec 08
Tate & Lyle	Mar 08, Dec 08, Jun 11	Jun 08, Mar 09
Taylor Wimpey		Mar 08
Thomas Cook Group		Jun 10
Tomkins	Sep 10	
TUI Travel	Dec 12	Jun 11
Weir Group	Sep 10	
Whitbread	Sep 09	Jun 09
Wolseley	Jun 09	Mar 09
Wood Group (John)	Apr 08, Mar 11, Sep 12	Dec 08, Sep 11, Sep 13
Yell Group		Mar 08

Source: FTSE International

INDEX PROFILES – INDUSTRY

The pie charts below show the profiles of the major UK stock market indices by industry. The size of the respective sectors in these charts is determined by the number of companies in the sector and not market capitalisation.

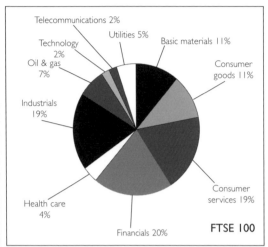

Telecommunications 2%
Utilities 5%
Technology 2%
Oil & gas 7%
Industrials 19%
Health care 4%
Basic materials 11%
Consumer goods 11%
Consumer services 19%
Financials 20%

FTSE 100

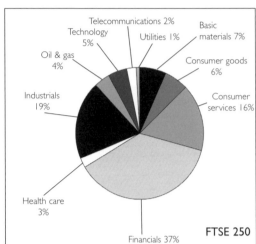

Telecommunications 2%
Technology 5%
Utilities 1%
Oil & gas 4%
Industrials 19%
Health care 3%
Basic materials 7%
Consumer goods 6%
Consumer services 16%
Financials 37%

FTSE 250

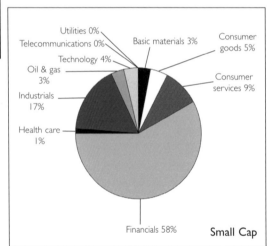

Utilities 0%
Telecommunications 0%
Basic materials 3%
Technology 4%
Oil & gas 3%
Industrials 17%
Health care 1%
Consumer goods 5%
Consumer services 9%
Financials 58%

Small Cap

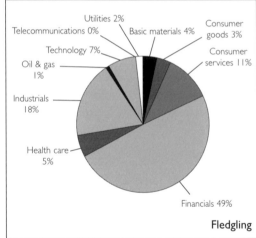

Utilities 2%
Telecommunications 0%
Basic materials 4%
Technology 7%
Oil & gas 1%
Industrials 18%
Health care 5%
Consumer goods 3%
Consumer services 11%
Financials 49%

Fledgling

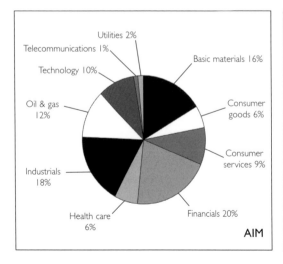

Utilities 2%
Telecommunications 1%
Technology 10%
Oil & gas 12%
Industrials 18%
Health care 6%
Basic materials 16%
Consumer goods 6%
Consumer services 9%
Financials 20%

AIM

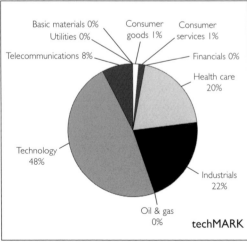

Basic materials 0%
Utilities 0%
Telecommunications 8%
Technology 48%
Oil & gas 0%
Consumer goods 1%
Consumer services 1%
Financials 0%
Health care 20%
Industrials 22%

techMARK

SECTORS

SECTOR ANNUAL PERFORMANCE

The table below shows the year-on-year percentage performance of the FTSE 350 sectors. The three best [worst] performing sectors in each year are highlighted in light grey [dark grey]. The table is ranked by the final column – the average annual return for the sector.

Sector performance 2003-2012 (percentage change YoY)

EPIC	Sector	2003	2004	2005	2006	2007	2008	2009	2010	2011	2012	Avg
NMX1750	Industrial Metals	639.9	68.3	16.8	79.8	-56.6	-83.9	307.3	72.4	-54.0	-29.4	96.1
NMX9570	Technology Hardware & Equipment	172.2	-9.9	5.5	-10.4	-1.2	-43.3	131.6	70.4	21.6	25.7	36.2
NMX2750	Industrial Engineering	37.1	14.4	27.6	19.8	-7.2	-31.1	83.1	78.2	3.2	14.7	24.0
NMX3760	Personal Goods	5.5	24.2	20.9	40.7	2.2	-42.9	105.8	76.1	-1.6	3.4	23.4
NMX1770	Mining	33.5	8.6	63.0	22.9	50.4	-55.7	108.5	27.8	-29.7	0.2	23.0
NMX0570	Oil Equipment Services & Distribution					38.1	-45.7	87.8	56.3	-10.4	6.2	22.1
NMX1350	Chemicals	-1.4	14.3	32.1	33.6	41.3	-37.8	43.8	58.5	-7.8	35.5	21.2
NMX3350	Automobiles & Parts	44.4	9.1	25.0	-3.5	1.4	-65.6	78.7	89.9	-17.6	25.0	18.7
NMX3780	Tobacco	12.1	23.4	31.0	14.8	34.0	-14.6	9.9	15.0	23.9	0.8	15.0
NMX2710	Aerospace & Defense	23.3	31.9	54.3	6.0	20.4	-27.6	15.8	7.7	1.1	16.9	15.0
NMX3530	Beverages	8.6	12.4	19.7	16.5	14.4	-11.6	28.9	15.6	9.3	25.8	14.0
NMX9530	Software & Computer Services	42.9	-6.1	16.7	-2.9	-7.5	-26.2	63.9	23.7	2.1	28.8	13.5
NMX2730	Electronic & Electrical Equipment	-30.8	-5.3	35.7	23.4	-5.5	-31.4	23.0	81.2	-6.6	41.8	12.6
NMX5750	Travel & Leisure	46.9	29.8	18.5	27.6	-15.9	-40.8	22.5	24.2	-15.9	25.2	12.2
NMX7530	Electricity	3.5	21.0	33.4	41.2	6.5	-16.2	-1.0	14.0	8.5	8.4	11.9
NMX2770	Industrial Transportation	23.6	15.3	25.7	49.9	-20.8	-61.2	52.3	25.7	-12.2	13.4	11.2
NMX2350	Construction & Materials	45.8	22.6	35.1	29.0	4.5	-35.7	-0.7	19.6	-13.1	0.3	10.7
NMX8770	Financial Services	28.2	7.3	25.9	37.9	2.0	-55.4	39.7	21.5	-28.5	23.5	10.2
NMX8980	Equity Investment Instruments	20.7	12.1	30.8	12.4	6.5	-36.1	31.3	18.5	-10.9	10.1	9.5
NMX7570	Gas Water & Multiutilities		24.8	13.9	31.0	7.3	-17.8	-0.6	7.9	2.8	13.2	9.2
NMX8530	Nonlife Insurance	-9.0	-5.4	44.6	28.6	-6.2	1.2	-1.7	17.6	-12.3	23.8	8.1
NMX1730	Forestry & Paper	11.7	2.8	6.6		-49.7	-52.1	64.4	53.3	-11.4	47.1	8.1
NMX2790	Support Services	12.1	-0.9	17.5	20.4	-9.7	-27.2	28.7	19.7	-2.4	20.2	7.8
NMX4530	Health Care Equipment & Services	29.6	5.8	4.0	-2.9	18.6	-36.3	47.0	7.5	-7.2	9.7	7.6
NMX5370	General Retailers	21.9	14.2	3.3	16.6	-25.9	-47.8	75.2	-2.5	-11.7	32.4	7.6
NMX3570	Food Producers	-5.2	10.7	12.1	9.8	12.9	-19.9	25.1	6.3	7.8	13.2	7.3
NMX8630	Real Estate Investment & Services								-2.0	-1.3	23.4	6.7
NMX8570	Life Insurance	7.4	17.9	17.1	18.5	-10.1	-43.3	26.5	2.0	-4.6	32.8	6.4
NMX5550	Media	15.7	4.9	6.0	4.0	0.2	-34.1	28.3	21.5	-1.9	19.2	6.4
NMX5330	Food & Drug Retailers	26.2	12.1	3.8	23.6	20.2	-22.5	12.5	1.8	-3.6	-12.0	6.2
NMX2720	General Industrials					-13.1	-30.0	23.2	37.6	-12.3	28.9	5.7
NMX0530	Oil & Gas Producers	4.9	12.5	25.6	-2.0	19.3	-16.0	13.3	0.5	4.8	-11.8	5.1
NMX6530	Fixed Line Telecommunications	22.2	4.9	-1.1	32.9	-5.4	-44.5	-1.7	19.8	-5.2	24.4	4.6
NMX6570	Mobile Telecommunications					32.9	-25.7	4.6	14.7	8.6	-12.5	3.8
NMX4570	Pharmaceuticals & Biotechnology	12.9	-12.1	28.7	-5.1	-9.5	8.0	4.2	-1.2	14.5	-7.0	3.3
NMX3720	Household Goods					-15.0	-28.6	30.9	1.0	-5.2	31.9	2.5
NMX8350	Banks	17.8	6.8	7.3	10.0	-21.3	-56.8	23.8	-0.1	-29.6	34.5	-0.8
NMX8670	Real Estate Investment Trusts				33.8	-36.5	-44.7	6.2	2.7	-12.6	25.7	-3.6

Observations

1. No sector has been in the top three best or worst performing sectors for more than two consecutive years.

2. Since 2003, 20 of the 38 sectors have never been in the top three performing sectors of the year.

3. The most volatile sector has been Industrial Metals, which has been one of the top three best or worst performing sectors in eight years since 2002.

SECTOR QUARTERLY PERFORMANCE

In the following pages there are four tables showing the performance of FTSE 350 sectors in the four quarters of the year.

Notes:

1. The tables are ranked by the final column – the average performance for each sector over the ten years.

2. For each year the top five performing sectors are highlighted in light grey, the bottom five in dark grey.

The general clustering of light grey highlights at the top of the table, and dark grey at the bottom, suggests that certain sectors consistently perform well (or badly) in certain quarters. This effect is strongest in the first quarter and weakest in the third.

The table to the right gives a subjective listing of the strong and weak sectors in each quarter (sectors with just one or two constituents have been left out).

Quarter	Strong	Weak
1	Industrial Engineering	Banks
	Industrial Metals	Food & Drug Retailers
	Oil Equip, Srvs & Dist	Pharm & Biotech
2	Electricity	Construction & Materials
	Fixed Line Telecoms	Household Goods
	Personal Goods	Industrial Metals
3	Life Insurance	General Retailers
	Software & Comp Srvs	Media
	Technology Hard & Equip	Oil & Gas Producers
4	Beverages	Banks
	Mining	General Industrials
	Tobacco	Real Estate Inv Trusts

First quarter

Sector	2004	2005	2006	2007	2008	2009	2010	2011	2012	2013	Avg
Industrial Metals	37.5	6.9	49.2	14.4	21.0	80.7	39.5	0.1	5.1	-18.5	23.6
Forestry & Paper	10.9	1.1			-1.6	-27.4	38.5	16.7	29.6	33.5	12.7
Industrial Engineering	3.4	5.1	14.1	9.6	3.2	10.2	21.0	1.6	7.8	17.3	9.3
Oil Equip Srvs & Dist				4.0	-0.3	19.6	11.1	2.5	20.1	3.1	8.6
Chemicals	3.8	5.9	13.9	10.0	7.4	-3.0	14.0	-4.1	25.5	6.7	8.0
Technology Hard & Equip	-0.3	-7.4	12.5	5.2	-28.1	27.1	19.7	22.9	8.2	19.4	7.9
Automobiles & Parts	-0.2	4.3	15.5	37.2	7.9	-29.6	17.9	-9.6	12.6	15.6	7.2
Electronic & Elect Equip	5.6	10.2	10.0	8.6	-2.0	-20.8	12.3	3.8	25.6	12.3	6.6
Household Goods				5.8	-4.4	3.6	5.6	-5.0	14.2	23.9	6.2
Construction & Materials	9.1	8.4	15.1	5.2	-2.7	-2.3	10.8	5.8	1.5	11	6.2
Industrial Transportation	4.1	3.6	20.1	-3.2	-12.6	3.2	19.7	3.0	15.8	7.5	6.1
Support Services	3.6	5.8	12.3	5.7	-4.8	-6.9	8.7	1.5	14.7	15.8	5.6
Aerospace & Defense	14.2	6.7	5.8	8.2	-9.4	-12.2	10.1	0.1	9.9	22.5	5.6
Personal Goods	6.3	6.0	6.6	2.7	-18.6	6.7	11.7	1.8	21.2	8.3	5.3
Real Estate Inv & Srvs							-0.6	2.8	5.9	11.9	5.0
Mining	-0.4	9.5	16.5	9.5	-0.9	13.4	11.5	-4.2	2.7	-10.1	4.8
Media	7.8	6.0	4.8	7.5	-13.5	-4.2	11.3	3.8	9.4	13.7	4.7
Financial Services	8.4	-2.6	22.5	4.6	-15.6	-2.9	-1.2	-4.0	17.5	18.2	4.5
Software & Comp Srvs	-1.0	-1.4	1.0	2.2	-11.7	10.8	15.8	0.9	14.5	11.5	4.3
General Industrials				5.9	-4.7	-20.6	12.6	5.9	21.1	9.6	4.3
Health Care Equip & Srvs	7.8	-6.0	-3.7	22.6	6.9	-2.3	2.1	3.1	1.2	9.9	4.2
Equity Inv Instruments	0.5	2.2	9.1	3.1	-5.8	-2.4	6.7	-0.1	7.7	9.6	3.1
General Retailers	2.2	-2.2	7.4	3.4	-19.1	20.6	-3.8	-9.0	19.9	7.3	2.7
Travel & Leisure	8.6	-0.6	2.5	4.2	-16.5	-6.5	17.8	-8.3	8.5	14.4	2.4
Tobacco	7.1	0.2	2.6	9.7	-7.9	-12.1	9.3	0.5	3.4	8.5	2.1
Nonlife Insurance	3.7	2.4	7.9	1.5	-10.4	-8.2	7.5	2.3	7.7	6.3	2.1
Beverages	0.6	0.3	7.4	1.2	-9.2	-15.5	3.9	-1.2	8.6	18.4	1.5
Life Insurance	2.1	5.4	16.2	-2.8	-10.7	-28.5	-4.6	9.5	15.3	11.3	1.3
Electricity	3.7	2.9	12.9	1.3	-7.0	-10.5	-3.3	2.1	2.5	5.7	1.0
Food Producers	3.7	4.6	1.6	6.7	-9.7	-15.6	2.6	-3.3	-2.0	17.5	0.6
Real Estate Inv Trusts			19.7	-5.0	1.8	-31.5	-2.1	4.8	9.6	0.5	-0.3
Oil & Gas Producers	-2.0	8.3	6.0	-3.4	-14.4	-7.2	2.6	5.7	-2.7	4.3	-0.3
Gas Water & Multiutilities	5.7	-1.8	4.0	5.3	-13.6	-18.6	1.0	1.5	5.1	8.6	-0.3
Mobile Telecom				-4.1	-19.6	-11.2	5.9	5.9	-3.4	20.8	-0.8
Banks	-4.2	-3.9	6.2	-3.1	-10.1	-27.4	6.7	-2.3	17.0	7.5	-1.4
Food & Drug Retailers	-3.1	-0.1	0.4	16.3	-19.3	-7.2	2.3	-7.6	-12.5	12.5	-1.8
Fixed Line Telecoms	-4.6	-0.3	-0.5	1.8	-19.9	-32.5	-4.6	-0.5	17.1	19.7	-2.4
Pharm & Biotech	-11.5	2.8	2.9	2.3	-15.3	-14.3	-0.7	-1.7	-5.5	14	-2.7

Second quarter

Sector	2004	2005	2006	2007	2008	2009	2010	2011	2012	2013	Avg
Personal Goods	15.4	-2.0	-6.9	5.0	-1.1	35.2	7.0	17.1	-11.5	0.8	5.9
Automobiles & Parts	10.0	1.9	-17.9	4.4	-26.7	81.7	-15.7	15.4	-12.4	13.9	5.5
Electricity	2.1	19.2	1.7	-0.8	6.8	2.8	-0.7	12.3	4.4	1.5	4.9
Fixed Line Telecoms	-3.8	1.0	6.4	10.0	-6.5	16.9	2.8	5.4	-2.9	8.7	3.8
Pharm & Biotech	1.8	10.8	4.2	-3.9	6.0	2.3	-2.8	10.4	2.2	2.5	3.4
Electronic & Elect Equip	-1.1	-14.5	-7.3	13.2	9.1	23.6	12.1	13.7	-4.6	-14.3	3.0
Beverages	6.3	10.5	-4.2	5.1	-5.2	13.9	-3.1	5.2	5.7	-8.9	2.5
Industrial Engineering	5.2	-2.3	-0.7	6.2	14.7	4.8	-1.2	8.7	-11.4	-5.4	1.9
Chemicals	3.2	-0.5	0.8	15.2	-6.5	7.6	-4.6	9.4	-3.4	-3	1.8
Real Estate Inv & Srvs							-14.5	8.6	1.2	11.8	1.8
Oil & Gas Producers	8.8	8.9	-1.4	15.1	16.4	1.4	-25.9	-3.2	-5.0	-2.2	1.3
Tobacco	2.6	12.0	-1.9	5.0	-7.8	2.8	-6.1	8.7	1.1	-3.6	1.3
Oil Equip Srvs & Dist			-7.8	8.4	21.0	21.8	-3.8	-1.3	-17.8	-10.7	1.2
Software & Comp Srvs	-6.7	5.4	-14.4	-3.5	7.1	20.8	-8.2	5.1	-0.5	4.4	1.0
Gas Water & Multiutilities	1.1	8.4	0.6	-3.8	-2.1	2.4	-5.4	2.7	5.4	-2.2	0.7
Mobile Telecom			-4.5	23.4	-0.7	-4.0	-8.3	-6.4	4.2	0.5	0.5
Industrial Transportation	0.9	3.0	10.0	-4.0	-19.0	14.6	-7.0	3.8	-6.8	5.5	0.1
Aerospace & Defense	10.4	10.6	-10.3	-1.5	-9.6	8.2	-9.5	1.7	0.4	0.6	0.1
Travel & Leisure	6.0	4.2	-0.9	-3.9	-7.6	6.3	-11.7	3.1	1.3	3.3	0.0
General Retailers	9.7	-3.6	-0.5	-8.8	-15.9	14.5	-10.3	9.8	-5.8	9.2	-0.2
Technology Hard & Equip	-0.9	-13.2	-6.4	14.5	-4.8	31.5	4.4	0.4	-15.2	-13.1	-0.3
Equity Inv Instruments	-0.9	5.3	-7.1	2.5	-2.7	10.7	-6.3	1.7	-4.7	-2.3	-0.4
Food Producers	4.6	2.1	-6.5	3.9	-13.1	7.2	-6.2	5.0	2.7	-4.7	-0.5
Mining	-6.5	2.1	0.5	18.5	16.9	17.2	-21.6	-2.0	-13.2	-18.3	-0.6
Financial Services	-8.9	2.9	-4.4	1.3	-3.6	21.7	-8.1	-1.5	-8.7	-0.1	-0.9
Nonlife Insurance	-4.2	6.5	-6.6	-6.5	-7.8	-3.3	0.4	5.8	3.8	1.7	-1.0
Life Insurance	4.9	-1.7	-9.2	-0.7	-18.5	31.8	-13.1	0.9	-6.5	0.6	-1.2
General Industrials			-8.9	-1.7	-1.8	13.1	-6.6	0.9	-6.2	1	-1.3
Banks	-1.0	3.4	-4.2	-1.0	-21.2	34.9	-11.9	-4.7	-7.6	-2.2	-1.6
Support Services	-2.1	0.3	-8.2	2.3	-9.4	11.0	-5.0	3.1	-4.8	-2.9	-1.6
Food & Drug Retailers	4.3	-0.7	2.1	-1.2	-3.4	2.9	-10.7	4.5	-6.3	-8.9	-1.7
Health Care Equip & Srvs	7.4	10.7	-17.7	-0.5	-22.0	6.8	-2.6	-4.3	0.9	-2.6	-2.4
Media	-1.0	-4.8	-3.9	3.2	-14.5	1.0	-5.8	3.1	-3.2	0.2	-2.6
Real Estate Inv Trusts			-5.0	-15.3	-21.7	15.9	-13.9	9.0	3.1	3.8	-3.0
Forestry & Paper	-3.6	-7.3			-29.1	39.9	-17.2	3.5	-7.5	-8.5	-3.7
Construction & Materials	-2.8	4.5	-8.2	14.4	-16.5	0.0	-17.8	-9.8	-1.7	-5.1	-4.3
Household Goods			-4.8	-6.3	-24.9	5.3	-15.3	7.1	-3.8	1.7	-5.1
Industrial Metals	-3.6	-22.2	3.7		-2.9	79.2	-25.0	-8.1	-29.4	-48.9	-6.4

Third quarter

Sector	2003	2004	2005	2006	2007	2008	2009	2010	2011	2012	Avg
Technology Hard & Equip	47.4	-19.8	15.2	-7.4	-6.0	6.5	23.2	29.8	-6.9	12.4	9.4
Automobiles & Parts	14.1	-14.3	12.9	5.2	-11.1	-12.2	35.9	45.7	-24.1	18.9	7.1
Life Insurance	10.5	-1.2	2.9	5.4	-2.2	-3.5	35.8	26.2	-21.4	10.7	6.3
Industrial Engineering	13.2	-4.5	12.0	-0.4	-1.7	-20.5	47.6	25.1	-20.4	11.5	6.2
Household Goods				10.4	-6.9	6.7	14.3	11.1	-6.4	8.2	5.3
Software & Comp Srvs	18.6	-7.6	1.7	2.3	3.6	-5.4	23.8	14.0	-7.1	9.3	5.3
Aerospace & Defense	9.8	1.1	17.3	5.9	8.2	-5.8	15.6	6.7	-12.4	3.5	5.0
Mining	17.6	17.2	31.1	-5.1	12.8	-44.1	26.5	19.1	-30.9	3.2	4.7
Food & Drug Retailers	9.5	-0.2	-2.7	9.3	1.9	4.0	12.3	12.7	-7.2	7.6	4.7
Chemicals	9.1	-3.7	14.8	6.7	2.1	-21.4	23.0	25.4	-20.3	9.8	4.6
Gas Water & Multiutilities	-4.2	10.1	0.8	13.9	1.6	3.8	6.7	9.1	-0.3	1.9	4.3
Oil Equip Srvs & Dist				4.6	7.1	-26.9	24.5	26.1	-22.3	14.5	3.9
Nonlife Insurance	-17.8	-7.5	13.3	13.9	3.8	18.3	16.5	8.5	-16.1	5.7	3.9
Banks	0.4	5.7	1.4	4.8	-8.5	-1.4	39.2	10.7	-24.1	7.8	3.6
Electricity	-2.6	9.8	10.6	8.1	1.4	-1.0	7.7	8.3	-6.7	-1.2	3.4
Mobile Telecom				6.3	5.3	-17.4	18.9	12.0	0.2	-1.4	3.4
Real Estate Inv Trusts				6.0	-9.4	4.4	27.8	13.2	-21.9	3.7	3.4
Beverages	3.6	-5.1	6.3	4.4	4.1	-1.0	15.2	5.4	-5.3	6.2	3.4
Pharm & Biotech	3.2	1.1	9.0	-2.4	-3.4	10.4	11.9	6.2	-2.7	0.2	3.4
Food Producers	3.5	-11.2	6.1	9.4	-11.3	-0.1	30.2	2.4	0.0	4.2	3.3
Electronic & Elect Equip	24.2	-18.7	22.6	4.0	-8.8	-18.1	24.4	22.0	-26.9	7.1	3.2
Tobacco	-7.0	-3.3	9.1	5.8	0.9	1.5	16.4	8.0	1.3	-3.2	3.0
Personal Goods	9.6	-12.6	4.7	18.9	-3.4	-7.9	20.3	35.8	-16.4	-21.2	2.8
General Industrials				-1.4	-3.8	-6.1	24.8	20.0	-21.2	5.7	2.6
Equity Inv Instruments	3.8	0.9	12.1	4.0	2.5	-14.4	16.5	8.5	-13.6	3.8	2.4
Construction & Materials	11.1	6.8	4.9	16.8	-0.6	-24.2	10.9	13.1	-15.7	-1.3	2.2
Fixed Line Telecoms	-0.5	4.7	6.9	11.4	-7.0	-14.1	21.5	2.9	-14.6	8.5	2.0
Travel & Leisure	6.0	0.5	2.6	7.8	-9.2	-11.2	22.1	8.5	-16.8	5.6	1.6
Forestry & Paper	0.6	-8.0	3.6		-45.0	-13.0	49.2	33.9	-23.7	15.6	1.5
Health Care Equip & Srvs	11.8	-12.5	-11.8	15.3	-5.8	5.6	24.6	-7.3	-12.0	6.6	1.5
Financial Services	7.2	-9.0	13.9	6.5	-4.0	-21.9	21.6	12.4	-21.8	7.2	1.2
Support Services	7.9	-8.6	2.5	5.9	-10.9	-10.5	19.4	8.8	-13.7	9.0	1.0
Media	1.9	-9.4	1.5	1.6	-5.2	-8.2	24.7	9.2	-16.1	7.5	0.8
Oil & Gas Producers	-3.4	6.5	12.7	-6.0	-2.5	-21.9	13.0	19.2	-12.2	0.1	0.6
General Retailers	3.0	0.5	-4.0	6.5	-10.7	-12.1	16.2	10.8	-10.8	5.1	0.5
Industrial Transportation	5.7	-2.7	7.6	3.0	-9.9	-19.1	26.9	7.1	-19.3	-1.3	-0.2
Real Estate Inv & Srvs								7.9	-18.8	6.7	-1.4
Industrial Metals	35.0	28.3	22.6	-15.0	-65.5	-60.8	10.9	30.6	-44.7	-7.5	-6.6

Fourth quarter

Sector	2003	2004	2005	2006	2007	2008	2009	2010	2011	2012	Avg
Beverages	14.1	10.7	1.5	8.5	3.4	3.8	16.3	9.0	11.0	3.3	8.2
Tobacco	14.5	16.0	7.0	7.7	15.4	-0.9	4.5	3.7	12.0	-0.4	8.0
Real Estate Inv & Srvs								6.8	8.8	7.8	7.8
Industrial Metals	48.1	-1.0	14.6	36.7	10.0	-65.0	13.5	26.3	-9.6	2.8	7.6
Mining	18.3	-0.4	11.2	10.6	2.7	-31.5	24.1	22.8	8.5	8.8	7.5
Personal Goods	4.2	15.8	11.3	19.2	-1.8	-23.0	18.7	8.6	-1.3	22.3	7.4
Food Producers	4.1	15.0	-1.0	5.6	14.9	2.2	6.1	7.9	6.2	7.8	6.9
Health Care Equip & Srvs	26.7	4.4	13.3	6.3	3.2	-27.6	13.1	16.7	6.7	0.8	6.4
Chemicals	5.5	10.7	9.2	9.1	9.2	-21.3	12.0	16.3	10.3	1.8	6.3
Travel & Leisure	13.9	12.3	11.5	16.6	-7.6	-13.6	0.9	10.0	6.9	7.9	5.9
Mobile Telecom				15.3	6.7	12.8	3.3	5.4	9.3	-11.8	5.9
Technology Hard & Equip	27.1	13.6	13.9	-8.1	-12.6	-22.2	12.5	5.0	5.9	22.0	5.7
Oil & Gas Producers	10.3	-0.9	-5.6	-0.3	10.1	8.1	6.5	11.0	16.6	-4.6	5.1
Food & Drug Retailers	8.2	11.2	7.6	10.2	2.7	-4.3	4.9	-1.1	7.5	-0.3	4.7
Gas Water & Multiutilities	9.4	6.0	6.2	9.9	4.3	-6.4	11.8	3.5	-1.1	0.3	4.4
Media	11.0	8.4	3.5	1.7	-4.7	-2.9	6.4	6.2	9.3	4.7	4.4
Construction & Materials	6.5	8.2	13.7	4.5	-12.6	4.3	-8.4	16.3	8.0	1.9	4.2
Aerospace & Defense	1.6	3.4	11.5	5.4	4.4	-6.2	5.4	1.3	13.3	2.3	4.2
Industrial Engineering	6.3	10.0	10.9	6.3	-18.8	-26.8	7.3	19.2	17.5	7.8	4.0
Oil Equip Srvs & Dist				23.8	14.5	-38.3	3.6	15.9	14.0	-6.1	3.9
Support Services	2.9	6.9	8.0	10.3	-6.3	-5.7	4.3	6.5	8.0	1.1	3.6
Financial Services	4.0	19.4	10.2	10.6	0.3	-29.5	-2.7	19.0	-3.2	7.4	3.5
Fixed Line Telecoms	14.6	9.3	-8.2	12.6	-9.2	-13.7	2.5	18.7	5.9	0.9	3.3
Equity Inv Instruments	7.5	11.5	8.5	6.6	-1.7	-18.6	4.3	9.3	1.5	3.3	3.2
Nonlife Insurance	2.9	2.9	17.0	12.0	-4.8	3.5	-5.0	0.4	-3.4	4.8	3.0
Electronic & Elect Equip	-16.2	11.4	17.4	16.3	-15.7	-21.6	1.1	18.0	8.2	10.5	2.9
Life Insurance	7.7	11.3	9.8	6.6	-4.8	-19.2	-1.1	-2.5	9.7	11.3	2.9
Electricity	6.3	4.1	-1.7	13.7	4.6	-14.8	-0.1	9.6	1.4	2.6	2.6
Household Goods				11.9	-7.9	-6.8	5.0	1.6	-0.5	11	2.0
General Retailers	2.7	1.4	14.1	2.6	-12.1	-12.9	9.2	2.0	-1.0	11.5	1.8
Industrial Transportation	6.5	12.9	9.6	10.2	-5.3	-32.2	1.5	5.3	1.7	6.4	1.7
Software & Comp Srvs	2.3	10.1	10.3	9.7	-9.5	-17.5	-1.1	2.0	3.6	3.3	1.3
Pharm & Biotech	4.0	-3.5	3.7	-9.3	-4.7	8.9	6.2	-3.6	8.4	-3.9	0.6
Automobiles & Parts	7.2	15.9	4.2	-3.2	-20.3	-50.4	2.9	31.2	4.0	6.5	-0.2
General Industrials				1.4	-13.2	-20.4	10.0	9.0	4.1	7.4	-0.2
Forestry & Paper	-1.8	4.5	9.8		-8.6	-21.0	8.4	-0.2	-3.9	6.3	-0.7
Banks	8.5	6.6	6.5	3.2	-10.3	-38.2	-9.2	-4.0	-0.3	15.4	-2.2
Real Estate Inv Trusts				11.0	-12.8	-33.6	4.7	7.6	-2.1	7.2	-2.6

SECTOR TRADING VALUE

The table on this page shows the average monthly trading value by sector for the first eight months of 2013. For example, over this period the companies in the Media sector traded on average £2681.4m each month.

The final three columns show the proportion of each sector's trade that was from companies in the three respective indices. In the case of the Media sector, 85% of the trade value was attributable to companies in the FTSE 100.

Code	Sector	Total FTSE All-Share (£m)	FTSE 100 (%)	FTSE 250 (%)	FTSE Small Cap (%)
1770	Mining	9,685.0	95	5	0
8350	Banks	8,201.9	100	0	0
530	Oil & Gas Producers	6,878.8	93	7	0
4570	Pharmaceuticals & Biotechnology	3,929.2	97	2	0
5750	Travel & Leisure	3,230.2	69	29	2
2790	Support Services	3,146.9	70	29	2
6570	Mobile Telecommunications	2,955.2	97	3	0
5550	Media	2,681.4	85	15	0
3530	Beverages	2,638.7	98	2	0
8570	Life Insurance	2,618.6	96	3	0
3780	Tobacco	2,497.6	100	0	0
7570	Gas, Water & Multiutilities	2,191.7	95	5	0
8770	General Financial	1,726.7	36	64	0
3570	Food Producers	1,699.7	97	2	2
3720	Household Goods	1,680.7	60	40	0
5330	Food & Drug Retailers	1,641.4	93	7	0
5370	General Retailers	1,532.2	70	29	1
2710	Aerospace & Defence	1,395.2	86	14	0
8670	Real Estate Investment Trusts	1,197.2	70	29	1
9570	Technology Hardware & Equipment	920.1	78	21	0
6530	Fixed Line Telecommunications	835.6	88	12	0
2750	Industrial Engineering	738.4	76	24	1
8530	Nonlife Insurance	716.7	50	50	0
2350	Construction & Materials	699.7	74	24	2
570	Oil Equipment, Services & Distribution	648.9	86	10	4
9530	Software & Computer Services	582.1	27	71	2
1350	Chemicals	554.3	74	25	1
7530	Electricity	527.6	85	15	0
2720	General Industrials	510.1	68	31	0
8980	Equity Investment Instruments	478.8	0	73	27
3760	Personal Goods	379.4	92	8	0
4530	Health Care Equipment & Services	236.3	94	4	2
3350	Automobiles & Parts	235.2	100	0	0
1750	Industrial Metals	220.7	55	44	1
2730	Electronic & Electrical Equipment	220.6	0	96	4
1730	Forestry & Paper	158.8	0	100	0
8630	Real Estate Investment & Services	153.2	0	82	18
2770	Industrial Transportation	26.5	0	74	26
3740	Leisure Goods	1.0	0	0	100
580	Alternative Energy	0.2	0	0	100

The proportion of sector trade from companies in the FTSE 100 and FTSE 250 is illustrated in the following chart.

Chart: average trading value on LSE by sector (Jan-Aug 2012)

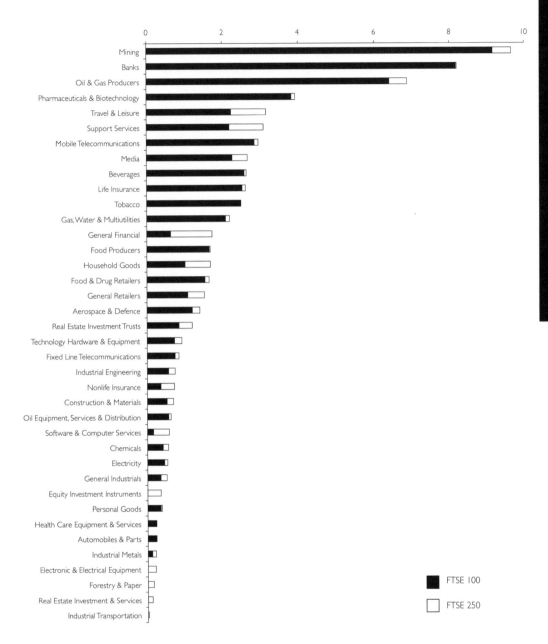

SECTOR PROFILES OF THE FTSE 100 AND FTSE 250

The chart below shows the sector weightings in the FTSE 100 and FTSE 250.

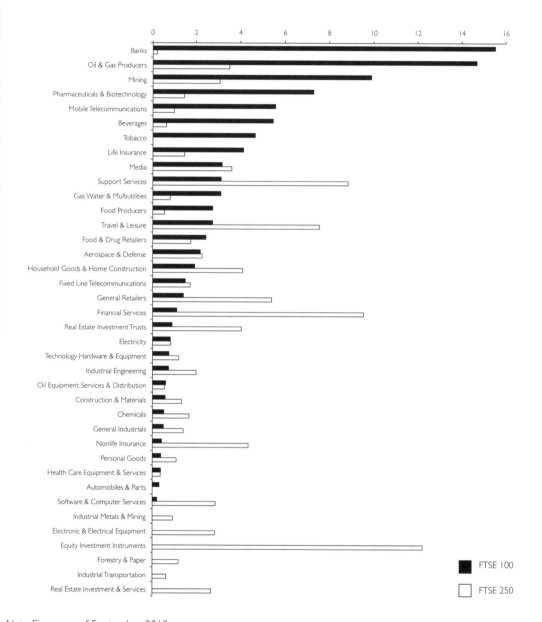

Note: Figures as of September 2013

Observations

1. The top four FTSE sectors (banks, oil and gas producers, mining and pharmaceuticals) together account for 47.4% of the total market capitalisation of the index. (In 2006, the top sectors accounted for 55% of the index capitalisation.)

2. In 1935 the FT 30 was dominated by engineering and machinery companies. Today, the sector isn't represented at all in the FTSE 100.

3. The FTSE 100 is still dominated by the old industries of oil, mining and banks, while the FTSE 250 has, proportionately, a greater representation of service (support, financial and computer) companies.

COMPANIES

COMPANY RANKINGS

On the following pages are tables with companies ranked according to various criteria. The tables are grouped into the following categories:

1. FTSE 350
2. FTSE 100
3. AIM
4. Investment Trusts

Table index

A summary of the tables is given below.

1. 10 largest companies by **market capitalisation**
2. 10 companies with largest average **daily trade value**
3. 5-year **share performance** 2008-2013 [FTSE 350]
4. 5-year **share performance** 2003-2008 [FTSE 350]
5. 10 companies with highest **turnover**
6. 10 companies with greatest **turnover growth** in 5 years to 2013 [FTSE 350]
7. 10 companies with greatest **turnover growth** in 5 years to 2008 [FTSE 350]
8. 10 companies with highest **ROCE** [FTSE 350]
9. 10 companies with highest **profits**
10. 10 companies with greatest **profit growth** in the 5 years to 2013 [FTSE 350]
11. 10 companies with highest **operating margins** [FTSE 350]
12. 10 companies with highest **EPS growth** in the 5 years to 2013 [FTSE 350]
13. 10 companies with highest **dividend growth** in the 5 years to 2013 [FTSE 350]
14. 10 companies with highest **dividend growth** in the 5 years to 2008 [FTSE 350]
15. 10 companies paying the most **tax** in last year
16. Best value **CEO** (best pay for performance)
17. Worst value **CEO** (highest excess remuneration)
18. 10 companies with largest **market capitalisation** [AIM]
19. 10 companies with largest **market capitalisation** (2007) [AIM]
20. 10 companies with largest **profits** [AIM]
21. 10 companies with largest **profits** (2007) [AIM]
22. 5-year **share performance** 2008-2013 [AIM]
23. 5-year **share performance** 2003-2008 [AIM]
24. 10 largest investment trusts by **capitalisation**
25. 10 **best performing** investment trusts 2008-2013
26. 10 **best performing** investment trusts 2003-2008
27. 10 investment trusts with highest average **daily trading value**

Note: All figures accurate as of 31 August 2013.

1. FTSE 350

Size, volume and performance

Table 1: 10 largest companies by market capitalisation

Rank	Rank (2007)	Company	TIDM	Capital (£m)
1	6	Royal Dutch Shell	RDSB	133,327
2	2	HSBC Holdings	HSBA	130,964
3	3	Vodafone Group	VOD	102,712
4	1	BP	BP.	83,318
5	4	GlaxoSmithKline	GSK	79,417
6	13	British American Tobacco	BATS	62,851
7	17	Lloyds Banking Group	LLOY	54,674
8	25	SABMiller	SAB	50,280
9	18	Diageo	DGE	50,244
10		Glencore Xstrata	GLEN	44,735

Table 2: 10 companies with largest average daily trade value

Rank	Company	TIDM	Average daily trade value (£m)
1	Vodafone Group	VOD	169
2	HSBC Holdings	HSBA	142
3	Rio Tinto	RIO	139
4	BHP Billiton	BLT	128
5	Barclays	BARC	124
6	GlaxoSmithKline	GSK	104
7	BP	BP.	101
8	Royal Dutch Shell	RDSB	88
9	British American Tobacco	BATS	84
10	Lloyds Banking Group	LLOY	81

Table 3: 5-year share performance 2008-2013 [FTSE 350]

Rank	Company	TIDM	5-yr change (%)
1	Sports Direct International	SPD	788
2	Ashtead Group	AHT	749
3	Howden Joinery Group	HWDN	740
4	Dialight	DIA	688
5	ARM Holdings	ARM	685
6	Rightmove	RMV	653
7	Xaar	XAR	628
8	Oxford Instruments	OXIG	539
9	Dunelm Group	DNLM	506
10	Hargreaves Lansdown	HL.	473

Table 4: 5-year share performance 2003-2008 [FTSE 350]

Rank	Company	TIDM	5-yr change (%)
1	Tullow Oil	TLW	854
2	Aveva Group	AVV	827
3	Cairn Energy	CNE	807
4	Hunting	HTG	670
5	Ashtead Group	AHT	489
6	Chemring Group	CHG	472
7	Centamin	CEY	465
8	Babcock International Group	BAB	441
9	Aggreko	AGK	363
10	SOCO International	SIA	355

Turnover

Table 5: 10 companies with highest turnover

Rank	Rank (2007)	Company	TIDM	Turnover (£m)
1	1	Royal Dutch Shell	RDSB	287,400
2	2	BP	BP.	231,100
3		Glencore Xstrata	GLEN	131,900
4	3	Tesco	TSCO	64,830
5	4	Vodafone Group	VOD	44,450
6	9	BHP Billiton	BLT	43,250
7	6	Unilever	ULVR	41,630
8	18	Rio Tinto	RIO	31,350
9	60	Imperial Tobacco Group	IMT	28,570
10	17	SSE	SSE	28,300

Table 6: 10 companies with greatest turnover growth in 5 years to 2013 [FTSE 350]

Rank	Company	TIDM	Turnover 5-yr growth (%)
1	Centamin	CEY	1000+
2	Petra Diamonds Ltd	PDL	1000+
3	IP Group	IPO	1000+
4	Londonmetric Property	LMP	1000+
5	Imperial Tobacco Group	IMT	771
6	Salamander Energy	SMDR	553
7	Pace	PIC	492
8	Randgold Resources Ltd	RRS	476
9	Melrose Industries	MRO	438
10	Playtech	PTEC	435

Table 7: 10 companies with greatest turnover growth in 5 years to 2008 [FTSE 350]

Rank	Company	EPIC	Turnover 5-yr growth (%)
1	Xstrata	XTA	1000+
2	Venture Production	VPC	1000+
3	CSR	CSR	1000+
4	Dana Petroleum	DNX	708
5	Tullow Oil	TLW	655
6	Tullett Prebon	TLPR	534
7	Big Yellow Group	BYG	510
8	Mouchel Parkman	MCHL	423
9	Helphire Group	HHR	389
10	Detica Group	DCA	375

Table 8: 10 companies with highest ROCE [FTSE 350]

Rank	Company	TIDM	ROCE (%)
1	888 Holdings	888	7,860
2	Rightmove	RMV	1,380
3	Imperial Tobacco Group	IMT	928
4	UBM	UBM	569
5	Atkins (W S)	ATK	474
6	De La Rue	DLAR	393
7	ITE Group	ITE	325
8	Moneysupermarket.com Group	MONY	279
9	Countrywide	CWD	276
10	William Hill	WMH	242

Profits

Table 9: 10 companies with highest profits

Rank	Rank (2007)	Company	TIDM	Profit (£m)
1	1	Royal Dutch Shell	RDSB	30,938
2	3	HSBC Holdings	HSBA	12,703
3	6	BHP Billiton	BLT	11,716
4	2	BP	BP.	11,571
5	5	GlaxoSmithKline	GSK	6,692
6	16	British American Tobacco	BATS	5,648
7	14	Unilever	ULVR	5,420
8	11	AstraZeneca	AZN	4,748
9	25	Standard Chartered	STAN	4,230
10	13	BG Group	BG.	3,916

Table 10: 10 companies with greatest profit growth in the 5 years to 2013 [FTSE 350]

Rank	Company	TIDM	5-yr profit growth (%)
1	British Sky Broadcasting Group	BSY	1000+
2	Aberdeen Asset Management	ADN	1000+
3	Centamin	CEY	1000+
4	KCOM Group	KCOM	1000+
5	Randgold Resources Ltd	RRS	949
6	Imagination Technologies Group	IMG	547
7	Fresnillo	FRES	510
8	Rank Group (The)	RNK	501
9	Tullow Oil	TLW	501
10	Oxford Instruments	OXIG	492

Table 11: 10 companies with highest operating margins [FTSE 350]

Rank	Company	TIDM	Operating margin (%)
1	Capital & Counties Properties	CAPC	265
2	Segro	SGRO	139
3	Daejan Holdings	DJAN	110
4	Hansteen Holdings	HSTN	89
5	IP Group	IPO	79
6	British Land Co	BLND	77
7	SOCO International	SIA	72
8	Rightmove	RMV	70
9	Land Securities Group	LAND	56
10	Big Yellow Group	BYG	55

Table 12: 10 companies with highest EPS growth in the 5 years to 2013 [FTSE 350]

Rank	Company	TIDM	EPS 5-Yr Growth (%)
1	Capital & Counties Properties	CAPC	1000+
2	Centamin	CEY	1000+
3	UNITE Group	UTG	1000+
4	Betfair Group	BET	1000+
5	Oxford Instruments	OXIG	953
6	Randgold Resources Ltd	RRS	862
7	International Personal Finance	IPF	631
8	Imagination Technologies Group	IMG	505
9	Fresnillo	FRES	451
10	Worldwide Healthcare Trust	WWH	389

Dividends

Table 13: 10 companies with highest dividend growth in the 5 years to 2013 [FTSE 350]

Rank	Company	TIDM	5-yr Div Growth (%)
1	RIT Capital Partners	RCP	950
2	BlackRock World Mining Trust	BRWM	600
3	Howden Joinery Group	HWDN	500
4	Petrofac Ltd	PFC	457
5	Worldwide Healthcare Trust	WWH	450
6	Randgold Resources Ltd	RRS	417
7	Booker Group	BOK	389
8	Londonmetric Property	LMP	367
9	Micro Focus International	MCRO	284
10	Rightmove	RMV	283

Table 14: 10 companies with highest dividend growth in the 5 years to 2008 [FTSE 350]

Rank	Company	EPIC	5-yr Div Growth (%)
1	Mouchel Parkman	MCHL	1000+
2	Topps Tiles	TPT	885
3	Sage Group (The)	SGE	735
4	BT Group	BT.A	655
5	ITE Group	ITE	600
6	Enterprise Inns	ETI	447
7	Vodafone Group	VOD	360
8	Aquarius Platinum Ltd	AQP	357
9	Capital & Regional	CAL	333
10	London Stock Exchange Group	LSE	329

Tax

Table 15: 10 companies paying the most tax in last year

Rank	Company	TIDM	Tax paid (£m)
1	Royal Dutch Shell	RDSB	14,400
2	BP	BP.	4,300
3	HSBC Holdings	HSBA	3,270
4	Vodafone Group	VOD	2,580
5	GlaxoSmithKline	GSK	1,950
6	BG Group	BG.	1,880
7	British American Tobacco	BATS	1,530
8	Unilever	ULVR	1,410
9	Centrica	CNA	1,170
10	Standard Chartered	STAN	1,160

2. FTSE 100

Table 16: Best value CEO (best pay for performance)

Rank	Company	TIDM	Excess remuneration (%)
1	Admiral	ADM	-93%
2	Hargreaves Lansdown	HL.	-89%
3	Vedanta Resources	VED	-85%
4	Severn Trent	SVT	-73%
5	Wolseley	WOS	-73%
6	Petrofac	PFC	-68%
7	GKN	GKN	-62%
8	IMI	IMI	-62%
9	Inmarsat	ISAT	-57%
10	Intertek	ITRK	-54%

Source: Obermatt

Table 17: Worst value CEO (highest excess remuneration)

Rank	Company	TIDM	Excess remuneration (%)
1	Reckitt Benckiser	RB.	1199%
2	Xstrata	XTA	391%
3	ICAP	IAP	388%
4	BG Group	BG.	322%
5	Tullow Oil	TLW	310%
6	Tesco	TSCO	226%
7	BHP Billiton	BLT	210%
8	GlaxoSmithKline	GSK	208%
9	Schroders	SDR	181%
10	Vodafone	VOD	102%

Source: Obermatt

3. AIM

Table 18: 10 companies with largest market capitalisation [AIM]

Rank	Name	TIDM	Capital (£m)
1	ASOS	ASC	4,310
2	Gulf Keystone Petroleum	GKP	1,866
3	Indus Gas Ltd	INDI	1,660
4	Energy XXI	EXXI	1,241
5	Coastal Energy Company	CEO	1,219
6	Songbird Estates	SBD	1,170
7	Abcam	ABC	937
8	Monitise	MONI	937
9	New Europe Property Investments	NEPI	878
10	Origin Enterprises	OGN	736

Table 19: 10 companies with largest market capitalisation (2007) [AIM]

Rank	Name	TIDM	Capital (£m)
1	Sibir Energy	SBE	1,616
2	Mecom Group	MEC	1,389
3	Nikanor	NKR	1,270
4	Clipper Windpower	CWP	898
5	Central African Mining & Exploration	CFM	811
6	Playtech Ltd	PTEC	810
7	Climate Exchange	CLE	793
8	Lamprell	LAM	783
9	Peter Hambro Mining	POG	769
10	Monsoon	MSN	701

Table 20: 10 companies with largest profits [AIM]

Rank	Name	TIDM	Profit (£m)
1	Coastal Energy Company	CEO	250
2	Songbird Estates	SBD	202
3	Gemfields	GEM	159
4	Asian Growth Properties Ltd	AGP	110
5	Highland Gold Mining Ltd	HGM	95
6	Datatec Ltd	DTC	84
7	Energy XXI	EXXI	83
8	Energy XXI (Bermuda) Ltd	EXXS	83
9	Asian Citrus Holdings Ltd	ACHL	77
10	Bankers Petroleum Ltd	BNK	61

Table 21: 10 companies with largest profits (2007) [AIM]

Rank	Name	EPIC	Profit (£m)
1	R.G.I International Ltd	RGI	88.4
2	Dawnay; Day Treveria	DTR	87.7
3	Songbird Estates	SBDB	77.2
4	Sportingbet	SBT	71.5
5	Sibir Energy	SBE	58.3
6	NETeller	NLR	56.8
7	Monsoon	MSN	53.5
8	Hotel Corporation (The)	HCP	51.2
9	RAB Capital	RAB	50.3
10	Abbey	ABBY	47.1

Table 22: 5-year share performance 2008-2013 [AIM]

Rank	Name	TIDM	5-yr share price (%)
1	Tricor PLC	TRIC	4,067
2	Mobile Streams PLC	MOS	3,643
3	Lo-Q	LOQ	2,061
4	Judges Scientific	JDG	1,426
5	Mar City PLC	MAR	1,285
6	Energy Technique PLC	ETQ	1,280
7	Dart Group	DTG	1,164
8	ASOS	ASC	1,094
9	Gable Holdings Inc	GAH	931
10	@UK PLC	ATUK	819

Table 23: 5-year share performance 2003-2008 [AIM]

Rank	Name	TIDM	5-yr share price (%)
1	ASOS	ASC	8,073
2	Redhall Group	RHL	1,976
3	RWS Holdings	RWS	1,094
4	IndigoVision Group	IND	900
5	Central African Mining & Exploration Company	CFM	879
6	CPL Resources	CPS	687
7	Desire Petroleum	DES	671
8	Pan African Resources	PAF	567
9	African Diamonds	AFD	552
10	IMPAX Asset Management Group	IPX	547

4. Investment Trusts

Table 24: 10 largest investment trusts by capitalisation

Rank	Rank (2007)	Investmet Trust	TIDM	Capital (£m)
1	1	Alliance Trust	ATST	2,446
2	4	Scottish Mortgage Investment Trust	SMT	2,283
3	2	Foreign & Colonial Investment Trust	FRCL	2,101
4	5	RIT Capital Partners	RCP	1,965
5	3	Templeton Emerging Markets Investment Trust	TEM	1,764
6	68	HICL Infrastructure Company Ltd	HICL	1,561
7	28	Murray International Trust	MYI	1,423
8	7	Mercantile Investment Trust (The)	MRC	1,397
9	8	Witan Investment Trust	WTAN	1,195
10	22	3i Infrastructure Ltd	3IN	1,189

Table 25: 10 best performing investment trusts 2008-2013

Rank	Investment Trust	TIDM	5-yr price change (%)
1	Biotech Growth Trust (The)	BIOG	223
2	Oxford Technology Venture Capital Trust	OXT	221
3	Aberdeen Asian Smaller Companies Inv Tr	AAS	216
4	Perpetual Income & Growth Investment Trust	PLIS	209
5	Acorn Income Fund Ltd	AIF	205
6	Scottish Oriental Smaller Co's Tr (The)	SST	180
7	Standard Life UK Smaller Companies Trust	SLS	155
8	Lindsell Train Investment Trust (The)	LTI	155
9	Baillie Gifford Shin Nippon	BGS	154
10	Aberdeen New Thai Investment Trust	ANW	154

Table 26: 10 best performing investment trusts 2003-2008

Rank	Investment Trust	EPIC	5-yr div growth (%)
1	City Natural Resources High Yield Trust	CYNW	808
2	Royal London UK Equity & Income Trust	RLU	533
3	Blue Planet Financials Growth & Inc IT No.1-No.10	BPFV	530
4	BlackRock Latin American Investment Trust	BRLA	421
5	JPMorgan Russian Securities	JRS	351
6	European Utilities Trust	EUT	294
7	Resources Investment Trust	REI	288
8	JPMorgan Indian Investment Trust	JII	286
9	New India Investment Trust	NIIW	281
10	BlackRock World Mining Trust	BRWM	279

Table 27: 10 investment trusts with highest average daily trading value

Rank	Investment Trust	TIDM	Average daily trade value (£m)
1	HICL Infrastructure Company Ltd	HICL	2.44
2	Templeton Emerging Markets Investment Trust	TEM	2.41
3	Alliance Trust	ATST	2.06
4	BlackRock World Mining Trust	BRWM	1.97
5	RIT Capital Partners	RCP	1.95
6	Scottish Mortgage Investment Trust	SMT	1.84
7	Murray International Trust	MYI	1.72
8	Merrill Lynch European Investment Trust	MLE	1.62
9	Foreign & Colonial Investment Trust	FRCL	1.37
10	Edinburgh Investment Trust (The)	EDIN	1.25

TEN BAGGERS

The term ten bagger was first used in relation to the stock market by Peter Lynch, the legendary manager of the Fidelity Magellan fund, in his book *One Up on Wall Street*. The phrase ten bagger comes from baseball but Lynch used it to describe stocks that rise ten times in value.

The table below shows the UK stocks that rose ten times or more in the ten years to September 2013.

UK ten baggers September 2003 to September 2013

Company	TIDM	Price increase (%)	Capital (£m)	PE	Sector
Ashtead Group	AHT	4,061	3,284	24	Support Services
Dragon Oil	DGO	1,950	3,046	8	Oil & Gas Producers
Xaar	XAR	1,897	580	39	Electronic & Electrical Equipment
First Quantum Minerals LD	FQM	1,624	6,724	5	Industrial Metals & Mining
Goodwin	GDWN	1,438	242	16	Industrial Engineering
Aveva Group	AVV	1,356	1,625	35	Software & Computer Services
Tullow Oil	TLW	1,158	9,668	25	Oil & Gas Producers
Domino's Pizza UK & IRL	DOM	1,068	997	24	Travel & Leisure
Babcock International Group	BAB	994	4,356	20	Support Services

Observations

1. The table above does not include those companies that rose ten times in the interim only to see their share prices fall back again. Of course, in the run up to the credit crunch this included quite a few companies.

2. Jim Slater's comment that "elephants don't gallop" would seem to hold true. Many of the above ten baggers were still small companies ten years ago. As Peter Lynch says, "The very best way to make money in a market is in a small growth company that has been profitable for a couple of years and simply goes on growing."

3. It can be seen that the ten baggers come from quite a wide range of sectors. In other words, it's not necessary to look for ten baggers in just a few glamour sectors.

HIGH-RETURN, LOW-VOLATILITY SHARES

The prices of shares can sometimes be so volatile that it is difficult to discern their overall trend. For example, take a look at the following ten-year chart of IAG; it's not immediately obvious if over the whole period these shares have been trending up or down.

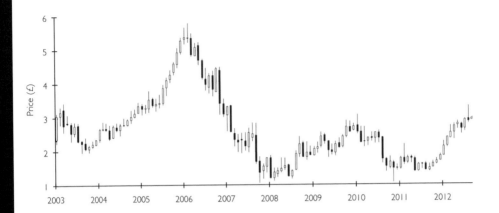

There are techniques to help eliminate the noise and get a clearer picture of any trend. For example, moving averages are a common technique used.

Another method can be to cut down on the amount of data and just look at share prices at the end of the year. The chart below plots the share prices of IAG for the end of each year – just 10 data points.

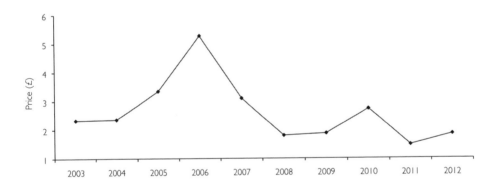

With this simple chart we can use regression analysis to add a line of best fit, as below.

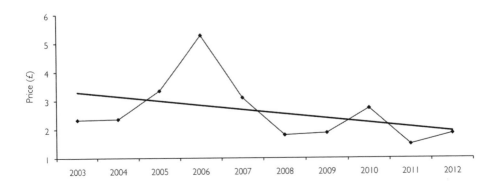

The regression line is sloping downwards which suggests the trend of the shares has been down over the period. Of course, investors are looking for shares with prices that trend upwards, such as that for RIO (chart below).

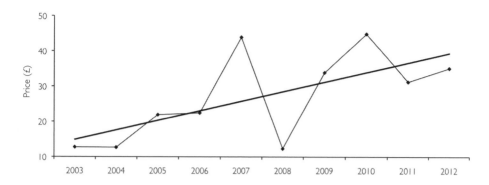

As can be seen in the above chart, the regression line has a positive slope – the trend has been up. Good.

However, an upward trend is not the only thing an investor might wish for. Even though the trend has been up, the shares of RIO have been very volatile; it would have been easy to lose money buying at the wrong time. The shares may have risen over the period as a whole, but the journey would have been a rocky and uncomfortable one for investors.

So, as well as an upward trend, investors would also like low volatility – such as SAB (chart below).

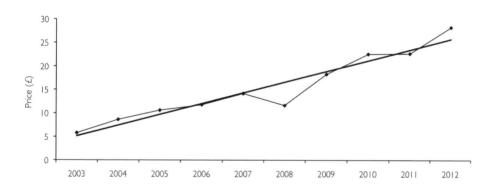

SAB shares would seem to satisfy well the two criteria:
1. **positive return** (positive sloping regression line), and
2. **low volatility** (prices keep close to the regression line).

Fortunately, regression analysis offers two statistics to quantify the criteria:
1. **gradient of the slope**: the higher the gradient of the slope the greater the return on the shares.
2. **R^2 (R-squared)**: a measure of how close the data points are to the regression line. The value ranges from zero to one, where one denotes the highest correlation. So here higher R^2 means lower volatility around the trend.

The gradient and R^2 figures for the three companies in the foregoing charts are given in the table to the right.

	Slope	R^2
IAG	-0.15	0.17
RIO	2.72	0.43
SAB	2.29	0.92

As seen in the chart, the slope of the regression line for IAG was down, as indicated by the negative value for the slope. RIO has a higher gradient value than SAB, but a much lower R^2 (i.e. RIO is more volatile).

LONG TERM

THE MARKET'S DECENNIAL CYCLE

The following table shows the annual performance of the FTSE All-Share since 1801. The table is arranged to easily compare the performance of the market for the same year in each decade.

For example, in the third year of the 1801 to 1810 decade (1803), the market fell 21.9%, while in the third year of the 1811 to 1820 decade (1813), the market fell 0.2%. Years are highlighted in which the market fell.

Decades	1st	2nd	3rd	4th	5th	6th	7th	8th	9th	10th
1801-1810	11.0	1.4	-21.9	10.3	8.5	0.7	3.5	4.7	10.4	-9.2
1811-1820	-14.6	-7.5	-0.2	2.4	-6.2	-12.2	32.6	5.5	-8.3	3.2
1821-1830	4.5	9.4	9.2	90.7	-22.7	-20.1	4.6	-14.5	3.3	-14.8
1831-1840	-15.7	2.2	16.5	-9.3	5.0	5.2	-8.5	-3.6	-12.7	3.1
1841-1850	-9.7	7.1	12.3	16.5	-2.1	-1.8	-13.9	-13.5	-7.3	14.4
1851-1860	-0.2	9.6	-6.8	-3.2	-3.4	5.4	-5.9	6.5	-2.0	11.1
1861-1870	3.1	16.6	12.8	5.0	1.4	-22.4	-2.2	6.8	7.4	8.6
1871-1880	18.9	4.0	3.6	-5.2	-7.9	-2.4	-9.6	-11.0	12.1	4.9
1881-1890	-0.6	-6.3	-5.0	-2.1	0.2	0.6	-3.6	5.8	13.1	-6.2
1891-1900	0.7	-0.1	1.6	6.0	11.2	22.0	5.2	0.3	-2.0	-0.9
1901-1910	-4.9	-1.3	-5.6	2.5	6.2	-0.4	-14.7	8.1	4.8	-2.5
1911-1920	0.3	-0.9	-6.7	-6.9	-5.1	0.5	-10.5	11.0	2.4	-13.3
1921-1930	-5.4	17.6	2.0	9.5	4.4	2.4	8.3	8.1	-7.4	-19.4
1931-1940	-23.5	5.6	27.2	8.3	7.8	13.9	-19.3	-14.3	0.8	-13.0
1941-1950	22.6	18.6	8.1	10.7	-0.6	18.1	-2.7	-4.0	-13.9	6.4
1951-1960	2.4	-5.1	16.0	34.5	1.6	-9.0	-3.3	33.2	43.4	-4.7
1961-1970	-2.5	-1.8	10.6	-10.0	6.7	-9.3	29.0	43.4	-15.2	-7.5
1971-1980	41.9	12.8	-31.4	-55.3	136.3	-3.9	41.2	2.7	4.3	27.1
1981-1990	7.2	22.1	23.1	26.0	15.2	22.3	4.2	6.5	30.0	-14.3
1991-2000	15.1	14.8	23.3	-9.6	18.5	11.7	19.7	10.9	21.2	-8.0
2001-2010	-15.4	-25.0	16.6	9.2	18.1	13.2	2.0	-32.8	25.0	10.9
2011-2020	-6.7	8.2								

ANALYSIS										
Since 1810										
Positive (yrs):	11	14	14	13	14	12	10	14	13	9
Average (%):	1.3	4.6	5.0	6.2	9.2	1.6	2.7	2.9	5.2	-1.2
Since 1921										
Positive (yrs):	5	7	8	6	8	6	6	6	6	3
Average (%):	3.6	6.8	10.6	2.6	23.1	6.6	8.8	6.0	9.8	-2.5
Since 1951										
Positive (yrs):	4	4	5	3	6	3	5	5	5	2
Average (%):	6.0	3.7	9.7	-0.9	32.7	4.2	15.5	10.6	18.1	0.6

Observations

1. Since 1801 the strongest years have been the 2nd, 3rd, and 5th years in the decades. The market has risen 14 out of the 21 decades in these years, with an average annual return over 4%. But the single year champion has got to be the 5th year in each decade which has risen an average of 9.2%.

2. The stand-out weakest year in the decade since 1801 has been the 10th – this is the only year to have risen below 10 times in the 21 decades and also the only year to have a negative average change (-1.2%).

3. Generally, performance in the more recent decades has not changed too much from the long-term picture. In the six decades since 1951, the strong years are still the 3rd and 5th years, although they are now also joined by the 7th and 9th years. The dominance of the 5th year is greater than ever – it is the only year to rise in every decade since 1951. And the 10th year continues to be weakest, increasing only twice in the past six decades.

CORRELATION BETWEEN UK AND US MARKETS

It's generally well known that the UK market closely follows the movements of the US market. But it hasn't always been like this – as the charts below show.

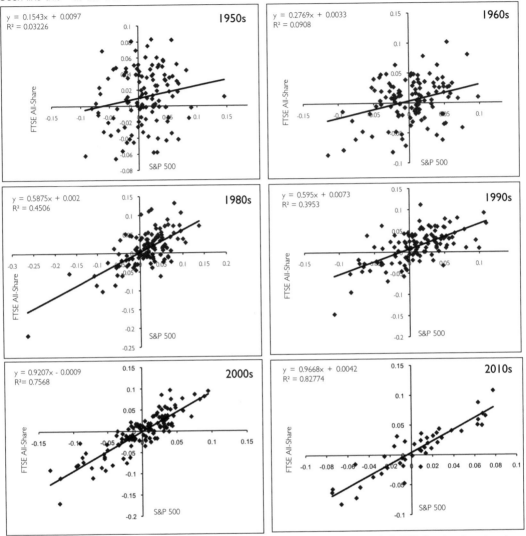

The charts show the correlation of monthly returns of the FTSE All-Share and S&P 500 for the decades since 1950 (except the 1970s).

Analysis

In the 1950s and 1960s there was negligible correlation between the UK and US markets on a monthly basis. The US market might rise one month and the UK would respond by rising or falling – there was no connection. In the 1970s some evidence of correlation can be seen for the first time – although it was still very weak. It was not until the 1980s that the correlation became statistically significant. There could be many reasons for this increase in correlation, but one contributing factor was undoubtedly the increasing presence of computers in trading rooms. And, of course, the October crash in 1987 would have alerted many for the first time to the scale of the inter-connectedness of worldwide markets.

Correlation stayed at a similar level in the 1990s to that reached in the previous decade. But it has been in recent years that the level of correlation has soared – to almost double the level seen in the 1990s. This can be clearly seen in the last two charts, where the points are closely aligned along the line of best fit. The level of correlation between the UK and US market is now so high that the usefulness of independent analysis of the larger-cap UK market indices is pretty much moot. Having said that, correlation has slightly dipped in the past year: R^2 (2010-2012) = 0.86; R^2 (2010-2013) = 0.83.

CORRELATION BETWEEN UK AND INT. MARKETS

The charts below show the correlation of monthly returns between the FTSE All-Share and six international indices since the year 2000.

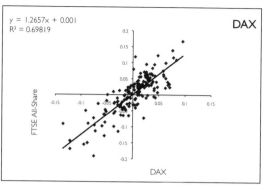

$y = 1.2657x + 0.001$
$R^2 = 0.69819$

DAX

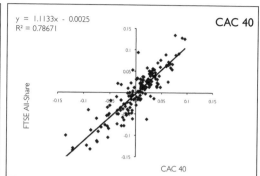

$y = 1.1133x - 0.0025$
$R^2 = 0.78671$

CAC 40

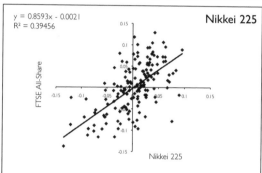

$y = 0.8593x - 0.0021$
$R^2 = 0.39456$

Nikkei 225

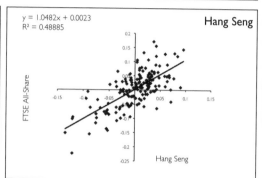

$y = 1.0482x + 0.0023$
$R^2 = 0.48885$

Hang Seng

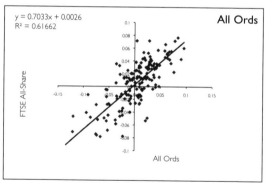

$y = 0.7033x + 0.0026$
$R^2 = 0.61662$

All Ords

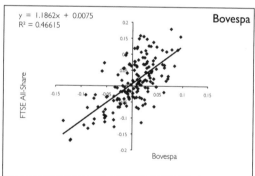

$y = 1.1862x + 0.0075$
$R^2 = 0.46615$

Bovespa

Analysis

The first thing to observe is that all the markets are positively correlated with the UK market. The next question is how closely correlated they are.

The table on the right summarises the R^2 values for the correlation between the FTSE All-Share and the six international indices. The higher the R^2 figure the closer the correlation (R^2 is a measure of how close the points are to the line of best fit).

By visual inspection it can be seen that in the charts of CAC 40 and DAX the points are more closely distributed around the line of best fit. This is confirmed in the table where it can be seen these two markets have the highest R^2 values (albeit lower than the value for the S&P 500).

Index	R^2
CAC 40	0.79
DAX	0.70
All Ordinaries	0.62
Hang Seng	0.49
Bovespa	0.47
Nikkei 225	0.39

The practical impact of this is that if a UK investor is looking to internationally diversify a portfolio they would do better by investing in markets at the bottom of the table (low R^2) than at the top.

SHARES, INTEREST RATES, STERLING & GOLD SINCE WWII

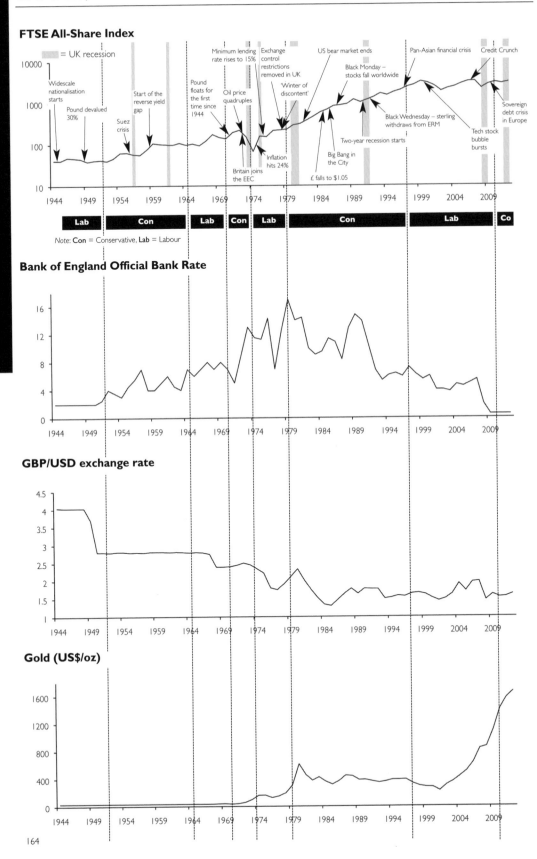

FTSE All-Share Index

= UK recession

Widescale nationalisation starts

Pound devalued 30%

Suez crisis

Start of the reverse yield gap

Pound floats for the first time since 1944

Oil price quadruples

Britain joins the EEC

Minimum lending rate rises to 15%

Exchange control restrictions removed in UK

'Winter of discontent'

Inflation hits 24%

US bear market ends

Black Monday – stocks fall worldwide

£ falls to $1.05

Big Bang in the City

Two-year recession starts

Black Wednesday – sterling withdraws from ERM

Pan-Asian financial crisis

Tech stock bubble bursts

Credit Crunch

Sovereign debt crisis in Europe

| Lab | Con | Lab | Con | Lab | Con | Lab | Co |

Note: **Con** = Conservative, **Lab** = Labour

Bank of England Official Bank Rate

GBP/USD exchange rate

Gold (US$/oz)

ULTIMATE DEATH CROSS

In the previous edition of the *Almanac* there was a chart with the FTSE All-Share poised to make an ultimate death cross (when the 50-month moving average moves down through the 200-month moving average). Readers were left hanging with the comment, "If the 50-month average does fall below the 200-month average will that signal lost decade(s) for the UK market as in Japan?"

So, what happened?

The chart below updates the action.

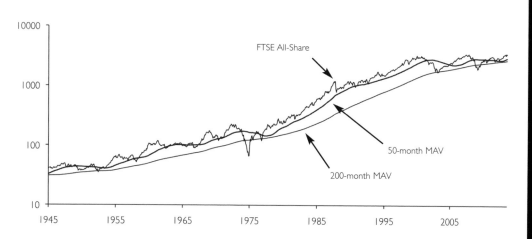

As can be (just) seen, the 50M MAV narrowly avoided crossing the 200M MAV. We were saved. And, in fact, the narrow avoidance of an ultimate death cross in the past has been a strong buy signal for an ensuing massive bull market.

The last time the FTSE All-Share made an ultimate death cross was 1945. So, this signal seems fairly rare. But has this always been the case? The following chart shows the FTSE All-Share with 50-month and 200-month moving averages for the period 1845 to 1945.

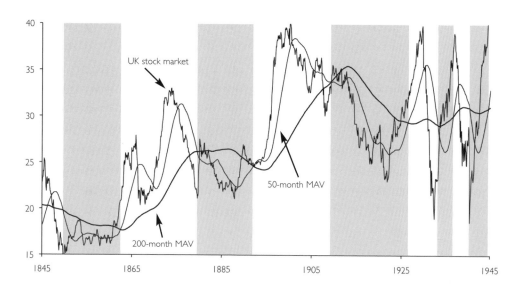

As can be seen for the 100 years prior to 1945, ultimate death crosses were not uncommon. In fact, the 50-month MAV was below the 200-month MAV (shaded in the chart) for 51 of the 100 years.

THE LONG, LONG TERM

The chart below plots a composite UK stock market index from 1693 to 2012. Yes, that's 1693 – a 319-year chart. To put the starting date of the chart in some context:

1. George Frederic Handel was eight years old,

2. six years later Thomas Savery demonstrated his first steam engine to the Royal Society, and

3. the English and French were fighting.

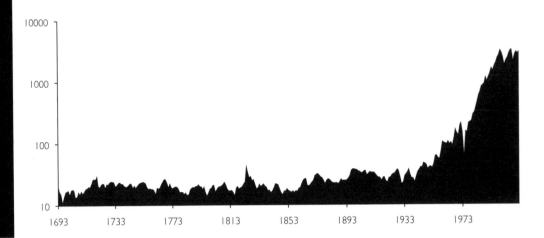

What can one do with data going back such a long way?

Two academics used the data history to check the persistency of monthly seasonality effects in the (very) long term. Their paper[1] has some interesting findings:

- Many months have under or outperformed for long periods but none have done so persistently over the whole 300 years.

- Of all the months, July and October displayed the greatest persistency of underperformance.

- December has the strongest record of outperforming the market. Before 1830 there was a very strong December effect, but this weakened, possibly as the January effect grew. Other strong months have been January, April and August.

- From having lower returns, after the 1850s January displayed stronger returns, which is attributed to the beginning of the celebration of Christmas as a public holiday from around 1835. The authors support this theory by their finding that stock markets in Christmas-celebrating countries significantly outperform stock markets in non-Christmas-celebrating countries around the turn of the year.

- In contrast to the monthly seasonality effects above, the six-month effect ("Sell in May…") has shown robustness over the whole 300-year period, and has been significantly strong since the 1950s.

- They attribute this six-month effect to vacation behaviour.

- They found that the stock market in the summer period underperformed the risk-free rate.

- A strategy based on the six-month effect beats the market more than 80% of the time over a 5-year time horizon, and over 90% of the time for a 10-year time horizon.

[1] Cherry Yi Zhang and Ben Jacobsen 'Are Monthly Seasonals Real? A Three Century Perspective', *The Review of Finance* (September 6, 2012).

THE LONG-TERM FORMULA

The chart below plots the FTSE All-Share from 1920 to the present day. Notes:

1. The Y-scale is logarithmic, which presents percentage (rather than absolute) changes better over long periods, and so is more suitable for long-term charts.

2. The straight line is a line of best fit calculated by regression analysis.

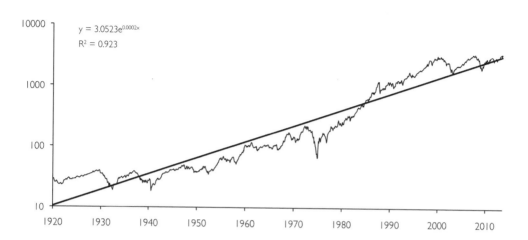

$$y = 3.0523e^{0.0002x}$$
$$R^2 = 0.923$$

Observations

1. The R^2 for the line of best fit is 0.92, which is quite high (i.e. the line of best fit fairly accurately approximates the real data points).

2. The FTSE All-Share traded below the long-term trend line (line of best fit) from 1938 to 1984, and then traded above the trend line until 2008 (having only just stayed above it in 2003). Currently the index is back above the trend line.

Forecasts

The equation of the line of best fit in the chart above is:

$$y = 3.052268823e^{1.000167454x}$$

The equation allows us to make forecasts for the FTSE All-Share. It is, in effect, the Holy Grail, the key to the stock market – as simple as that!

For example, at the time of writing the FTSE All-Share is 3,507, while the above equation forecasts a value today (according to the long-term trend line) of 3,199. This suggests the index is currently overpriced relative to the long-tem trend line. But as can be seen in the above chart the index can spend long periods trading above or below the long-term trend line.

Now, if we think that the trend of the market in the last 90 years will broadly continue, we can use the equation to forecast the level of the FTSE All-Share in the future. And this is what has been done in the table to the right. Forecasts for the FTSE 100 have also been given.

Date	FTAS Forecast	FTSE 100 Forecast	Chng (%)
Dec 2018	4,422	8,299	+26
Dec 2023	6,003	11,267	+71
Dec 2033	11,067	20,772	+215
Dec 2063	69,324	130,111	+1,876

- The equation estimates that the FTSE 100 will be at 8,299 in December 2018 (26% above the current level).

- Looking forward 10 years, to 2023, the forecast is for a FTSE 100 level of 11,267 (+71%).

- And in 50 year's time (well, why not?) the FTSE 100 is forecast to be 130,111 (+1,876%).

Now's the time to place those 50-year spread bets.

MARGINAL UTILITY

PONTIFICAL ANALYIS

The leader of the Catholic Church has a number of official titles, including: Bishop of Rome, Vicar of Jesus Christ, Successor of the Prince of the Apostles, Supreme Pontiff of the Universal Church, Primate of Italy, Archbishop and Metropolitan of the Roman Province, Sovereign of the Vatican City State, and Servant of the servants of God. Missing from that list is *pope* – it's not an official title apparently.

Anyway, 2013 saw the first resignation of a pope since 1415, and Jorge Mario Bergoglio became Bishop of Rome, Successor of the Prince… and Pope Francis. This prompted some analysis of the (undoubted) close links between pontifical turnover and the stock market.

Hence, the following chart. This plots the FTSE All-Share from 1700 (log scale) and the years of new popes (indicated by the vertical bars).

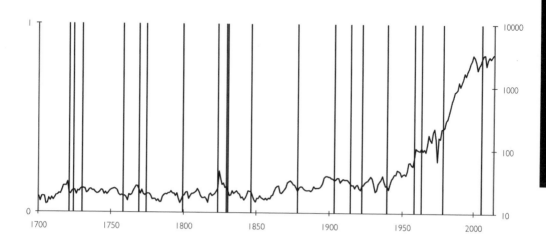

As can be (clearly) seen on the chart, significant turning points in the stock market often coincide with changes in pope. Few readers will need reminding of the dramatic end of the 1824 bull market that coincided with Leo XII replacing Pius VII as pope.

But papal influence extends far beyond stock market turning points. The chart also shows that pontificates of long duration have tended to coincide with strong equity markets. During the pontificate of John Paul II (1978 to 2005) the UK market rose 2800%. Whereas periods of short duration pontificates have coincided with weak or flat equity markets. This suggests that long popes are good for long positions and short popes are good for short positions.

UNDER PRESSURE

Readers of last year's *Almanac* may remember the desperate, expensive and ultimately futile attempt to discover some relationship between the amount of sun in a day and stock market returns. The following chart summarises the miserable effort.

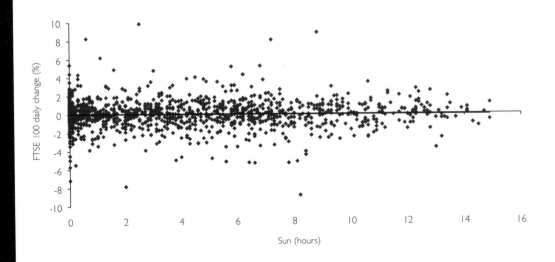

No correlation – hopeless.

But we might have been barking up the wrong tree.

Background

To recap briefly, it has long been thought that there is some connection between the weather and stock returns. That when the sun shines, investors feel happy, they take on more risk and prices rise; and when the weather is gloomy, investors feel likewise and prices fall.

Many academic studies have looked into this, but findings have been inconsistent.

One of the most extensive surveys was conducted by Hirshleifer and Shumway in their paper 'Good Day Sunshine: Stock Returns and the Weather'.[1] The authors did find a positive correlation between equity market returns and the amount of sunshine, but not for any other weather conditions (e.g. rain or snow).

Pressure

But the author of a more recent paper[2], Michael Schneider, decided to take a new approach.

Schneider took as his starting point the idea that investors have to directly experience the weather to be affected by it. For example, investors sitting in a neon-lit trading room can be largely unaware of whether it is raining outside or not. But what all people can be affected by, wherever they are, is barometric pressure.

Elsewhere, psychological studies have shown that high barometric pressure can induce positive moods, and vice versa.

Hence, Schneider ran his tests and found there was indeed a strong correlation between barometric pressure and stock returns.

Further:

1. The barometric effect was greater for smaller, riskier stocks.

2. The result was economically as well as statistically significant.

Controlling for all weather variables, Schneider found that it was only barometric pressure that affects equity returns.

---

[1] David A. Hirshleifer and Tyler Shumway, 'Good Day Sunshine: Stock Returns and the Weather', *Journal of Finance*, Vol. 58 (June 2003), pp. 1009-1032.
[2] Michael Schneider, 'Under Pressure: Stock Returns and the Weather' (25 June 2013).

THE WIMBLEDON INDICATOR

Lawn tennis was invented in the 1870s by Major Walter Clopton Wingfield and was originally called sphairistike. In 1876 tennis was added to the activities of the The All England Croquet Club and a year later the first Lawn Tennis Championship was played at Wimbledon.

For many years the men's singles champion was, naturally, a Briton. This was upset in 1907 when an Australian, Norman Brooks, became champion. The natural order of things was re-established in 1934 when Fred Perry won the first of three consecutive men's finals (all three against the German Gottfried Alexander Maximilian Walter Kurt Freiherr von Cramm).

Nothing much then happened at Wimbledon until 2013 when Andy Murray beat Novak Djokovic in the final 6-4, 7-5, 6-4 (easy).

And the connection with the stock market is...?

I'm glad you asked. How about this:

- After the Great Crash of 1929, the UK market bottomed in June 1932; **49 months later** Fred Perry won Wimbledon.
- After the Credit Crunch of 2007, the UK market bottomed in March 2009; **51 months later** Andy Murray won Wimbledon.

We need to look at this on a chart.

The following chart shows the performance of the FTSE All-Share for January 2007 to July 2013 overlaid on the index for January 1930 to December 1939. The index has been rebased to 100 in both cases.

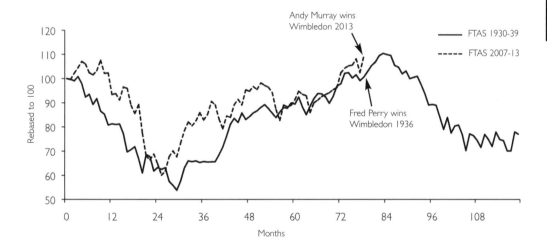

Of course, correlation is not causation… but spooky, no?

If the market today continues to follow the Fred Perry market of the 1930s, we can expect the UK market to be strong for another five months (to around December 2013) and after that experience a big sell-off.

Wimbledon stats	
The last year wooden racquets were used	1987
Number of matches played each tournament	650
Average number of balls used each tournament	54,000
Prize money in 2013	£22,560,000

Note: the Wimbledon Indicator is not to be confused with the Wimbledon Effect, which is the observation that an institution or industry can be successful without strong domestic participation or ownership. This effect applies to Wimbledon itself and the financial industry in the City (which is dominated by overseas companies).

CHINESE CALENDAR AND THE STOCK MARKET

When we look at the annual performance of the stock market we naturally take our start and end points as 1 January and 31 December. For example, a long-term chart of an index will normally plot the index values on 31 December for each year.

But using different start and end points may be interesting. While the overall performance of the market will obviously not change, the path to the final point may show up differently, and thus possibly reveal a pattern of behaviour not previously noticed.

The start of the Chinese Year moves around (on the Western calendar) from year to year, but always falls between 21 January and 21 February. The calculation of the actual date of the Chinese New Year is sinologically complex. For example:

> Rule 5: In a leap suì, the first month that does not contain a zhongqì is the leap month, rùnyuè. The leap month takes the same number as the previous month.

That quote comes from a 52-page academic paper 'The Mathematics of the Chinese Calendar'.[1] However, we shall skip lightly over such details and focus on a key aspect of the Chinese calendar which is the sexagenary cycle. This is a combination of 10 heavenly stems and the 12 earthly branches. The branches are often associated with the sequence of 12 animals. (At last – the animals!) Cutting to the chase, the Chinese calendar encompasses a 12-year cycle where each year is associated with an animal.

Can we detect any significant behavioural patterns in the stock market correlated with the sexagenary cycle? In other words, are there monkey years in the market?

The following chart plots the average performance of the stock market[2] for each animal year since 1950. For example, Ox years started in 1961, 1973, 1985, 1997, 2009; the average performance of the market in those (Chinese) years was +14.0%.

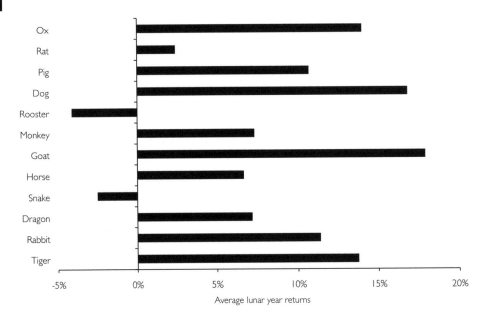

Average lunar year returns

As can be seen the best performing market animals have been the goat and dog. And, coincidentally (or, is it?), the worst performing animals have been the rooster (perhaps a mistranslation for turkey?) and snake.

The Chinese New Year starting 10 February this year is the year of the horse.

As the famous Chinese proverb says:

> *If the wind comes from an empty cave, it's not without a reason.*

---

[1] Helmer Aslaksen, 'The Mathematics of the Chinese Calendar', www.math.nus.edu.sg/aslaksen (2010).
[2] The S&P 500 was used for this study; as the correlation between the US and UK markets is so high this index is a sufficient proxy for the UK market for the purposes here.

SINCLAIR NUMBERS

FTSE 100 INDEX DAILY PERFORMANCE

Date	Up (%)	Avg Change (%)	Std Dev
2 Jan	59	0.4	1.2
3 Jan	71	0.3	1.1
4 Jan	57	0.2	1.4
5 Jan	45	-0.1	1.0
6 Jan	60	0.3	0.9
7 Jan	29	-0.2	1.0
8 Jan	43	-0.1	0.6
9 Jan	43	-0.1	1.0
10 Jan	38	-0.1	0.8
11 Jan	38	-0.2	0.7
12 Jan	40	-0.3	0.7
13 Jan	35	-0.2	0.9
14 Jan	57	-0.1	1.5
15 Jan	62	0.2	1.3
16 Jan	57	0.2	0.9
17 Jan	57	0.2	0.9
18 Jan	62	0.2	1.1
19 Jan	40	-0.2	0.8
20 Jan	30	-0.5	0.8
21 Jan	43	-0.5	1.3
22 Jan	48	0.0	1.3
23 Jan	38	-0.3	0.9
24 Jan	62	0.5	1.2
25 Jan	38	-0.2	0.7
26 Jan	80	0.7	1.1
27 Jan	50	0.2	1.3
28 Jan	57	0.1	1.1
29 Jan	43	-0.2	1.0
30 Jan	57	0.3	1.1
31 Jan	62	0.2	0.8
1 Feb	67	0.7	1.0
2 Feb	75	0.3	0.9
3 Feb	50	0.3	1.2
4 Feb	43	-0.3	1.1
5 Feb	48	-0.1	1.2
6 Feb	62	0.0	0.9
7 Feb	52	0.0	1.1
8 Feb	57	0.2	1.0
9 Feb	55	0.0	0.7
10 Feb	35	-0.3	0.8
11 Feb	62	0.4	1.0
12 Feb	38	-0.1	1.2
13 Feb	67	0.2	0.6
14 Feb	43	0.0	0.7
15 Feb	62	0.1	0.7
16 Feb	45	0.2	1.1
17 Feb	75	0.4	0.9
18 Feb	40	0.0	0.7
19 Feb	48	0.0	1.1
20 Feb	43	-0.3	1.1
21 Feb	43	-0.1	0.8
22 Feb	43	-0.1	0.6
23 Feb	45	-0.2	1.0
24 Feb	40	-0.1	0.9
25 Feb	71	0.4	1.1
26 Feb	57	0.2	0.9
27 Feb	48	-0.1	0.9
28 Feb	48	-0.2	1.1
29 Feb	40	-0.1	1.4
1 Mar	67	0.3	1.0
2 Mar	50	-0.1	1.4
3 Mar	55	0.1	1.0
4 Mar	57	0.4	1.2
5 Mar	52	0.1	1.3
6 Mar	52	0.2	1.0
7 Mar	48	-0.2	0.8
8 Mar	67	0.1	0.7
9 Mar	45	0.0	0.8
10 Mar	70	0.3	1.3
11 Mar	48	-0.2	1.0
12 Mar	43	-0.3	1.3
13 Mar	43	0.1	1.6
14 Mar	62	0.3	1.3
15 Mar	48	0.1	1.0
16 Mar	45	0.0	1.3
17 Mar	55	0.0	1.4
18 Mar	48	0.1	1.1
19 Mar	62	0.1	0.8
20 Mar	48	0.1	1.0
21 Mar	45	0.0	1.0
22 Mar	43	-0.4	1.1
23 Mar	45	0.1	1.0
24 Mar	50	-0.2	1.4
25 Mar	45	0.2	1.1
26 Mar	57	0.2	0.9
27 Mar	50	0.0	1.0
28 Mar	39	-0.3	0.7
29 Mar	56	0.2	0.8
30 Mar	45	-0.4	1.2
31 Mar	44	0.1	1.4
1 Apr	75	0.5	1.2
2 Apr	68	0.7	1.2
3 Apr	41	-0.3	1.1
4 Apr	50	0.0	0.9
5 Apr	67	0.2	0.8
6 Apr	63	0.2	0.7
7 Apr	45	0.2	1.1
8 Apr	26	-0.3	0.7
9 Apr	67	0.3	0.8
10 Apr	55	0.3	1.7
11 Apr	41	-0.2	0.9
12 Apr	55	0.1	0.7

Date	Up (%)	Avg Change (%)	Std Dev
13 Apr	59	0.2	0.6
14 Apr	28	-0.3	0.9
15 Apr	62	0.3	0.9
16 Apr	55	0.1	1.2
17 Apr	56	0.0	1.1
18 Apr	48	0.0	1.0
19 Apr	55	0.2	0.7
20 Apr	58	-0.1	1.2
21 Apr	39	-0.1	0.5
22 Apr	45	0.1	0.8
23 Apr	41	-0.1	1.0
24 Apr	52	0.1	1.1
25 Apr	62	0.1	0.5
26 Apr	68	0.3	0.6
27 Apr	50	-0.2	1.1
28 Apr	50	0.1	1.1
29 Apr	50	0.3	0.8
30 Apr	55	0.1	0.7
1 May	53	0.1	0.8
2 May	76	0.5	0.9
3 May	61	-0.2	1.1
4 May	53	-0.1	1.2
5 May	50	0.0	1.0
6 May	63	0.3	1.0
7 May	41	-0.4	0.9
8 May	52	0.1	1.1
9 May	41	-0.1	0.7
10 May	45	0.3	1.4
11 May	52	0.1	1.1
12 May	55	0.0	0.9
13 May	57	0.2	0.9
14 May	36	-0.5	1.4
15 May	55	0.2	0.9
16 May	41	0.1	0.6
17 May	50	-0.2	1.3
18 May	57	0.2	0.9
19 May	55	-0.2	1.4
20 May	52	-0.1	1.0
21 May	59	0.0	0.8
22 May	55	0.0	1.0
23 May	41	-0.4	1.2
24 May	41	-0.1	0.8
25 May	53	-0.2	1.1
26 May	56	0.3	0.8
27 May	41	0.0	1.1
28 May	56	0.2	0.8
29 May	65	0.2	0.9
30 May	22	-0.4	1.3
31 May	56	0.1	0.6
1 June	62	0.4	1.1
2 June	50	0.2	1.0

Date	Up (%)	Avg Change (%)	Std Dev
3 June	60	0.1	0.8
4 June	55	0.1	1.0
5 June	52	0.0	1.0
6 June	55	0.0	1.0
7 June	50	0.0	0.8
8 June	38	-0.1	0.9
9 June	45	0.2	0.8
10 June	48	-0.1	0.7
11 June	50	-0.1	1.0
12 June	41	-0.2	0.9
13 June	55	-0.2	0.8
14 June	45	-0.1	1.1
15 June	48	-0.1	1.0
16 June	65	0.2	0.5
17 June	67	0.3	0.9
18 June	41	-0.3	0.7
19 June	45	-0.1	1.0
20 June	36	-0.4	1.0
21 June	55	0.0	0.8
22 June	43	-0.3	0.9
23 June	35	-0.3	0.8
24 June	38	-0.4	0.9
25 June	59	0.1	0.8
26 June	41	-0.5	1.0
27 June	59	0.2	0.8
28 June	64	0.2	0.9
29 June	57	0.1	1.2
30 June	60	0.0	0.9
1 Jul	67	0.3	1.5
2 Jul	55	0.0	1.1
3 Jul	64	0.2	1.2
4 Jul	55	0.4	1.0
5 Jul	43	0.1	1.0
6 Jul	52	0.1	1.0
7 Jul	60	0.4	1.0
8 Jul	25	-0.2	0.9
9 Jul	57	0.1	0.8
10 Jul	38	-0.4	0.9
11 Jul	52	-0.2	1.4
12 Jul	33	-0.2	0.8
13 Jul	71	0.3	0.9
14 Jul	60	0.3	1.0
15 Jul	45	-0.1	1.7
16 Jul	48	0.1	0.8
17 Jul	62	0.3	1.3
18 Jul	38	-0.2	1.1
19 Jul	52	-0.1	1.2
20 Jul	43	-0.1	0.8
21 Jul	45	-0.1	0.9
22 Jul	45	-0.5	1.5
23 Jul	57	0.0	1.1

Date	Up (%)	Avg Change (%)	Std Dev
24 Jul	43	-0.4	1.1
25 Jul	43	0.1	1.2
26 Jul	57	0.1	1.0
27 Jul	57	0.1	1.0
28 Jul	75	0.2	0.6
29 Jul	75	0.5	1.4
30 Jul	57	0.3	0.9
31 Jul	43	0.2	1.0
1 Aug	57	-0.2	1.4
2 Aug	76	0.6	1.1
3 Aug	43	-0.1	1.2
4 Aug	30	-0.4	0.9
5 Aug	50	-0.2	1.3
6 Aug	43	-0.2	1.4
7 Aug	67	0.3	0.9
8 Aug	62	0.1	1.3
9 Aug	57	0.1	1.0
10 Aug	29	-0.6	1.3
11 Aug	45	0.0	1.3
12 Aug	70	0.4	1.1
13 Aug	57	0.2	1.1
14 Aug	71	0.3	1.0
15 Aug	57	0.0	1.2
16 Aug	57	-0.1	1.1
17 Aug	62	0.1	1.2
18 Aug	55	0.0	1.5
19 Aug	45	-0.3	1.3
20 Aug	52	0.1	0.7
21 Aug	67	0.2	1.2
22 Aug	52	0.2	1.0
23 Aug	52	0.0	0.8
24 Aug	71	0.2	0.9
25 Aug	69	0.0	1.0
26 Aug	44	-0.1	0.8
27 Aug	56	0.2	1.1
28 Aug	47	-0.3	1.4
29 Aug	47	0.0	0.8
30 Aug	71	0.3	1.0
31 Aug	59	0.2	1.0
1 Sep	65	0.3	1.2
2 Sep	50	0.0	1.0
3 Sep	57	0.0	1.5
4 Sep	57	0.0	1.0
5 Sep	48	-0.4	1.1
6 Sep	67	0.1	1.1
7 Sep	52	0.1	1.4
8 Sep	40	0.0	1.1
9 Sep	30	-0.3	0.8
10 Sep	38	-0.3	1.1
11 Sep	30	-0.1	0.9
12 Sep	43	-0.2	1.2

Date	Up (%)	Avg Change (%)	Std Dev
13 Sep	52	0.1	0.8
14 Sep	57	0.0	1.4
15 Sep	50	-0.2	1.4
16 Sep	60	-0.1	1.2
17 Sep	48	0.1	1.6
18 Sep	48	-0.1	1.4
19 Sep	52	0.2	2.3
20 Sep	48	-0.1	1.3
21 Sep	33	-0.4	0.9
22 Sep	50	-0.3	1.4
23 Sep	35	-0.2	1.1
24 Sep	38	-0.1	1.3
25 Sep	48	0.0	1.1
26 Sep	52	0.2	1.5
27 Sep	76	0.7	1.1
28 Sep	52	0.1	1.2
29 Sep	45	-0.3	1.3
30 Sep	45	-0.2	1.3
1 Oct	76	0.4	1.5
2 Oct	38	-0.1	1.2
3 Oct	57	0.2	1.0
4 Oct	62	0.1	1.1
5 Oct	76	0.3	1.7
6 Oct	55	0.3	2.4
7 Oct	50	0.0	0.7
8 Oct	43	-0.3	1.5
9 Oct	43	-0.2	1.2
10 Oct	43	-0.3	2.2
11 Oct	62	0.3	1.3
12 Oct	48	0.2	1.2
13 Oct	60	0.7	2.0
14 Oct	45	0.1	1.1
15 Oct	48	-0.3	2.1
16 Oct	43	-0.8	2.0
17 Oct	67	0.4	1.5
18 Oct	52	-0.1	0.8
19 Oct	48	-0.2	1.7
20 Oct	50	-0.2	3.3
21 Oct	60	0.4	1.9
22 Oct	33	-0.6	1.7
23 Oct	57	-0.1	1.4
24 Oct	48	-0.2	1.5
25 Oct	38	-0.3	0.8
26 Oct	43	-0.3	1.6
27 Oct	55	0.0	1.3
28 Oct	65	0.1	1.3
29 Oct	52	0.6	2.2
30 Oct	67	0.4	1.4
31 Oct	76	0.4	1.1
1 Nov	57	-0.1	0.9
2 Nov	57	0.2	0.9

Date	Up (%)	Avg Change (%)	Std Dev
3 Nov	55	0.2	1.2
4 Nov	40	0.4	1.6
5 Nov	62	-0.1	1.1
6 Nov	62	-0.1	1.4
7 Nov	48	-0.2	1.0
8 Nov	57	0.1	0.7
9 Nov	43	-0.2	1.1
10 Nov	50	0.0	0.6
11 Nov	55	0.1	1.5
12 Nov	57	0.3	1.2
13 Nov	48	-0.1	1.0
14 Nov	52	0.2	0.8
15 Nov	57	0.1	0.7
16 Nov	62	0.1	0.9
17 Nov	40	-0.2	1.1
18 Nov	60	0.1	0.8
19 Nov	33	-0.5	1.6
20 Nov	52	0.0	1.2
21 Nov	52	-0.1	1.3
22 Nov	48	-0.1	1.0
23 Nov	57	0.3	1.3
24 Nov	55	0.6	2.3
25 Nov	60	0.0	1.0
26 Nov	48	-0.2	1.1
27 Nov	62	0.2	0.8
28 Nov	48	0.1	1.2
29 Nov	71	0.1	0.7
30 Nov	43	-0.2	1.5
1 Dec	55	0.1	1.9
2 Dec	50	0.1	0.9
3 Dec	52	0.1	0.8
4 Dec	33	-0.1	0.7
5 Dec	57	0.3	1.2
6 Dec	52	-0.1	0.7
7 Dec	43	0.0	0.7
8 Dec	60	0.4	1.6
9 Dec	50	0.1	0.9
10 Dec	38	-0.2	0.7
11 Dec	43	-0.1	1.0
12 Dec	48	-0.2	0.9
13 Dec	67	0.0	1.0
14 Dec	52	-0.1	0.9
15 Dec	50	0.0	0.7
16 Dec	75	0.6	0.8
17 Dec	43	-0.1	1.0
18 Dec	67	0.2	0.9
19 Dec	57	-0.1	0.9
20 Dec	62	0.1	0.9
21 Dec	57	0.4	1.0
22 Dec	70	0.3	0.6
23 Dec	80	0.4	0.6

Date	Up (%)	Avg Change (%)	Std Dev
24 Dec	81	0.2	0.6
27 Dec	85	0.4	1.2
28 Dec	62	0.2	0.5
29 Dec	75	0.4	1.2
30 Dec	60	0.2	0.9
31 Dec	53	0.0	1.1

The rows for the ten strongest [weakest] days are highlighted light grey [dark grey].

FTSE 100 INDEX WEEKLY PERFORMANCE

Week	Up (%)	Avg Change (%)	Std Dev
1	69	1.2	2.6
2	28	-0.5	1.8
3	48	-0.3	2.6
4	55	0.0	1.8
5	66	0.9	2.0
6	59	0.3	2.0
7	62	0.4	1.3
8	52	0.0	2.3
9	55	0.6	2.0
10	55	-0.1	2.4
11	55	0.2	2.3
12	45	0.2	2.6
13	45	0.0	1.8
14	66	0.7	2.1
15	47	0.1	2.2
16	63	0.5	1.5
17	53	0.0	1.7
18	63	0.4	2.3
19	60	0.3	2.1
20	57	-0.2	2.4
21	43	-0.3	2.0
22	40	0.3	1.9
23	60	0.2	1.8
24	57	-0.3	2.1
25	33	-0.9	1.8
26	47	-0.1	1.9
27	70	1.0	2.0
28	38	-0.6	2.4
29	55	0.2	2.4
30	38	-0.4	2.3
31	79	0.6	2.6
32	52	0.0	2.4
33	59	0.1	2.2
34	76	0.4	1.9
35	55	0.4	2.3
36	45	-0.5	2.3
37	41	-0.5	2.3
38	41	-0.3	2.9
39	48	0.3	2.6
40	66	0.8	2.5
41	59	-0.4	4.5
42	62	0.2	2.7
43	45	-0.8	4.1
44	55	0.7	3.3
45	66	0.1	2.1
46	59	0.3	1.6
47	48	-0.2	3.2
48	59	1.0	3.2
49	48	-0.2	2.5
50	48	0.0	2.2
51	76	0.8	1.6
52	76	1.0	1.5
53	80	-0.6	2.1

The rows for the ten strongest [weakest] weeks are highlighted light grey [dark grey].

FTSE 100 INDEX MONTHLY PERFORMANCE

Month	Up (%)	Avg Change (%)	Std Dev
January	59	0.5	5.2
February	59	1.0	4.1
March	59	0.7	3.4
April	69	1.8	3.6
May	47	-0.2	4.5
June	40	-0.8	3.6
July	55	0.8	4.3
August	59	0.6	4.8
September	48	-1.0	5.8
October	76	0.7	6.8
November	59	0.7	3.8
December	86	2.5	3.0

3

REFERENCE

CONTENTS

STOCK INDICES

FT Ordinary Share Index (FT 30)

The FT 30 was first calculated in 1935 by the *Financial Times* newspaper. The index started at a base level of 100, and was calculated from a subjective collection of 30 major companies – which in the early years were concentrated in the industrial and retailing sectors.

For a long time the index was the best known performance measure of the UK stock market. But the index become less representative of the whole market. Also the index was price-weighted (like the DJIA), and not market-capitalisation-weighted. Although the index was calculated every hour, the increasing sophistication of the market needed an index calculated every minute and so the FT 30 has been usurped by the FTSE 100.

FTSE 100

Today, the FTSE 100 (sometimes called the "footsie") is the best known index tracking the performance of the UK market. The index comprises 100 of the top capitalised stocks listed on the LSE, and represents approximately 80% of the total market (by capitalisation). It is market capitalisation weighted and the composition of the index is reviewed every three months. The FTSE 100 is commonly used as the basis for investment funds and derivatives. The index was first calculated on 3 January 1984 with a base value of 1000.

The FTSE 100, and all the FTSE indices, are calculated by FTSE International – which started life as a joint venture between the *Financial Times* newspaper and the London Stock Exchange, but is now wholly owned by the LSE.

FTSE 250

Similar in construction to the FTSE 100, except this index comprises the next 250 highest capitalised stocks listed on the LSE after the top 100. The index is sometimes referred to as the index of "mid-cap" stocks, and comprises approximately 18% of the total market capitalisation.

FTSE 350

The FTSE 350 is an index comprising all the stocks in the FTSE 100 and FTSE 250 indices.

FTSE Small Cap

Comprised of companies with a market capitalisation below the FTSE 250 but above a fixed limit. This lower limit is periodically reviewed. Consequently the FTSE Small Cap does not have a fixed number of constituents. In mid-2013, there were 269 companies in the index, which represented about 2% of the total market by capitalisation.

FTSE All-Share

The FTSE All-Share is the aggregation of the FTSE 100, FTSE 250 and FTSE Small Cap indices. Effectively it is comprised of all those LSE listed companies with a market capitalisation above the lower limit for inclusion in the FTSE Small Cap. The FTSE All-Share is the standard benchmark for measuring the performance of the broad UK market and represents 98% to 99% of the total UK market capitalisation.

FTSE Fledgling

This index comprises the companies that do not meet the minimum size requirement of the FTSE Small Cap and are therefore outside of the FTSE All-Share. There are fewer than 200 companies in the FTSE Fledgling.

FTSE All-Small

This consists of all the companies in the FTSE Small Cap and FTSE Fledgling indices.

FTSE TMT

Reflects the performance of companies in the Technology, Media and Telecommunications sectors.

FTSE techMARK All-Share

An index of all companies included in the LSE's techMARK sector.

FTSE techMARK 100

The top 100 companies of the FTSE techMARK All-Share, under £4bn by full market capitalisation.

FTSE AIM UK 50

Comprises the 50 largest UK companies quoted on the Alternative Investment Market (AIM).

FTSE AIM 100

Comprises the 100 largest companies quoted on the Alternative Investment Market (AIM).

FTSE AIM All-Share

All AIM-quoted companies.

STOCK INDICES – INTERNATIONAL

Dow Jones Industrial Average Index (DJIA)

The DJIA is the oldest continuing stock index of the US market and probably the most famous stock index in the world. Created in 1896, it originally comprised 12 stocks, but over the years the index has expanded to reach the point where today it includes 30 stocks. The index is weighted by price, which is unusual for a stock index. It is calculated by summing the prices of the 30 stocks and dividing by the divisor. Originally the divisor was 30, but this has been adjusted periodically to reflect capital changes such as stock splits, and is currently about 0.13. This means that companies with high stock prices have the greatest influence on the index – not those with large market values. The longest established company in the index is General Electric, which joined the index in 1907.

Standard & Poor's 500 (S&P 500)

This is the main benchmark index for the performance of the US market. The index is weighted by market value and constituents are chosen based upon their market size, liquidity and sector. The index was created in 1957, although values for it have been back-calculated several decades.

NASDAQ 100

This index tracks the performance of the 100 largest stocks listed on the NASDAQ exchange. The index is calculated using a modified capitalisation weighting method ("modified" so that large companies like Apple don't overwhelm the index). NASDAQ companies tend to be smaller and younger than those listed on the NYSE and although there is no attempt to select technology stocks, it is regarded as the tech stock index. The index can be traded as there's an ETF associated with it (the most actively traded ETF in the US). The ETF has the symbol QQQ and is sometimes referred to as the "Qs" or "Qubes".

Nikkei 225

The Nikkei 225 is owned by the Nihon Keizai Shimbun ("Nikkei") newspaper. It was first calculated in 1949 (when it was known as the Nikkei-Dow index) and is the most widely watched stock index in Japan. It is a price-weighted index of 225 top-rated Japanese companies listed in the First Section of the Tokyo Stock Exchange. The calculation method is therefore similar to that of the Dow Jones Industrial Average (upon which it was modelled).

TOPIX

The TOPIX is calculated by the Tokyo Stock Exchange. Unlike the Nikkei 255, TOPIX is a market capitalisation-weighted index. TOPIX is calculated from all members of the First Section of the Tokyo SE, which is about 1500 companies. For these reasons, TOPIX is preferred over the Nikkei 225 as a benchmark for Japanese equity portfolios.

Hang Seng

The Hang Seng was first calculated in 1964. Today it has 48 constituents representing some 60% of the total Hong Kong market by capitalisation.

CAC 40

The CAC 40 is the main benchmark for Euronext Paris (what used to be the Paris Bourse). The index contains 40 stocks selected among the top 100 by market capitalisation and the most active stocks listed on Euronext Paris. The base value was 1000 at 31 December 1987.

DAX

The DAX 30 is published by the Frankfurt Stock Exchange and is the main real-time German share index. It contains 30 stocks from the leading German stock markets. The DAX is a total return index (which is uncommon), whereby it measures not only the price appreciation of its constituents but also the return provided by the dividends paid.

EPIC, TIDM, SEDOL, CUSIP AND ISIN CODES

This page describes the common codes associated with securities.

EPIC

Some time ago the London Stock Exchange devised a system of code names for listed companies. These codes provide a short and unambiguous way to reference stocks.

For example, the code for Marks & Spencer is MKS. This code, MKS, is easier to use than wondering whether one should call the company Marks & Spencer, Marks and Spencer or Marks & Spencer plc.

These codes were called EPIC codes, after the name of the Stock Exchange's central computer prior to 1996.

TIDM

After the introduction of the Sequence trading platform, EPIC codes were renamed Tradable Instrument Display Mnemonics (TIDMs), or Mnemonics for short. So, strictly, we should now be calling them TIDMs or Mnemonics – but almost everyone still refers to them as EPIC codes.

SEDOL

SEDOL stands for Stock Exchange Daily Official List Number. These are seven digit security identifiers assigned by the London Stock Exchange. They are only assigned to UK-listed securities.

CUSIP

CUSIP (Committee on Uniform Securities Identification Procedures) codes are nine-character alphanumeric identifiers used for Canadian and US securities.

ISIN

ISIN stands for International Securities Identification Number. These are 12-digit alphanumeric identifiers assigned by the International Standards Organisation (ISO) in order to provide standardisation of international securities. The first two letters represent the country code; the next nine characters usually use some other code, such as CUSIP in the United States or SEDOL in Great Britain, with leading spaces padded with 0. The final digit is the check digit.

DAILY TIMETABLE OF THE UK TRADING DAY

The table displays the basic structure of the UK trading day, with some comments from a trader.

07.00	**Regulatory News Services open** The period before the market opens at 08.00 is the most important hour of the day. By the time the opening auction begins at 07.50 traders will have a clear idea at what price any particular major stock should be opening at. Scheduled announcements are normally in the Regulatory News. Having a good idea of what companies are reporting for the forthcoming week is essential. Quite a few banks, brokers and websites provide comprehensive forward diaries. As well as checking the movement of the major stock indices overnight, check the early show for the futures contracts on the main indices, as well as any US company results that were released after hours. Unlike the UK, in the US it is common for companies to release results after the markets close.
07.50-08.00	**Pre-market auction** There are fewer opportunities in the opening auction than the closing auction, partly because there are lower volumes in the opening auction. It is safer to trade against an 'at-market' order than against several orders from several other participants that appear to be at the wrong price – almost certainly they have seen something that you haven't. Despite representing only a small proportion of the total day's volume, the opening uncrossing trade will often be (or very close to) the high or low trade of the day for that stock.
08.00	**UK market and FTSE 100 Index Futures open** By 08.00 as the UK market opens you should be fully prepared for the day's trading.
08.00-16.30	**Continuous trading** Trading is continuous until 16.30. During the day there is a calendar of key economic figures to look out for, as well as both ad-hoc and scheduled announcements. Some company-scheduled trading figures come out at midday, particularly companies that are dual-quoted. US index futures should be monitored throughout the day as well as other influential continental indices such as Germany's DAX. Traders will often concentrate on watching the high volatility shares as these provide the most trading opportunities, although many will add 'guest' stocks to their watch list and go to where the day's action is and join 'event' traders. Stocks to watch during the day include the biggest movers on the day (both risers and fallers), those experiencing high volume and constant gainers (popular with momentum players).
14.30	**US markets open** The US markets usually open at 14.30 UK time, although at certain times of the year, due to daylight saving, it may be an hour earlier or later. As the futures contracts on the US markets trade throughout morning trading in the UK, traders will always have a good idea where the US markets are due to open, subject to the release of economic figures at 13.30 UK time.
16.30-16.35	**Post-market auction** There can often be opportunities in the closing auction, particularly on the last business day of the month or when there are index constituent changes. The general strategy is to take the other side of a large 'at-market' order that is forcing the uncrossing price away from the day's trading range, in the anticipation that the stock will revert to the previous ('normal') level the following day.
17.30	**FTSE 100 Index Futures close**
18.30	**Regulatory News Services close** A number of key announcements can come out after the market close and although most newspapers will pick up any significant stories, it is worth scanning through the day's late announcements before the start of trading the following day.

Source: *The UK Trader's Bible* by Dominic Connolly

FT 30 INDEX 1935 – WHERE ARE THEY NOW?

The FT 30 Index was started by the *Financial Times* on 1 July 1935. Today the most widely followed index is the FTSE 100, but for many years the FT 30 (originally called the *FT Ordinaries*) was the measure everyone knew. The table below lists the original companies in the FT 30 Index in 1935 – a time when brokers wore bowler hats and share certificates were printed on something called paper. It's interesting to see what became of the stalwarts of UK PLC from over 70 years ago.

Company	Notes
Associated Portland Cement	The name was changed to Blue Circle Industries in 1978, and then left the index in 2001 when it was bought by Lafarge.
Austin Motor	Left the index in 1947. In 1952 Austin merged with rival Morris Motors Limited to form The British Motor Corporation Limited (BMC). In 1966 BMC bought Jaguar and two years later merged with Leyland Motors Limited to form British Leyland Motor Corporation. In 1973 British Leyland produced the Austin-badged Allegro... (the story is too painful to continue).
Bass	Left the index in 1947. In 1967 merged with Charrington United Breweries to form Bass Charrington. In 2000 its brewing operations were sold to Interbrew (which was then instructed by the Competition Commission to dispose parts to Coors), while the hotel and pub holdings were renamed Six Continents. In 2003 Six Continents was split into a pubs business (Mitchells & Butlers) and a hotels and soft drinks business (InterContinental Hotels Group).
Bolsover Colliery	Left the index in 1947. The mines were acquired by the National Coal Board on nationalisation in 1947. Bolsover Colliery closed in 1993.
Callenders Cables & Construction	Left the index in 1947. Merged with British Insulated Cables in 1945 to form British Insulated Callender's Cables, which was renamed BICC Ltd in 1975. In 2000, having sold its cable operations, it renamed its contruction business Balfour Beatty.
Coats (J & P)	Left the index in 1959. Traded as Coats Patons Ltd after the takeover of Patons & Baldwins, then as Coats Viyella, finally as Coats plc. Finally taken over by Guinness Peat Group in 2004.
Courtaulds	Demerged its chemical and textile interests in the 1980s, with the former eventually being bought by Akzo Nobel and the latter by Sara Lee. Left the index in 1998.
Distillers	Purchased by Guinness in the infamous bid battle of 1986 when it left the index.
Dorman Long	Left the index in 1947. Joined British Steel following nationalisation in 1967.
Dunlop Rubber	Left the index in 1983 and was bought in 1985 by BTR (which became Invensys).
Electrical & Musical Industries	In 1971 changed its name to EMI and later that year merged with THORN Electrical Industries to form Thorn EMI but then de-merged in 1996. In 2007 EMI Group plc was taken over by Terra Firma Capital Partners but following financial difficulties ownership passed to Citigroup in 2011.
Fine Spinners and Doublers	Fell out of the index in 1938, and was later bought by Courtaulds in 1963.
General Electric	General Electric was re-named Marconi in 1999, suffered disastrous losses in the dot-com crash and was bought by Ericsson in 2006.
Guest Keen & Nettlefolds	Guest Keen is better known as GKN and is still in the FT 30 today.
Harrods	Left the index in 1959 when it was bought by House of Fraser, and then later by Mohamed Al Fayed.
Hawker Siddeley	Left the index in 1991, and was then bought in 1992 by BTR (which became Invensys).
Imperial Chemical Industries	Spun out Zeneca in 1993, and the rump (called ICI) was sold to Akzo Nobel in 2007.
Imperial Tobacco	Still going strong.
International Tea Co Stores	Fell out of the index in 1947, was acquired by BAT Industries in 1972 and ended up as Somerfield in 1994.
London Brick	Replaced in the index by Hanson which bought it in 1984.
Murex	Left the index in 1967 due to "poor share performance". Acquired by BOC Group in 1967.
Patons & Baldwins	Left the index in 1960 when bought by J&P Coats.
Pinchin Johnson & Associates	Left the index in 1960 when bought by Courtaulds.

Company	Notes
Rolls-Royce	In 1971 RR was taken into state ownership, the motor car business was floated separately in 1973, and RR returned to the private sector in 1987.
Tate & Lyle	Still going strong, although its sugar refining and golden syrup business was sold to American Sugar Refining in 2010.
Turner & Newall	Left the index in 1982. The company was heavily involved with asbestos production, so it is not surprising that things ended badly. In 1998 the business was acquired by Federal-Mogul, which soon after filed for Chapter 11 protection as a result of asbestos claims.
United Steel	Left the index in 1951. The iron and steel works on nationalisation became part of British Steel Corporation (and now part of Tata Steel); while the mining interests passed to the National Coal Board (now closed).
Vickers	Left the index in 1986. Bought by Rolls-Royce in 1999.
Watney Combe & Reid	Left the index in 1972 when it was bought by Grand Metropolitan, which itself became part of Diageo.
Woolworth (FW)	Left the index in 1971. Bought by the forerunner of Kingfisher in 1982, and then de-merged and re-listed in 2001. But the remaining Woolworths stores all closed by January 2009.

Of the 30 companies only four exist today as listed companies: GKN, Imperial Tobacco, Rolls-Royce and Tate & Lyle (all of which are in the FTSE 100 Index). And only GKN and Tate & Lyle are in today's FT 30.

The star performer from the original line-up has been Imperial Tobacco.

It's interesting to note the complete lack of representation of the four sectors that dominate the UK market today – no banks, telecom, oil or drug companies.

Index performance

Since 1935 the FT 30 has risen 1935% (which is a rather odd coincidence!); by comparison the FTSE All-Share over the same period has risen 8936%. The following chart plots the year-end values of the FT 30 against the FTSE All-Share (the latter has been rebased to start at the same value as the FT 30).

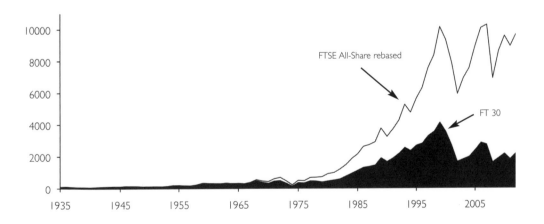

One of the reasons for the very large difference in performance is that the FT 30 is a price-weighted index (as are the Dow Jones Industrial Average and Nikkei 225), whereas most indices today (including the FTSE All-Share and FTSE 100) are weighted by market-capitalisation. When the FTSE 100 was introduced in 1984, if it had been price-weighted and performed in line with the FT 30, today it would have a value around 2805.

FTSE 100 INDEX – 1984

The FTSE 100 Index was started on 3 January 1984 with a base level of 1000. The table below shows the original companies in the index. Of the initial 100 companies only 18 remain in the index today (indicated in bold in the table, and with their new names in brackets) – a sign of the great changes in UK PLC in under 30 years.

Allied – Lyons	Ferranti	Plessey Co.
Associated British Foods	Fisons	**Prudential Corporation [Prudential]**
Associated Dairies Group	General Accident Fire & Life	RMC Group
Barclays Bank [Barclays]	General Electric	Racal Electronics
Barratt Developments	Glaxo Holdings	Rank Organisation
Bass	Globe Investment Trust	**Reckitt & Colman [Reckitt Benckiser Group]**
BAT Industries	Grand Metropolitan	Redland
Beecham Group	**Great Universal Stores [Experian]**	**Reed International [Reed Elsevier]**
Berisford (S. & W.)	Guardian Royal Exchange	**Rio Tinto – Zinc Corporation [Rio Tinto]**
BICC	Guest Keen & Nettlefolds	Rowntree Mackintosh
Blue Circle Industries	Hambro Life Assurance	**Royal Bank of Scotland Group**
BOC Group	Hammerson Prop.Inv. & Dev. 'A'	Royal Insurance
Boots Co.	Hanson Trust Harrisons & Crossfield	**Sainsbury (J.)**
Bowater Corporation	Hawker Siddeley Group	Scottish & Newcastle Breweries
BPB Industries	House of Fraser	Sears Holdings
British & Commonwealth	Imperial Chemical Industries	Sedgwick Group
British Aerospace	Imperial Cont. Gas Association	**Shell Trans. & Trad. Co. [Royal Dutch Shell]**
British Elect. Traction Co.	Imperial Group	Smith & Nephew Associated Co's.
British Home Stores	Johnson Matthey	Standard Chartered Bank
British Petroleum [BP]	Ladbroke Group	Standard Telephones & Cables
Britoil	**Land Securities**	Sun Alliance & London Insurance
BTR	**Legal & General Group**	Sun Life Assurance Society
Burton Group	**Lloyds Bank [Lloyds Banking Group]**	THORN EMI
Cable & Wireless	Lonrho	Tarmac
Cadbury Schweppes	MEPC	**Tesco**
Commercial Union Assurance [Aviva]	MFI Furniture Group	Trafalgar House
Consolidated Gold Fields	**Marks & Spencer**	Trusthouse Forte
Courtaulds	Midland Bank	Ultramar
Dalgety Distillers Co.	National Westminster Bank	**Unilever**
CJ Rothschild	Northern Foods	United Biscuits
Edinburgh Investment Trust	P & O Steam Navigation Co.	Whitbread & Co. 'A'
English China Clays	**Pearson (S.) & Son [Pearson]**	Wimpey (George)
Exco International	Pilkington Brothers	

The following table compares the market capitalisations of the top five largest companies in the index in 1984 and today.

Rank (1984)		Capital (£m)	Rank (2012)	Capital (£m)
1	British Petroleum Co.	7,401	Royal Dutch Shell	133,327
2	Shell Trans. & Trad. Co.	6,365	HSBC Holdings	130,964
3	General Electric Co.	4,915	Vodafone Group	102,712
4	Imperial Chemical Industries	3,917	BP	83,318
5	Marks & Spencer	2,829	GlaxoSmithKline	79,417

Oil is still there today, but industrial, chemical and retail have been replaced by bank, telecom and pharmaceutical.

In 1984 the total market capitalisation of the index was £100bn; in 2012 the total market capitalisation is £1,824bn. It's interesting to note that Shell's market cap. today is 33% larger than the whole FTSE 100 in 1984.

REFERENCE

194

ALSO FROM HARRIMAN HOUSE

Free Capital

How 12 private investors made millions in the stock market

By Guy Thomas

Available in paperback and eBook

How to Value Shares and Outperform the Market

A simple, new and effective approach to value investing

By Glenn Martin

Available in paperback and eBook

The 17.6 Year Stock Market Cycle

Connecting the Panics of 1929, 1987, 2000 and 2007

By Kerry Balenthiran

Available in paperback and eBook

The Search for Income

An investor's guide to income-paying investments

By Maike Currie

Available in paperback and eBook

ALSO FROM HARRIMAN HOUSE

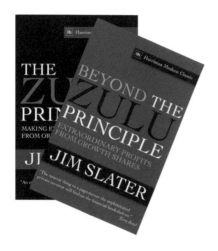

The Zulu Principle
Making extraordinary profits from ordinary shares

Beyond The Zulu Principle
Extraordinary Profits from Growth Shares
Both by Jim Slater
Available in paperback and eBook

101 Ways to Pick Stock Market Winners
By Clem Chambers
Available in paperback

The Financial Spread Betting Handbook
The definitive guide to making money trading spread bets
By Malcolm Pryor
Available in paperback and eBook

The Sterling Bonds and Fixed Income Handbook
A practical guide for investors and advisers
By Mark Glowrey
Available in paperback and eBook